SIGNS AND WONDERS

The Relationship Between

Synchronicity and the Miraculous in

Depth Psychology and Religion

David C. Asomaning

Originally submitted in partial fulfillment of the requirements for the degree of Doctor of Philosophy Union Theological Seminary New York City March 2003

Reproduced with minor edits and omissions.

Cover designed by Emily Armstrong of Starling Memory Designs
Internal design by Sandra Seymour of Howson Books

David C. Asomaning
Visit my website at www.SynchroMind.com
SynchroMind - The Leadership Development Co
5601 Spanish River Road
Fort Pierce, FL 34951 USA
First Printing 2108
Name of Company

ISBN-13: 978-1-7335213-0-7

ACKNOWLEDGMENTS

I AM DEEPLY GRATEFUL to the all family members, friends, colleagues, clients, partners, mentors, teachers, and advisors who have supported and assisted me patiently during the odyssey of this doctoral project.

I would like specially to thank the members of my committee, Professors Ann B. Ulanov, Harry W. Fogarty, Frederick W. Weidmann, and Vincent L. Wimbush for their wisdom, insights, guidance, support, and friendship. I am very grateful for the gracious manner, and the many ways in which they played a part in keeping my hope alive as I wrestled to achieve my dream of completing this project, even when the obstacles, adversities, and trials and tribulations of life or my own limitations with regard to it often seemed insurmountable. I am also deeply grateful to Professor Randall G. Styers for his guidance on the subjects of magic and semiotics in the early stages of my writing.

I would like to thank Professor Vincent L. Wimbush who, in addition to participating on my dissertation committee, included me in The African Americans and the Bible Research Project, of which he has been the director. My participation in the project was a profound and synchronistic watershed experience for me and my work. I am grateful for the immeasurable ways in which the book has benefited from the investigative processes I developed in the social sciences consulting group of the project, where we focused on the preparation of the project's national ethnographic strategy. I am grateful to have been invited to prepare a paper for the project which I entitled, "African Americans and Miraculous Healing: Toward a Depth Psychological, Biblical, and Semiotic Hermeneutic," and which I delivered at the culminating conference of the project in 1999 at Union Theological Seminary. I am also deeply grateful that I was invited to revise this paper, which is now entitled "African American Social Cultural Formation, the Bible, and Depth Psychology," and which appears in the volume, *African Americans and the Bible*, New York: Continnum, 2000, ed. Vincent L. Wimbush, along with the wealth of other conference papers gathered together under the auspices of the research project. It has been rewarding to see the chapter for The African Americans and the Bible Project evolve into Chapter Five of this book.

I would also like to express my deepest gratitude to Otema B. Yirenkyi, Jacob Miller, Shannon Ayers, Twila Perry, and Kerstin Spitzl for being significant dialogue partners, and for providing invaluable editorial support along the way. They each showed me how I had accumulated blind spots from being immersed in my subject for so long, blind spots which tended to make me hard on my readers. Their help, together with the superb guidance of my advisors, brought me out of the many literary and conceptual thickets I entered.

In sustaining the lengthy effort and dedication needed to develop the skills and tools to be an effective scholar, teacher, healer, and leader at the crossroads of theology, depth psychology, and contemporary social cultural formation, my commitment has been possible because of both the support of others, and the amazing never-ending renewal of the Spirit in my life ever since my first true awakening in December of 1980. It has been a wonderful journey so far, and I am excited and inspired about what is yet to come.

And so, I dedicate this book to all I have traveled with thus far on my journey. I dedicate this book to the remainder of the journey, and to all I am yet to meet on it. Also, I dedicate this work to the Great Spirit who leads, supports, and loves us all equally and infinitely on the way.

CONTENTS

INTRODUCTION

THIS STUDY IS ABOUT how synchronicity can help us to understand the miraculous better, and how at the same time, the miraculous can help us to understand synchronicity better. Synchronicity, at its simplest, is meaningful coincidence which can result when a person's ego opens more fully in some way through and past unconscious barriers to the Self, the psyche's center, often with attendant increases in insight and awareness. The miraculous, at its simplest, can be described as resulting from the opening up and the aligning of a person's soul with the infinite power of God, which can result in amazing experiences[1] of supernatural power of freedom or healing or discovery.

---

[1]In Chapter One I provide fuller definitions of both synchronicity and the miraculous. See further on in this introduction for discussions of the ego-Self and soul-God frameworks underlying synchronicity and the miraculous. While my focus in this study is largely on positive forms of synchronicity and the miraculous, it must be noted here – and this raises many additional questions beyond the scope of the present study - that sometimes a miracle for one person has positive consequences, while that same miracle has negative consequences for another. As an example of such a miracle, take the parting of the Red Sea which had positive consequences for the Israelites while it had negative ones for the Egyptians; compare this to the feeding of the multitudes, the unexpected catch, and the transformation of water to wine, which had positive consequences for all those involved. There are also such nuanced differences in types of synchronicity: some are positive for those involved (see the example of Jung and the scarab beetle in Chapter Three); others reveal more negative circumstances (see the example of the servitor explaining to

The rigors involved in undertaking this study have challenged me, unlike anything else I have ever done, to confront the many mistakes I have made in my life. These mistakes have been both of a psychological and theological nature. I chose this topic on synchronicity and the miraculous in order to understand better how to make the difficulties and problems of my life and those of my clients more manageable and even transformative, through both the healing power of depth psychology, and the salvation from evil provided us through theology. However, initially at least, instead of getting the psychological and theological easement of some of my harshest problems that I expected from this study, life actually became harder for me as I pursued this study.

I believe that one of the reasons life became harder during this doctoral process was that I continued to make certain mistakes because, often, I did not realize that I was behaving in a way driven by various inner unresolved psychological conflicts. In other words, I was unconscious of various self-defeating patterns in my life, and as a result I have repeated certain mistakes over and over again. In technical terms one could say that at the level of the ego, I have been unaware of, and thus incapable of resolving, the unconscious dynamics driving my repeated mistakes. This study is concerned, in part then, with the fuller opening up of the ego to unconscious self-defeating dynamics, as well as to the resolving of such self-defeating dynamics, especially as this process of resolution is accompanied by synchronicities.

At the same, theologically I have also made many mistakes in my life because, frequently, I have not lived according to God's will for my life. In other words, often, I have violated God's precepts and

the empress how her psychology is afflicting her empire, in Chapter One); others still are meaningful for one person while relatively meaningless for another (see the example of Jung and Freud regarding loud noises from a sideboard during a visit they were having with each other in Chapter Three).

principles based on my personal whim, idiosyncrasy, unawareness, or even willful rebellion and sin. This sinfulness on my part has often led to dire results for me. Therefore, in addition to a focus on synchronicity, this study also focuses on the opening up of the soul to God more fully, as well as to the resolution of the soul's sinful state before God, especially as this process is accompanied by the miraculous.[2]

---

[2]These two dimensions of looking at our mistakes, the depth psychological one involving the ego in relation to unconscious dynamics, and the theological one which involves the moral culpability of the soul before God, can be applied as follows to a couple of examples – the example of gossiping and that of child molestation. In gossiping, we could speculate that for some people this type of behavior might have its origins in early childhood in the following way: let us say that a person perceives that he or she can escape negative consequences from parents for his or her own bad behavior by putting the spotlight for the bad behavior on any available siblings. This early childhood defense subsequently becomes unconscious and is used in adulthood every time one feels threatened by negative consequences from one's own behavior. In other words, one uses gossip as an opportunity to make others look bad by distracting oneself and others from one's own mistakes. One of the main problems here in this mistaken behavior, is that it involves a psychological defense in which there is a lack of awareness about this pattern. From a theological perspective, divine law tells us that one shall not bear false witness against one's neighbor, and so the problems in the mistake here are those of moral culpability before God for violating a commandment while doing harm to another person as well. In the case of a child molester, the perpetrator may be psychologically unaware that he was victimized as a child, and that is why he keeps repeating the pattern of molesting others; on the other hand the perpetrator may not be aware of his culpability before God for harming another, or for the sexual sin involved, and so on. If to err is human, then the unflinching exploration of my own personal mistakes, psychological and theological, helps me to assist those in my care more effectively, and hopefully makes a contribution to how other helps address their mistakes as well. The Bible demonstrates the dimension of awareness depth psychology strives for in places like this: "You hypocrite, first take the log out of your own eye, and then you will see clearly to take the speck out of your neighbor's eye" (Matthew 7:5). The Bible also demonstrates that lack of awareness makes us morally culpable before God: "Then Jesus said, "Father, forgive them; for they do not know what they are doing" (Luke 23:34).

I illustrate various points of view throughout this study using autobiographical material drawn from my own psychological and theological development. In doing this, I employ the facts that I grew up in Ghana, West Africa, until the age of seventeen, and that I am biracial and bicultural.[3] Also, I use personal and theoretical references to my family, my parents in particular, and to my African background.[4]

This study has been tortured and arduous for me because of my own ego resistance to my unconscious, as well as because of my having been encumbered by sin to the detriment of my soul's connection to God. For instance, in the early stages of working on this project, I was much more focused on the pride of accomplishing a heroic and challenging personal life goal. I was not so focused on the unconscious dynamics related to my actual quest. It now seems apparent that my path was made more difficult for me because I was unaware that this personal ambition was very wrapped up in many unresolved psychological and spiritual conflicts.

The connections between my work on this study and my relationship with my father are one way to illustrate how I have made ego-Self mistakes on the one hand, as well as soul-God mistakes on the other. The on-going struggle to open up to my unconscious has been supported over and over again by the synchronicities that have come my way and urged me on as I have attempted to surface and resolve my various conflicts, as I will show later on.

At the same time, as I have wrestled seriously with various areas of sinfulness in my life, it has become more and more clear to me that my own rebellion – conscious or unconscious - from God's will

---

[3] See section on social cultural formation below and Chapter Five.

[4] See Chapter Two on Ananse, a children's story I grew up with in Ghana.

and direction for me – has slowed me down, and at times even stopped me completely, from finishing this study. More specifically, if I return to the example of my father, it appears I became alienated, hostile, and even disrespectful towards him, and other authority figures in my life, for what I felt was a lack of understanding and support towards me regarding my very difficult doctoral process.

This behavior on my part amounts to sinfulness, at least in so far as one of the soul's requirements before God in the Ten Commandments, is that we honor our parents. The deepening regard for my soul's connection to God's imperatives has blossomed over time into a deep regard for, and belief in, the resurrection of Jesus. In fact, through this study, it has become my strong personal belief that a fervent and alive acceptance of the resurrection of Jesus is the supreme imperative of my soul as a Christian before God. The supreme miracle of the resurrection of Jesus, and the belief of the Christian in this resurrection through faith, I believe, neutralizes all of our sins before God and makes everything about us new again.[5] However, this belief in the resurrection, is not to be merely as a symbolic reference to living a good or better life, but that we are raised from the dead in every

---

[5]While the term "miracle" is never used in the New Testament to refer to the resurrection of Jesus, "The resurrection of Jesus is related to the miracles of Jesus in the sense of identifying and confirming the truth that 'God was with him' (Acts 10:38)," Colin Brown, *Miracles and the Critical Mind*, (Grand Rapids, Mich.: Wm. B. Eerdmans Publishing Company, 1984), 289. Also, see *Resurrection*, Journal for the Study of the New Testament Supplement Series 186, (Sheffield: Sheffield Academy Press, 1999), eds., Stanely E. Porter, Michael A. Hayes, and David Tombs; The *Resurrection: An Interdisciplinary Symposium on the Resurrection of Jesus,* (New York: Oxford University Press, 1997), eds., Stephen T. David, Daniel Kendall, and Gerald O'Collins; and *The Fear of Freedom: A Study of Miracles in the Imperial Church*, University Park: The Pennsylvania State University Press, 1989), Rowan A. Greer. Taken together, these works provide rich perspectives on a history-of-ideas approach to the resurrection and the miraculous.

aspect of our lives, and in every conceivable way, by participating in the death and resurrection of Jesus, through faith.

THE THESIS

THE THESIS OF THIS STUDY is that it is of the utmost importance for depth psychologists and pastoral theologians to embrace broader and deeper understandings of synchronicity and the miraculous simultaneously. This simultaneous embrace is important because of the benefits to the people in the care of these practitioners that result from enhanced clinical work and pastoral care when understandings about synchronicity are used to deepen approaches to the miraculous, and when understandings of the miraculous are used to strengthen an appreciation of synchronicity. As will be explained more fully in this study, the benefit an awareness of synchronicity brings to how we address the miraculous, is in providing a depth psychological awareness of the psyche's role in the miraculous. For example, let us consider that on a conscious level, I may have forgiven my father for neglecting me, and no longer feel any conscious anger towards him, and that I therefore experience God's miraculous power more fully in my life as a result because I am honoring him according to the commandments. However, in spite of my conscious forgiveness of my father, I may be continuing to get into conflicts with other dominant people in my life, which could be a tell-tale indicator that I still have unresolved unconscious conflicts with my father which are blocking even greater soul-God connections for me. These unconscious conflicts, were they to be resolved more fully, might, in turn, lead to enhanced experiences and understandings of the miraculous in my life. In other words, here we are bringing depth psychology's understanding of how to resolve unconscious conflicts into the service of the soul-God relationship and the miraculous.

On the other hand, the benefit an awareness of the miraculous brings to how we address synchronicity, is in providing the ego with a theological awareness of the benefits to the soul of believing in God. To illustrate this using the example of my father, let us say that I have resolved many of my unconscious conflicts with my father in such a way that I feel well adjusted to most other dominant figures whom I encounter. This is pretty good from an ego-Self perspective, and yet from a theological soul-God approach, I could still benefit from what the resurrection of Jesus might imply for a more profound and complete resurrection of the synchronistic aspects of my ego-Self relationship to my father. Let us try to go even further now, in pinning down what the resurrection really brings to us. The resurrection pledges to bring us total and thorough redemption from whatever the problem might be in a way which depth psychology does not. Depth psychology brings us enhanced awareness of the conflict, and even deepening ability to avoid it from repeating. However, I have heard people say to me, that even with all the awareness they have obtained through depth psychology, it alone is not able to give them the total and complete promise of eternal salvation from sin, evil, and God's judgement that is promised to us as we exercise our faith in the resurrection of Jesus. In other words, synchronicity helps us in our approach to the miraculous to attend to unconscious dynamics, and the miraculous aids in our approach to synchronicity to attend more rigorously to God's utterly redemptive role through the resurrection. A simultaneous approach to the role of the unconscious regarding synchronicity in the psyche, as well as God's role regarding the miraculous in the soul, provides us with a much more powerful way of attending to, and resolving, the mistakes of the human condition.[6]

---

[6]Nonetheless, there is cross-over between depth psychology and theology, as for

Understanding this simultaneous embrace theoretically helps practitioners care for those they are responsible for in practical ways as follows: depth psychologists are able to encourage clients to bring in stories of synchronicity in order to explore how they enrich the faith of patients with regard to the miraculous, and specifically with regard to the resurrection; pastoral care givers are able to encourage believers to delve into stories of the miraculous while harnessing their synchronistic experiences to help such stories take on new life. Without this simultaneous embrace what is more likely to happen is that clinicians minimize the faith life of patients in favor of looking solely at unconscious dynamics, even to the extent of possibly interpreting patients' synchronistic experiences as neurotic and pathological especially when patients evince strong faith.

On the other hand, pastoral care givers, without this simultaneous embrace, might minimize clients' unconscious dynamics solely in favor of urging them to embrace a faith confession about the power of traditional Christian concepts like the creeds, prayer, worship, and even the resurrection of Jesus. In overlooking or minimizing the synchronistic depth psychological dimensions revealed in faith positions towards the miraculous on the part of clients, pastoral care-givers convey the subtle message that the inner wholeness of the psyche does not have much

---

instance when Jesus on the cross says, "Father, forgive them; for they do not know what they are doing," Luke 23:34. One could say that these words that Jesus speaks are about the issues of lack of awareness that depth psychologists are typically concerned with. On the other hand, depth psychologists do make moral pronouncements as in courts cases involving issues of mental competence. Also, one might be led to ask whether or not there is a hierarchy between the depth psychological and theological approaches offered up here. My initial response would be to say that Jesus can both save us and help us towards greater insight, while depth psychology which is expert at insight, cannot provide the ultimate salvation we get through Jesus.

relevance to the experience of the miraculous – all that is needed is a good understanding of the doctrines and practices of the faith tradition. As will be demonstrated more fully through this study, the simultaneous embrace of synchronicity and the miraculous helps us to avoid these twin pitfalls and thereby supports fuller richer lives.

METHOD

THE METHOD USED to advance the thesis of this study, that there is tremendous benefit to us in exploring how we might embrace broader and deeper understandings of synchronicity and the miraculous simultaneously, is a method of integration. This method of integration is used to join understandings of synchronicity based on the ego-Self framework from depth psychology, with understandings of the miraculous based on the soul-God framework from theology, in a manner akin to my illustrations above regarding my psychological and theological mistakes, but with much more of an emphasis on exploring synchronicity and the miraculous in the context of personal transformation towards greater psychological and theological wholeness.

This method of integration also brings different disciplines and subdisciplines into "conversation" with one another. I aim to integrate various contexts of discourse that are usually ignored, or kept isolated from one another. This method shares common qualities with what Carol Newsom describes as Mikhail Bakhtin's conception of dialogic conversation.

[An] important feature is the embodied, almost personal quality of dialogic truth in contrast to the abstraction characteristic of monologism. Again, the

paradigm of the conversation is illustrative. The participants in a conversation are not propositions or assertions but the persons who utter them.[7]

Newsom recognizes that writing and texts are not necessarily the best vehicles for conversations, but, nonetheless, along with Bakhtin, she affirms that in literary productions, it is possible to come close to

---

a genuine dialogue, a model of writing [Bakhtin] called polyphonic....[T]he author must give up the type of control exercised in monologic works and attempt to create several consciousnesses....[I]n a polyphonic text the dialogic play of ideas is not merely a function of plot and character but is the motive of the entire work.[8]

As will be illustrated throughout this study, the method of integration used here is concerned with addressing the polyphonic nature of the psyche and soul.

The dimension of this method concerned with praxis, includes standard clinical work (doing insight-oriented analytic psychotherapy with individuals, couples, families, and groups), and yet also extends to practical theology[9] with a more broadly useful social character. To this end, one of the focuses of this method is on

---

[7]Carol A. Newsom, "Bakhtin, the Bible, and Dialogic Truth," *The Journal of Religion* 76, no. 2 (1996), 294.

[8]Ibid., 295-6.

[9]Gijsbert D. J. Dingemans, "Practical Theology in the Academy: A Contemporary Overview," *The Journal of Religion* 76, no. 1 (1996): 82-95, offers a nuanced treatment of "the praxis of practical theology" by describing the field in terms of empirical-analytical versus hermeneutical approaches to clerical, church, liberation, and individual paradigms of praxis. He includes an examination of integrative approaches to the diverse subdisciplines in the field, and describes two such integrative perspectives as "coalescence of approaches," and "complementarity of methods.

healing efficacy, in African American social cultural formation with regard to the Bible and biblical psychotherapy. This involves exploring the relationships, resonances, and dissonances in depth psychology and theology, with particular emphasis on the experiences of African Americans as they have appropriated and applied their own distinctive hermeneutical approaches to transpersonal experiences of liberation and healing.

There are additional dimensions in which the praxis element of this method is hermeneutical and dialogical, and this concerns the use of language and communication, and indeed an entire scope of rhetorical strategies, as instruments of meaning-making in the quest for liberation from various forms of oppression. The Ghanaian philosopher, Ato Sekyi-Otu notes that Franz Fanon, the black psychiatrist and anticolonialist theoretician, in his rhetorical strategies,

ultimately gives psychoanalytic language no more and no less than an analogical and metaphoric function, as distinct from a foundational or etiological one, in accounting for the condition of the colonized and their dreams: above all, their dreams, their manifest dreams. To the Lacanian dictum that "the unconscious is structured like a language," Fanon might have responded that the dreams of the colonized may well be structured like the language of neurosis but that they are occasioned by the language of political experience. It is with Fanon's interpretation of these dreams and this language that this book is centrally concerned.

My intuition that this interpretation is most revealingly read as framed by a dramatic narrative structure led me to pay close attention to the linguistic acts of Fanon's texts. I discerned in these linguistic acts so many subtle and surrogate dramaturgical devices: stage directions, signals of imminent plot twists and complications, markers of incipient ironies and reversals, choric commentaries and points of strategic complicity or critical difference between protagonal utterance and authorial stance.[10]

This citation not only reflects Sekyi-Otu's implied appreciation of the Bakhtin-like polyphony embedded in Fanon's writing through the interplay of literary devices such as "protagonal utterance" and "authorial stance;" it also emphasizes the role of various linguistic acts as liberative tactics. The method of this study is concerned not only with the polyphony of the psyche as manifested in various texts, but in Sekyi-Otu's terms, also with the way in which various literary devices, such as those related to biblical texts are used as liberative tools in the face of oppression.[11]

As will be unfolded throughout this study, the integration of ego-Self and soul-God frameworks leads us to a consideration of the integration of the dynamics involving the simultaneous embrace of synchronicity and the miraculous that go on within individual persons which we will call the intra level; the dynamics that go on between people which we will call the inter level; and the dynamics that go on between people and the transcendent which we will call the trans level.

Also, as will be demonstrated in this study, the method of integration leads us to derive benefits from exploring the

---

[10]Ato Sekyi-Otu, *Fanon's Dialectic of Experience* (Cambridge, MA: Harvard University Press, 1996), 8. See also Hussein Abdilahi Bulhan's, *Franz Fanon and the Psychology of Oppression*, New York: Plenum Press, 1985, and *Fanon: A Critical Reader*, Cambridge MA: Blackwell Publishers, 1996, ed. by Lewis R. Gordon, T. Denean Sharpley-Whiting and Renee T. White.

[11]Sources for such praxis-oriented rhetorical strategies might include interviews, speeches, monographs, literature, autobiography, music, poetry, film, and art, to name a few. This multidisciplinary approach, shades into bricolage, i.e., using whatever materials are at hand, which is also an aspect of the method being presented here. See Henry Louis Gates, Jr., *Figures in Black: Words, Signs, and the "Racial" Self* (New York: Oxford University Press, 1987), xviii, for an approach to bricolage in literature, and Claude Levi-Strauss, *The Savage Mind* (Chicago: University of Chicago Press, 1966), 16-36, on the bricoleur in mythology. See also, Grey Gundaker's *Signs of Diaspora; Diaspora of Signs: Literacies, Creolization, and Vernacular Practice in African America*, New York: Oxford University Press, 1998.

integration of the intra, inter, and trans levels within depth psychology, within theology, and within African American social cultural formation as these levels pertain to the simultaneous embrace of synchronicity and the miraculous.

One of the significant learnings from this study has been that in order to gain the maximum benefits from this process of integration, it is of the utmost importance vigilantly to avoid collapsing the various categories we are integrating with one another. Thus, synchronicity does not simply become the miraculous in another guise; the ego-Self framework is not the same thing as the soul-God framework; nor are the intra, inter, and trans levels simply the same thing in each of the various discourses explored here. By maintaining a rigorous discipline of understanding the parallels between synchronicity and the miraculous rather than collapsing them into one another, their distinctions reveal themselves more clearly, and these distinctions then become the basis for the benefit in integrating them.

Method: Integrating the Ego-Self Framework and the Soul-God Framework

The method of integration underlying this study is used to join understandings of the ego-Self framework from depth psychology with the soul-God framework from theology because by joining these two frameworks, we are also in a sense joining our understandings of synchronicity and the miraculous, given that, as has been pointed out above, the opening of the ego to the unconscious is often accompanied by synchronicity, and the opening of the soul to God is often accompanied by the miraculous. Let us now look more fully at descriptions of the ego-Self framework and the soul-God framework.[12]

---

[12]In Chapter One there is a fuller elucidation of the 6 parallels between

The Ego-Self Framework

Jung pioneered the development of a comprehensive theoretical depth psychological framework which can be said to pivot around his discernment within the psyche of two different centers. Jung says the ego is the center of consciousness, the part of the psyche we are conscious of. The other center, the Self, is the center of the whole of the psyche: it is both ego consciousness and the rest of the psyche, of which we remain unconscious.

The ego tries to maintain an experience of itself as the center of the entire psyche, and is often resistant to the role of the Self as the center of the entire psyche. The Self seeks admission into the life of the ego, and very often when the Self gains such entry over our egocentricity, meaningful coincidence or synchronicity is the result. Synchronicity refers to experiences of meaningful coincidence which we register as profoundly meaningful, and through which we glimpse a larger orderedness and wholeness of reality that transcends our usual divisions of matter and psyche, of past, present, and future, of boundaries of space and time, and of inner and outer worlds.

Jung's ego-Self framework is a useful tool for investigating how people's actions may reflect a certain ego resistance to synchronicity, or a yielding to it as well on the other hand, because synchronistic events can be seen as a reflection of the ego's surrender or not to the Self or of the Self's access to the ego.

The Soul-God Framework

From a religious perspective, a theological framework also exists for Christians which can be said to consist of the relationship

synchronicity and the miraculous based on the definitions of these terms in relation to the two frameworks, and it is these parallels, which pave the way for a richer and fuller integration of synchronicity and the miraculous.

between the human soul and the Creator of this soul, God. The soul is answerable to the Creator about questions of ultimate meaning in both our being, and our becoming, more fully what God intends for us. In this regard the soul is finite and God is infinite.

The soul on its own is incapable of pleasing God its Creator, or of living in accordance with God's ultimate purposes, and yet the soul, unaided by God, persists in a state of darkness and death about God's purposes for it. This state of darkness and death, our utter deviation from God's purposes for us, is a total state of perpetual errors and mistakes which is referred to as a state of sin, and makes us morally culpable before God. This sinful deviation from God is not mild and benign, but rather is strong and often willful.

God seeks to awaken the sin-deadened soul, and to flood it with Grace, love, and correction. For the Christian, the total surrender to Jesus as Savior and Redeemer, as Master and Lord, as the crucified and miraculously risen One who takes away the sin of the world, this Jesus, is the One through whom access to God's ultimate purposes becomes possible and actualized.

When the soul opens to God through Jesus, by accepting Him as the crucified and miraculously risen One who takes away the sin of the world, the Christian's inner life experiences a flowering of virtues and gifts of God's Spirit, and is open to nurture by the sacraments of the Church, and is nurtured above all through prayer, in which unusual phenomena - miracles – which might seem to be reserved for mystics alone, can become the provenance of every Christian.[13]

---

[13]This approach in which the miraculous can belong to every Christian rather than just the extraordinary ones known as mystics has been made clear to me in Stephen Fields' introduction to Anselm Stolz's *The Doctrine of Spiritual Perfection*, New York: The Crossroad Publishing Company, 2001. According to Fields, in Stolz's view, both psychology and theology have a distorted understanding when they assume that "extraordinary phenomena – voices, visions, ecstasies, and stigmata – are

Method: Integrating the Intra, Inter, and Trans Levels

The method of integration in this study involves an emphasis on a holistic approach to the processes that go on within a person, between persons, and between a person and the transcendent. While these three dimensions will be addressed and integrated much more fully further on in this study, suffice it to say here again for now that the processes that go on within a person whether depth psychological or theological are referred to in this study as being on the intra level; the processes psychological and theological which go on between persons are referred to as being on the inter level; and the processes which go on between persons and the transcendent are referred to as being on the trans level. However, this is not to collapse these various levels into one another; rather, this aspect of the method provides us with an effective nomenclature for easily referring to our work of integration with these different levels as needed. For example, we can say that we are referring to the trans level in theology and making a parallel between it and the trans level in depth psychology, or that we are

essential [exclusive] to mysticism. By contrast, Stolz seeks to integrate the mystical life into the central dogmas of the Catholic faith and thus to recover it as the perfection of grace available to *all* Christians....Since mysticism is the flowering of virtues and gifts of the Spirit implanted by the sacraments and nurtured in prayer, a proper understanding of it provides a paradigm for understanding the nature and goal of every Christian's inner life. Stolz does not accept the strong distinction between mysticism and the usual modes of Christian prayer. Developing a balanced reciprocity between these, he locates their common essence in the human person's being created in the image and likeness of God," v-vi. In a similar manner, it is my view that synchronicity and miraculous as addressed simultaneously can be a part of the experience of most everyday Christians. I say all of these things as a Christian of a particular sort, understanding that other Christians might have other views, and that other religious systems, such as Buddhism, Judaism, or Islam might have different things to say about the miraculous as well.

referring to the intra level in depth psychology and making a parallel between it and the intra level in theology.

Also, this method is used to explore the ways in which people either do or do not embrace synchronicity and the miraculous simultaneously. In this study when we examine the simultaneous embrace of synchronicity and the miraculous we are looking for the ways in which people, in their speech, written output, or in their other behaviors, are more or less conscious of synchronicity and the miraculous together in an integrated way, and of the relationship between them being advanced in this study. We are also examining how the ego-Self framework from depth psychology and the soul-God parallel to it from theology are in evidence or not in the discourses being analyzed here.[14]

Method: Integrating Across Four Audiences

In this study my intended audiences are the people working in these four areas: academic study on the interface between religion and depth psychology; active church ministry on the same interface; pastoral psychotherapy in contemporary society at large, and also pastoral psychotherapy with a particular focus on contemporary African American social cultural formation in relation to the Bible.

---

[14]This process of looking for a simultaneous and integrated or holistic approach to synchronicity and the miraculous can be likened to the manner in which an analyst, in standard analysis, looks for and interprets the latent content in the manifest content of a client's expressions. In standard analytic settings, while we are often looking for latent sexual and aggressive dynamics, and interpreting for the client the barriers of repression set up against these unconscious forces, the interpretive process I am advancing here, includes a person's various manifest and latent expressions of the ego-Self framework, of the soul-God framework, and of the synchronicity-miraculous parallel as crucial features of the analytic and interpretive process.

The method of integration used in this study is seen as a response to a number of conceptual gaps that are apparent in discourses within and among these four audiences. While I understand that integration is compelling to me for a variety of personal and professional reasons which are addressed in this study, I am cautious about imposing this system of integration on the work of others for whom this has not been a primary goal. My own approach to integration in this study is less as a criticism of the work of others where these conceptual gaps occur, and more as an extension of the work that others have done.

Additional Conceptual Gaps in Connection with these Four Audiences

While this study addresses depth psychology, theology, and African American social cultural formation with regard to synchronicity and the miraculous, the study has interdisciplinary implications far beyond the conceptual gaps that exist in these three fields of study. Although a deeper consideration of these additional fields is beyond the scope of this study, here now follows a brief description of several of the interdisciplinary conceptual gaps in various fields which could be addressed by the methods of this study.

The wealth of literary-critical scholarship[15] on postmodern discourse often refers abundantly to Freudian and neo-Freudian lineages[16], but less often to Jungian ideas. In turn, in the recent past, the Jungian world has dealt less frequently with issues related

---

[15] For example, Sue Vice, ed. *Psychoanalytic Criticism: A Reader*, (Cambridge, UK: Polity Press, 1996).

[16] For example, Anthony Elliot, *Psychoanalytic Theory: An Introduction* (Cambridge, MA: Blackwell Publishers, 1994); Edith Wyschogrod, David Crownfield, and Carl A. Raschke, eds. *Lacan and Theological Discourse* (Albany, NY: State University of New York, 1989), 18.

specifically to critical postmodern discourse, although now there is more being done here.[17] Also there does not appear to be much deliberate overlap between Jungian studies and religious studies on the miraculous[18] when Jungian approaches focus on the supernatural, the occult, or synchronicity, although there are many interdisciplinary ways in which it would seem that these areas could be linked.[19]

In religious studies, the miraculous is treated primarily through anthropology, sociology, the historical-critical method, or philosophy, with little reference to depth psychology, especially in its transpersonal and transcendent dimensions.[20] There is some

---

[17]For example, Irena R. Makaryk, ed. *Encyclopedia of Contemporary Literary Theory: Approaches, Scholars, Terms* (Toronto: University of Toronto Press, 1993).

[18]An exception to this, is Morton Kelsey's comprehensive companion articles "Miracles an Overview," and "Miracles: Modern Perspectives," in *The Encyclopedia of Religion*, ed. Mircea Eliade (New York: Macmillan Publishing Company, 1987), 541-52, where there is a deliberate, albeit brief, linking of miracles and synchronicity in the latter article.

[19]For example, Robert E. Aziz, *Jung's Psychology of Religion and Synchronicity* (Albany: State University of New York Press, 1990). See also Barry Ulanov's chapters on Myth, Literary Theory, and Philosophy, in *Jung and the Outside World*, (Wilmette, IL: Chiron Publications, 1992), in which he touches briefly on synchronicity; George Devereux, ed. *Psychoanalysis and the Occult* (New York: International Universities Press, Inc., 1953).; Robert L. Moore, ed. *Carl Jung and Christian Spirituality* (Mahwah, NY: Paulist Press, 1988).; Edward F. Edinger, *Ego and Archetype: Individuation and the Religious Function of the Psyche* (Boston: Shambhala, 1972); W. W. Meissner, *Psychoanalysis and Religious Experience* (New Haven: Yale University Press, 1984), asserts that "As long as the reality of a supernatural order of existence is included in the schema, adequate ego functioning must be measured to some degree against the demands imposed by that dimension of reality. Here we are dependent on theology, since it makes explicit what revelation tells us about the character of the supernatural" 210.

[20]For example, Robert Bruce Mullin, *Miracles and the Modern Religious Imagination* (New Haven: Yale University Press, 1996).; Rene Latourelle, *The Miracles of Jesus and*

evidence that certain transpersonal approaches to depth psychology are more interdisciplinary.[21]

When philosophy addresses itself to the related issues of progress, power, and social theory and other aspects of postmodern discourse, while depth psychological conceptions related to Freud are abundant, there is little of Jung on synchronicity, or the miraculous in a theological register present.[22]

In science, the new physics is frequently popularized to emphasize its parallels with certain aspects of Eastern religion and mysticism, and to elucidate the concept of synchronicity, but rarely to pursue similar aims with regard to the miraculous in biblical religion.[23]

the Theology of Miracles, trans. Matthew J. O'Connell (Mahwah, New York: Paulist Press, 1988).; Bruce Kaye and John Rogerson, Miracles and Mysteries in the Bible (Philadelphia: The Westminster Press, 1978).; Herman Hendrickx, The Miracle Stories of the Synoptic Gospels (San Francisco: Harper & Row, Publishers, 1987).

[21]In Bruce W. Scotton, Allan B. Chinen, and John R. Battista, eds. Textbook of Transpersonal Psychiatry and Psychology (New York: BasicBooks, 1996), synchronicity is referred to on p. 41, and miracles are referred to on p. 190, in connection with psi phenomena, although synchronicity and miracles are not linked directly in these discussions.

[22]Jurgen Habermas, The Philosophical Discourse of Modernity: Twelve Lectures, trans. Frederick Lawrence (Cambridge, MA: The MIT Press, 1987); Thomas Docherty, ed. Postmodernism: A Reader (New York: Columbia University Press, 1993); in a related vein, T. Byram Karasu, Deconstruction of Psychotherapy (Northvale, NJ: Jason Aronson Inc., 1996), borrowing from Fukuyama's The End of History and the Last Man, says, "the end of history can also lay the groundwork for a universal foundation that surpasses all of its successive events and ideas. Just as Fukuyama is concerned with the long-term effects of rival ideologies, and with the 'final forms' that mark the [end of humanity's evolutionary progress] so I am anticipating here the final fate of psychotherapy and the psychotherapist's ideological as well as practical endpoint – the so-called last therapist....The final surviving clinician is the one who shall endure all of the conceptual schisms and schemas that predated him [or her]," 131-2.

[23]F. David Peat, Synchronicity: The Bridge Between Matter and Mind (New York:

Also, in popular culture, there is a well-spring of interest in angels, psychic and other paranormal phenomena, mind-body medicine, and non-traditional alternatives to education, healing, and self-help, which frequently involve the miraculous and synchronicity. Such trends are not yet being fully addressed in mainstream scholarly discourse.[24]

In addition to the conceptual gaps outlined above, there exist serious epistemological conflicts over truth claims regarding the supernatural, the occult, and the paranormal, whether the context is depth psychology or religion.[25] The book seeks to begin to address, in a fuller and more overarching way, integrated approaches to some of the disjunctions, absences, omissions, minimizations, or repressions on the depth psychology-religion interface. Let us now

Bantam Books, 1987).

[24]For example, *A Course in Miracles*, 3 vols. (Mill Valley: CA: Foundation for Inner Peace, 1992), and the various writings of Deepak Chopra.

[25]Jerome Frank's *Persuasion and Healing: A Comparative Study of Psychotherapy*, offers sociological and phenomenological perspectives on natural-scientific and religio-magical psychotherapeutic healing. His distinctions between scientific and religious approaches to healing help us to continue to find ways to honor, harness, and extend both scientific and religious systems for psychotherapeutic applications in a more integrated manner. Mircea Eliade's classic, *Shamanism: Archaic Techniques of Ecstasy*, looks at distinctly religious and magical approaches to healing based on anthropological and phenomenological understandings.

William James' method of pragmatism is a guiding beacon supporting the adoption of whatever works from the domains of science, psychology, and religion in the healing endeavor, as opposed to an approach based in one or another single constricting ideology in science, religion, or psychology. My experience of fragmentation in this area, and my subsequent determination to pursue synthesis, started as an undergraduate, when I tried as a biology major, to integrate science and spirituality in my senior thesis entitled "Split-brain Research as it Elucidates the Concept of Mental Unity." Admittedly this now seems like a feeble attempt from my current perspective, but at the time it seemed heroic (although perhaps quixotic) in view of the unrelenting and exclusionary devotion to empiricism and logical positivism in the science department of my college at the time. See fuller autobiographical treatment in Chapter Two.

take a closer look at my focus on African American social cultural formation.

African American Social Cultural Formation

As a special focus within the audience concerned with pastoral psychotherapy, I devote Chapter Five of this study to African American social cultural formation in relation to biblical psychotherapy and synchronicity and the miraculous. African American social cultural formation is a significant context in which one can find the four arenas noted above – culture, academia, the church, and clinical work – in microcosm, all interacting at the same time.

Vincent L. Wimbush sharpens the focus on the significance of attending to African American social cultural formation in relation to the Bible in the following manner:

> The fathoming of the functions and understandings and uses of the Bible in contemporary African American society and culture should direct more attention upon an analysis of the problematics of the interaction of society and culture and sacred texts in general. The very broaching of the African American experience should cause dis-ease, a shaking of the historicism and, in all too many places old and new, the theological foundationalism that has been the hallmark of biblical studies. From the perspective of the African experience in the Americas nothing now seems natural or given. Now everything requires explanation, argument, a rationale. Sacred text? The Bible? These very categories now require more sharply critical consideration. If not the categories themselves, are the phenomena behind the categories universal? Or are the matters basically western? Addressing the issue is important. With African Americans in the foreground the addressing of the issue is critical; it is where the probing must begin. So – the Bible and African American society and culture? The "Bible" here to begin with clearly cannot be understood as a transcendent, ahistorical force; it must be seen as a decidedly sociocultural, political, historical construction but as such a nonetheless dangerous and powerful

force. The danger and power and volatility of the construction are such that those dominant peoples most intimately associated with and clearly defined by the construction could never really decide whether those they enslaved and

defined as "other" should be thoroughly inculturated through the agency of the Bible or should be kept far away from it. African slaves, for the most part, were also wary of and hesitant about the locus of power that the whites called "the Scriptures."[26]

As will be demonstrated in Chapter Five, approaching the pastoral care endeavor in the context of African American social cultural formation and the Bible, on the intra, inter, and trans levels yields rich results.[27]

I have chosen African American social cultural formation in relation to the Bible and biblical psychotherapy as a significant aspect of my investigation because I am an African American; because I was raised in Ghana until the age of seventeen; and because I am fluent in the Akan language, and familiar with the Akan world-view, one of many belonging to the people of Ghana (see fuller autobiographical presentation in Chapter Two).

Also, given that my mother is a white American and my father is a black African, I struggle to appropriate and integrate white European and American depth psychological and theological

---

[26]Vincent L. Wimbush, "Reading Darkness, Reading Scriptures," in *African Americans and the Bible: Sacred Texts and Social Textures*, (New York: Continuum, 2000), ed. Vincent L. Wimbush, 14-5; see also Wimbush's *The Bible and African Americans: A Brief History*, Minneapolis: Fortress Press, 2003, and also "The Bible and African Americans: An Outline of an Interpretive History," in *Stony the Road We Trod: African American Biblical Interpretation*, ed. Cain Hope Felder (Minneapolis: Fortress Press, 1991).

[27]Ever since Professor Wimbush invited me into the discourse on African American social cultural formation in relation to the Bible, I have been exploring the connections this discourse and synchronicity and the miraculous on the intra, inter, and trans levels.

traditions using my method, without being untrue to my black African identity and heritage. This struggle for a more personal and professional integration, harmonization, and balance between black and white traditions in my methodological formation has been especially important for me to be involved in because white European

and American depth psychological and theological traditions have been dominant in most of my formal training.

Also, I focus on African American social cultural formation because of my own direct personal experiences of oppression through white anti-black racism. Also, I maintain this focus as a student of broader institutional trends towards non-racist Pan-Africanism,[28] on the part of people of African descent who, while being race-conscious, do not want to be guilty of black anti-white racism.[29]

There are several additional questions related to African American social cultural formation that, while important, cannot be addressed here, although they serve as a backdrop to the topic. What can depth psychology learn regarding how to address questions of race and racism from the rich resources of black psychological, biblical, and theological discourse? How can depth psychology be adapted from a primarily white enterprise into one that is a more trustworthy tool of healing change in, and for, black

---

[28]Kwame Anthony Appiah, *In My Father's House: Africa in the Philosophy of Culture* (New York: Oxford University Press, 1992), ix, provides me with this understanding of non-racist Pan-Africanism. Also, I believe my method of integration is motivated by multidetermined drives to reconcile opposites of all sorts in my life. Also see *It's the Little Things: Everyday Interactions that Anger, Annoy, and Divide the Races*, (New York: Harcourt, 2000), by Lena Williams.

[29]See description of the synchronistic dream in Chapter Two, related to Professor Wimbush, which further clarified the amazing and miraculous quality for me of my being included in The African Americans and the Bible Research Project, and which has been a such watershed for my work.

communities? How can depth psychology enrich the approaches of black psychological, theological, and biblical discourse? What are some of the approaches used by African American communities when it comes to understanding synchronicity and miraculous healing? What can we learn about the relationship between depth psychology and African American religious experiences of synchronicity and the miraculous as signs of God's liberating action in the face of racial oppression and injustice?[30] Have the combination of various African religious backgrounds and the distinctive experiences of oppression and injustice that African Americans have suffered caused African Americans to give more credence to the miraculous?[31] Also, has this combination of religion

---

[30]Charles H. Long, *Significations: Signs, Symbols, and Images in the Interpretation of Religion* (Philadelphia: Fortress Press, 1986).

[31]One of the interesting challenges of this study has been that, often, I have experienced two extreme reactions from various dialogue partners along the way regarding the African American social cultural formation focus on synchronicity and the miraculous: one reaction is that it must be obvious to me that Africans, and therefore African Americans, are more invested in the supernatural world and therefore are more invested in the miraculous. At present, I do not necessarily agree or disagree with this observation. It just has not been the main question of interest to me – this frequently surprises my dialogue partners. My actual interest is in an intuition that if one must generalize here, then I would say that "white" cultures probably resist the supernatural and the miraculous and synchronicity in ways that appear more obvious than "black" cultures, in favor of the scientific and that this imbalance needs to be corrected; at the same time I would say that "black" cultures resist the scientific in favor of the supernatural, the miraculous, more obviously than white cultures do, and that this imbalance also needs to be corrected. In other words, just as depth psychology has something valuable to offer theology and vice versa, and as synchronicity has something valuable to offer the miraculous and vice versa, so also, do black cultures have something valuable to offer white cultures and vice versa regarding synchronicity and the miraculous. The way the discussions usually go, however, my dialogue partners tend to try and privilege the supernatural experience of Africans and African Americans – this usually feels like a form of resistance by white dialogue partners to the true miraculous for themselves because

31

and oppression led to greater dependence on miracle-tinged pathways to deliverance in these communities? How can the insights garnered from these investigations be applied to the even further refinement of strategies for improved and healthier functioning in African American and other communities?[32]

It is one of the significant findings of this study that there have been no major studies or practical systems of psychological and theological helping focused on the integration of synchronicity from a depth psychological perspective with the miraculous from a theological perspective in mainstream academia, the church world, or the clinical world. Another finding of this study is that, if there is an absence of integration regarding synchronicity and the miraculous for the mainstream arenas described above, it is even more true with regard to pastoral psychotherapy in relation to the Bible and African American social cultural formation. One of the major purposes of this study has been to provide a workable system for responding to these findings.

it feels as though they are saying the supernatural belongs exclusively to primitive exotic black people; at the same time black dialogue partners resist the integrated focus I am advancing by pridefully assuming for themselves and black people an inside track regarding the supernatural and the miraculous. Neither of these fairly commonly held positions is what I am interested in advancing here; nor is it really the main thrust of my interest in this study – integrating the benefits from the two cultural perspectives is what is essentially of interest to me.

[32] Such strategies for improved functioning are needed for problems arising from racism; abuses of power by various leaders; family and relational dysfunctions; sexism and conflicted and unintegrated sexual experience; and economic disempowerment and meaningless work to mention but a few areas. See Delores S. Williams, *Sisters in the Wilderness: The Challenge of Womanist God-Talk* (Maryknoll, NY: Orbis Books, 1993). Virginia Fabella and Mercy Amba Oduyoye, ed. *With Passion and Compassion: Third World Women Doing Theology* (Maryknoll, NY: Orbis Books, 1996). Mercy Amba Oduyoye, *Hearing and Knowing: Theological Reflections on Christianity in Africa* (Maryknoll, NY: Orbis Books, 1986).

In other words, much to my surprise, my research for this study has not uncovered significant mainstream or African and African American approaches to the questions about the integrated relationship between synchronicity and the miraculous I am most interested in pursuing from the perspectives of depth psychology and theology presented here. As a result this study addresses the question of how an integrated approach to synchronicity and the miraculous can be created, and what it might begin to look like?

African American Social Cultural Formation, the Bible, and Psychotherapy

My involvement in The African Americans and the Bible Research Project under the leadership of Professor Vincent L. Wimbush[33], from 1998 to 2000, helped me focus my work not only on the study of synchronicity and the miraculous as this pertains to my academic and clinical work in general, but deepened my interest in making a contribution to understanding how a focus on synchronicity and the miraculous is engaged in by African American scholars, clinicians, and patients who are actively exploring and even wrestling with their relationship to the Bible.

As I explored whether or not such a focus on synchronicity and the miraculous exists with regard to African Americans and the Bible in psychotherapy, I discovered that I would need to do so in a

---

[33]For me, Professor Wimbush and my work for him in the project, as well as my involvement in the large community of African and African American scholars participating in the project were the manifestations and embodiments of the promises I received from a wisdom figure in a synchronistic dream, promises that I could learn richly about my African heritage, and that I would also be led into a deeper understanding of synchronicity and the miraculous at the same time. See Chapter Two for an account of the dream in which this wisdom figure – appearing as Professor Wimbush – came to me, and for a fuller description of The African Americans and the Bible Research Project.

more explicitly psychodynamic framework, and so I began to use the phrase "African American biblical psychotherapy" to refer to just such a framework. This is a phrase I use to refer to psychodynamic psychotherapy practiced by African American psychotherapists with African American clients in which the Bible is a central source of understanding regarding the healing process for both the psychotherapists and clients. By "psychodynamic" I am referring to counseling and psychotherapy based on an understanding and acceptance of a full range of unconscious processes in the psyche.

It would be going too far for me to say that this is currently a broadly recognizable school of psychotherapy, although there are models of psychology, counseling, and psychotherapy that are strongly based on the Bible which are predominant in conservative and primarily white conservative Christian circles. These tend not to be strongly psychodynamic.

There are also many fundamentalist, pentecostal, and evangelical Bible-based African American counseling systems which again are not deeply psychodynamic.[34] African American biblical psychotherapy refers then to psychodynamic understandings of, and approaches to, psychotherapy in which African American psychotherapists and clients employ the Bible in central ways in the therapeutic process.[35]

---

[34]These understandings of the absence of psychodynamic thinking and practice in the more conservative circles of Christian ministry are based on my experiences as a teacher at the Blanton-Peale Graduate Institute. There we had many black and white conservative students in the Pastoral Studies Program for whom the program was the first serious exposure to psychodynamic thinking in relation to Christian counseling.

[35]Also, because the limited literature on African American biblical psychotherapy contains almost nothing about synchronicity and the miraculous (a significant finding of this study in and of itself), I decided to use my method to try and understand the reasons for this absence, and also to see if these phenomena were

STRUCTURE

IN CHAPTER ONE, in order to provide a context in which to explain and explore the thesis of this study more completely, we must start with comprehensive descriptions of synchronicity and the miraculous. In this chapter we also explore a simultaneous and integrated embrace of synchronicity and the miraculous based on six major parallels between synchronicity and the miraculous.

In Chapter Two, I describe three conversion experiences which touch on the supernatural, as well as on synchronicity and the miraculous, using the ego-Self framework and the soul-God framework. It is these personal experiences and this evolution which serve as major original reasons for my interest in this topic. The focus in this chapter is also on how disciplined attention to personal coincidences, synchronicities, and the miraculous can build up into a passion for learning and teaching about synchronicity and the miraculous simultaneously in a way that is relevant to others.

The remainder of the book explores for the presence or absence of integrated approaches to the intra, inter, and trans levels based on the ego-Self framework in depth psychology and the soul-God framework in theology. We are also looking for the presence or absence of evidence of an awareness of the *simultaneous* relationship between synchronicity and the miraculous, i.e., the exploration of how people employ or omit these various elements.

In Chapter Three, I explore more fully the intra, the inter, and the trans levels of theory in depth psychology as these relate to synchronicity and the miraculous simultaneously. This is done through the work of Freud, Klein, Winnicott, Kohut, Stern, Jung, and Ulanov.

actually being addressed but in disguised or muted ways.

Chapters Four and Five follow a format similar to that of Chapter Three. In Chapter Four, the focus shifts to an exploration of the intra, inter, and trans levels in relation to synchronicity and the miraculous using the work of Feuerbach, Kelsey, Kee, Hume, Easton, and Ulanov.

Chapter Five addresses African American social cultural formation, the Bible, and psychotherapy through an exploration of intra, inter, and trans levels in relation to synchronicity and the miraculous. [36] This is done through four African American interpretive processes – those of Cleage, Wimberly, Walker, and

---

[36]Also, I include this chapter on African American social cultural formation because I am looking to create an integrated depth psychological and theological model that might appeal to Africans and African Americans who otherwise would be suspicious of depth psychological and theological model of treatment dominated by Euro-American perspectives. Put another way, I have included in this study, a treatment of synchronicity and the miraculous in relation African American social cultural formation, the Bible, and psychotherapy, first of all, as my own response to the following query: "What is the relationship between African, American, and European elements in African American self-identity when it comes to the use of synchronicity and the miraculous in African culture in general, and psychotherapy involving the Bible in particular?" This question is adapted from Cornell West's *Prophecy Deliverance! An Afro-American Revolutionary Christianity* (Philadelphia: Westminster Press, 1982), 24, as he is cited by Theophus H. Smith in *Conjuring Culture: Biblical Formations of Black America* (New York: Oxford University Press, 1994), 140-1: "Precisely because magical categories are so vexed or problematic in contemporary academic discourse, I have chosen the expedient of framing this philosophical discussion in terms of the wisdom traditions of African and African American oral cultures. Before proceeding, however, it is illuminating to note how the African American philosopher Cornel West has addressed such problems of discourse in black studies. For his part, West is not as optimistic as many 'Afrocentric' scholars about efforts 'to articulate a competing Afro-American philosophy based principally on African norms and notions.' In West's judgment, 'it is likely that the result would be theoretically thin,' not, however, because African cultures lack the materials for discursive depth, but because African American thought is ineluctably more American than African' " While Smith seeks to answer the question posed above about African, American, and European elements in African American self-identity through the convergence of Afro-American and Euro-American trajectories in black America's cognitive styles and sensibilities with regard to conjure, I frame an initial response to the same question in this study, but in relation to synchronicity and the miraculous, African and African American social cultural formation, and the Bible in psychotherapy." Also see *Postcolonial African Philosophy: A Critical Reader*, Cambridge, MA: Blackwell Publishers, 1997, ed., Emmanuel Chukwudi Eze.

Lee. It is expected that the explorations in this chapter can make a distinctive contribution to African and African American depth psychology, in a manner that is theologically and spiritually alert and informed. [37]

---

[37]In African American social cultural formation with regard to the Bible and biblical psychotherapy, while there is much attention in Christian theology, to the hand of God in setting captives free from slavery and racism, there is little in the way of specific explicit attention to the rich possibilities of linking African and African-derived understandings about divination and the supernatural to Western depth psychological and religious approaches to synchronicity and the miraculous. At the same time, further work is needed about the distinctions between forms of divination and the miraculous which are biblically acceptable and those which are not. See M.G. Easton's treatment of the biblically true and false, the acceptable and unacceptable, with regard to divination in the following excerpt, and on various categories of the supernatural ("signs and wonders," "prophet," "seer," "soothsayer," "sorcerer," "stargazers," "witchcraft," "wizard," and the like) throughout Easton's Dictionary of the Bible, Illustrated Bible Dictionary, Third Edition, Thomas Nelson, 1897: "Of false prophets (Deut. 18:10, 14; Micah 3:6, 7, 11), of necromancers (1 Sam. 28:8), of the Philistine priests and diviners (1 Sam. 6:2), of Balaam (Josh. 13:22). Three kinds of divination are mentioned in Ezek. 21:21, by arrows, consulting with images (the teraphim), and by examining the entrails of animals sacrificed. The practice of this art seems to have been encouraged in ancient Egypt. Diviners also abounded among the aborigines of Canaan and the Philistines (Isa. 2:6; 1 Sam. 28). At a later period multitudes of magicians poured from Chaldea and Arabia into the land of Israel, and pursued their occupations (Isa. 8:19; 2 Kings 21:6; 2 Chr. 33:6). This superstition widely spread, and in the time of the apostles there were "vagabond...exorcists" (Acts 19:13), and men like Simon Magus (Acts 8:9), Bar-jesus (Acts 13:6, 8), and other jugglers and impostors (Acts 19:19; 2 Tim. 3:13). Every species and degree of this superstition was strictly forbidden by the law of Moses (Ex. 22:18; Lev. 19:26, 31; 20:27; Deut. 18:10, 11). But beyond these various forms of superstition, there are instances of divination on record in the Scriptures by which God was pleased to make known his will. (1.) There was divination by lot, by which, when resorted to in matters of moment, and with solemnity, God intimated his will (Josh. 7:13). The land of Canaan was divided by lot (Num. 26:55, 56); Achan's guilt was detected (Josh. 7:16-19), Saul was elected king (1 Sam. 10:20, 21), and Matthias chosen to the apostleship, by the solemn lot (Acts 1:26). It was thus also that the scape-goat was determined (Lev. 16:8-10). (2.) There was divination by dreams (Gen. 20:6; Deut. 13:1, 3; Judg. 7:13, 15; Matt. 1:20; 2:12, 13, 19, 22). This is

The book closes in Chapter Six, with a review of the most significant results of the entire exploration, and with indications of where further work can be pursued most profitably.

illustrated in the history of Joseph (Gen. 41:25-32) and of Daniel (Dan. 2:27; 4:19-28). (3.) By divine appointment there was also divination by the Urim and Thummim (Num. 27:21), and by the ephod. (4.) God was pleased sometimes to vouchsafe direct vocal communications to men (Deut. 34:10; Ex. 3:4; 4:3; Deut. 4:14, 15; 1 Kings 19:12). He also communed with men from above the mercy-seat (Ex. 25:22), and at the door of the tabernacle (Ex. 29:42, 43). (5.) Through his prophets God revealed himself, and gave intimations of his will (2 Kings 13:17; Jer. 51:63, 64)."

1. DEFINITIONS AND PARALLELS

SYNCHRONICITY

JUNG,[38] VON FRANZ[39], and Aziz refer to synchronicities as the meaningful parallels of inner and outer events for the experiencer, parallels in which these inner and outer events have not caused one another. In particular, Jung provides the following meanings of synchronicity:

> I would like to call attention to a possible misunderstanding which may be occasioned by the term "synchronicity." I chose this term because the simultaneous occurrence of two meaningfully but not causally connected events seemed to me an essential criterion. I am therefore using the general concept of synchronicity in the special sense of a coincidence in time of two or more causally unrelated events which have the same or a similar meaning, in contrast to "synchronism," which simply means the simultaneous occurrence of two events.

---

[38]Carl Gustav Jung (1875-1961) "ranks in importance only to Freud in the history of psychoanalysis....Born in Switzerland, Jung received his medical degree from the University of Zurich where he wrote a dissertation on the pathology of occult phenomena," http://www.apsa-co.org/ctf/pubinfo/bios/jung.html.

[39]"Marie-Louise von Franz, Ph.D. (1915-1998), worked closely with Jung from 1934 until his death in 1961. She is the author of many books on Jungian psychology," http://www.innercitybooks.net/.

Synchronicity therefore means the simultaneous occurrence of a certain psychic state with one or more external events which appear as meaningful parallels to the momentary subjective state.[40]

Von Franz adds to these meanings as follows:

synchronicity is constituted by the coincidence or simultaneity of two psychic states, that is, a normal psychic state that can be adequately explained causally and another, not derivable from it, that is the critical experience which is not causally connected with the first and the objectivity of which can only be verified later.[41]

Aziz elaborates yet further by stating the following:

Synchronicity, it will suffice to say...describes the meaningful paralleling of inner and outer events. These events, which by definition are not causally related to each other, are understood to be manifestations of a type of orderedness in nature itself – an acausal orderedness, to be sure, that transcends space and time. As a simple example of a synchronistic experience we could take the following. An individual dreams that a friend, someone whom he has not seen or heard from in many years, comes to his house to visit with him. The next day, having received no previous notice of his friend's planned trip with the exception of the dream, that same individual finds his friend at his front door. This is what Jung described as a synchronistic experience, for there is a meaningful paralleling of two causally unrelated events – the inner event being the dream image, the corresponding external event being the arrival of the friend.[42]

---

[40]C. G. Jung, *Synchronicity: An Acausal Connecting Principle*, trans. R. F. C. Hull, 1973 ed., Bollingen Series (Princeton, N.J.: Princeton University Press, 1960), 25.

[41]Marie-Louise von Franz, *Psyche and Matter* (Boston: Shambhala Publications, Inc., 1992), 23-4.

[42]Robert Aziz, C. G. Jung's *Psychology of Religion and Synchronicity*, (Albany, N.Y.:

In addition to their definitions of synchronicity above, Jung, von Franz, and Aziz emphasize the *connection* between synchronicity and psychological transformation towards wholeness. For instance, according to von Franz,

> In the course of observing the effects of activated archetypes or patterns of psychological reactions in his patients, Jung again and again encountered cases where rare outer chance events tended to coincide meaningfully with archetypal dream images. Such cases seem to occur only when an archetype is activated producing highly charged conscious and unconscious emotions. The following may serve as an illustration. A woman with a very strong power complex, and a "devouring" attitude toward people, dreamt of seeing three tigers seated threateningly in front of her. Her analyst pointed out the meaning of the dream and through causal arguments tried to make her understand the devouring attitude which she thus displayed. Later in the day the patient and her friend, while strolling along Lake Zurich, noticed a crowd gazing at three tigers in a barn – most unusual inhabitants for a Swiss barn!

Taken separately, the causal background of the two events seems clear. The power display in the woman probably brought about her tiger dream as a warning illustration of what was constellated in her. The three real tigers were in that barn because a circus was spending the night in town. But the highly improbable coincidence of the inner and outer three tigers in this woman's life seems to have no common cause, and therefore it inevitably struck her as "more than mere chance" and somehow as "meaningful."[43]

State University of New York Press, 1990), 1. Robert Aziz, Ph.D. was a therapist in private practice in London, Ontario, at the time this book was published. At that time, he was also, a sessional lecturer in the faculty of Part-Time and Continuing Education at the University of Western Ontario where he taught Jungian Psychology.

[43]Von Franz, 298-9.

In such a way synchronicities can get our attention about things we need to transform in order to change towards greater wholeness.

THE MIRACULOUS

THE OXFORD DICTIONARY of the Christian Church says the following about conceptions related to the term miracle:

> *According to the traditional view, a miracle is a sensible fact...produced by the special intervention of God for a religious end, transcending the normal order of things usually termed the Law of Nature. The possibility of miracles began to be questioned with the rise of modern science in the 17th and 18th centuries with its ever growing tendency to regard the world in which we live as a closed system, subject to the laws of nature, and to exclude all interference from a higher power. Neither pantheism which identifies God with the Law of Nature, nor Deism which separates God from the world, nor 18th century thought as represented by the skepticism of D. Hume[44], accorded a place to supernatural intervention. Thus the miracles of Scripture and Church history were normally regarded as facts within the sphere of natural explanation, misrepresented by credulous contemporaries, and the term "miracle" came to be treated as a cover for human ignorance....*
>
> *In support of the traditional belief it is argued that on a genuinely theistic view miracles are not only possible but even probable, for if God is held to be the supreme First Cause responsible for, but not subject to, the Laws of Nature, it would be likely that He [sic] should from time to time, act directly without the intervention of secondary causes. The latest developments in the field of science, which move further and further away from a hard-and-fast determinism, may indicate an approaching reconciliation between Christian tradition and modern scientific research.*

---

[44]Chapter Four takes up a much closer and nuanced assessment of Hume on the miraculous.

> *Whereas Protestant orthodoxy normally confines itself to belief in the miracles recorded in Scripture, Catholic orthodoxy claims that miracles have at all times occurred within the pale of the Church. The reputed cures at Lourdes are among the best known, and according to Roman Catholic canon law, two to four well-authenticated miracles after death are required for the beatification of a saint, though belief in any of these miracles is not demanded of the faithful.*[45]

Geddes MacGregor, in a similar vein, yet with some nuanced differences, says of the term "miracle," that it

> *Is from the Latin miraculum, meaning simply a wonder: any extraordinary occurrence. The Greek words used in the New Testament for what has been traditionally rendered "miracle" are semeion (a sign, visible indication of secret power or divine truth) and teras (a wonder, an extraordinary act or happening), for example in Acts 14:3: semeia kai terata (signs and wonders). Modern translators, seeing that "miracle" has become too "loaded" a word in English, generally prefer to use "sign." Traditionally, a miracle was interpreted as an act or event transcending the "laws" of nature. Such a possibility was denied not only by Hume but by Spinoza and Hegel and by the 18th century deists whose mechanistic universe caused them to see miracles as God's tinkering with the machine he [sic] had created, as though he must have botched it in the first place. Although some Christians today insist on upholding the traditional understanding of miracle as a suspension of the laws of nature, many educated Christians prefer to see the universe as portrayed by modern physicists as providing scope for accommodating the miraculous. Modern parapsychology, moreover, can interpret some events that would have been in the past accounted miraculous in ways that do not introduce a conflict between "science" and religion. For example, hypnotism and telepathy are widely recognized phenomena. Alexis Carrel, an eminent French medical man and Nobel laureate testifies to seeing at Lourdes a cancerous sore shrivel to a scar before*

---

[45]F.L Cross and E.A. Livingstone, ed., *The Oxford Dictionary of the Christian Church*, (New York: Oxford University Press, 1983), 920.

his eyes, in the course of prayer for healing. This sort of event need not call for belief in suspensions of the "laws" of nature. It may call, rather for a deeper perception of the presence of spiritual dimensions within the universe that are ordinarily untapped.[46]

The study of signs is central to the study of miracles in the Bible. According to *The Interpreter's Dictionary of the Bible* the word-combination "signs and wonders"

Appears many times in the Bible and may be called a traditional formula....Of the approximately thirty-five occurrences of the word 'wonder' in the [Old Testament], eighteen instances are parallel to, and nine are practically synonymous with, the word sign, for the meanings of the word overlap....Israel's confession of faith, as expressed in the ancient cultic credo, included the affirmation that Yahweh brought his people out of Egypt 'with signs and wonders'....This formula, which witnesses to Israel's faith in Yahweh as the Lord of history...is found again and again....In the [New Testament] the word 'wonder'...never occurs by itself but always as a plural form in conjunction with 'signs'....[47]

Furthermore, according to the The Interpreter's Dictionary of the Bible,

---

[46]Geddes MacGregor, *Dictionary of Religion and Philosophy*, (New York: Paragon House, 1991), 416-7. He has been a minister of the Church of Scotland, with doctorates from the Sorbonne and from Oxford, and has been Rufus Jones Professor of Philosophy and Religion at Bryn Mawr College and Dean of the Graduate School of Religion at the University of Southern California, http://theologytoday.ptsem.edu/jul1960/v17-2-bookreview13.htm. See also, David Ray Griffen, *Parapsychology, Philosophy, and Spirituality: A Postmodern Exploration*, (Albany: State University of New York Press, 1997), and C. E. M. Hansel, *ESP and Parapsychology: A Critical Reevaluation*, (Buffalo: Prometheus Books, 1980).

[47]A. G. Buttrick, ed. *The Interpreter's Dictionary of the Bible*, (Nashville: Abingdon Press, 1986), 348.

The frequent association of biblical words for 'wonder' with signs suggests another characteristic of biblical miracles. Not only do they witness to the wonderful character of God's actions, but they also have the effect of confirming the word of God, spoken in threat or promise, disfavor or favor. A sign stands in close, but subordinate, relation to the prophetic word, adding a kind of evidential support in experience....A sign makes an impact upon the senses, especially the sense of sight. In the [Old Testament] the word [sign] is used with a variety of meanings, such as a marker, signal, token, ensign, omen, etc. A common denominator among all these meanings is that a sign is characterized by visibility or historical concreteness. When used in connection with 'miracle,' a sign is a visible indicator which points to the invisible power and activity of God in the world. Frequently signs are given in connection with a divine commission, as evidence of God's promise: "I will be with you."[48]

Here, we see the linkages between the terms "sign," "wonder," and "miracle." When the earlier definitions of synchronicity are juxtaposed with these definitions of the miraculous, we can begin to discern a resonance between both synchronistic events and miracles, although such resonances between synchronicity and the miraculous are rarely been studied systematically.[49]

---

[48]Ibid., 349.

[49]Additional Definitions: while the terms below are all relevant to the study of synchronicity and the miraculous, their relevance is beyond the scope of this particular study. It must be sufficient for now to define them briefly in order to keep each one of them apart from our definitions of synchronicity and the miraculous. The Supernatural – invisible powers that influence human reality but are normally beyond our everyday natural powers of perception. The Occult – secret knowledge by which those in the know harness the power of the supernatural for their purposes. Magic – the use of techniques such as charms, spells, and rituals for harnessing supernatural forces to achieve specific aims such as healings or attacks on others; it can also refer to the creation of illusions by trickery. Superstition – the ignorant attribution of effects to wrong causes, often thought to be supernatural, and usually based on lack of informed scientific understanding. The Paranormal – unusual psychological phenomena such as telepathy, clairvoyance, and psychokinesis. Parapsychology – the scientific investigation of evidence for paranormal phenomena.

SIX PARALLELS

THIS STUDY PRESENTS six main parallels between synchronicity and the miraculous which are derived from the definitions above. These parallels are as follows:

1) in experiences of synchronicity as well as in experiences of the miraculous, the **inner and outer realities** of the experiencer correlate;

2) in both types of experiences, the experiencer is engaged in something felt to be **very meaningful and the experiencer responds with great amazement**;

3) concepts about **acausality regarding synchronicity are analogous to concepts about God in definitions of the miraculous**;

4) in both kinds of experiences, after either a synchronicity or miracle, there are often **significant disruptions in understanding** for the experiencer;

5) in synchronicity and the miraculous, **often significant transformations in a positive direction** occur for the experiencer; and

6) in experiences of synchronicity **the ego-Self framework is a parallel to the soul-God framework** in experiences of the miraculous.

The First, Second, and Third Parallels Between Synchronicity and the Miraculous

That there are major parallels between synchronicity and the miraculous, beyond my own initial hunches that this might be so, first became evident to me through comparisons of definitions from Ann Ulanov and Paul Tillich. There are three main parallels to be discerned by comparing Ulanov's and Tillich's definitions of synchronicities and miracles: 1) in both synchronicities and miracles, there is an alignment between inner and outer reality for the experiencer; 2) this alignment creates deep meaning for the experiencer in a synchronicity, and in a miracle creates amazement for the experiencer; and 3) synchronicities arise from the acausal dimension of the psyche according to Jung, von Franz, and Aziz. I see this acausal dimension in synchronicities as a parallel to God's role in the miraculous, or what Tillich puts forth as the "giving side of the revelatory experience" in miracles.

Parallel 1: Let us now take a closer look at the definitions of Ulanov and Tillich in order to capture these three parallels more fully. Ulanov illuminates our understanding of synchronicity in a depth psychological context by explaining that

> *Examples of synchronistic events occur frequently in analysis of unconscious contents where meaningful parallelism between psychic and physical events takes place. A dream may refer to life events which happen after the dream rather than before it. Similar or identical thoughts or dreams may occur in different places at the same time.* [50]

Ann Ulanov is of further help in explicating the connection between inner psychological events and outer physical ones in synchronicities, and she also suggests something of the subjective hermeneutic mindset needed to interpret such experiences as meaningful. Commenting on Jung's approach to synchronicities, Ulanov says the following:

> *In his study of the Self as it is increasingly manifest in the individuation process, Jung formulated the concept of synchronicity which postulated an acausal*

---

[50] Ann Belford, "A Consideration of C. G. Jung's Psychology of the Feminine and Its Implications for Christian Theology" (Ph.D. diss., Union Theological Seminary, 1967), 108.

connecting principle between meaningful coincidences. Causality which functions within spatio-temporal dimensions does not apply to unconscious processes, particularly when the objective psyche has been activated

The determination of the event as synchronistic depends on whether or not it is experienced as meaningful, which is an individual subjective response. The empirical material from which conclusions are drawn are just these subjective experiences. On this subjective basis it is known that synchronistic events occur often with profound effect on the individual.[51]

Paul Tillich gives the following definition of the miraculous:

The sign-events in which the mystery of being gives itself consists in special constellations of elements of reality in correlation with special elements of the mind. A genuine miracle is first of all an event that is astonishing, unusual, shaking, without contradicting the rational structure of reality. In the second place, it is an event which points to the mystery of being, expressing its relation to us in a definite way. In the third place, it is an occurrence which is received as a sign-event in an ecstatic experience. Only if these three conditions are fulfilled can one speak of a genuine miracle.[52]

Juxtaposing the definitions of synchronicity and the miraculous highlights their similarities, especially when we note that Ulanov refers to synchronicities as "events [which] occur frequently in analysis of unconscious contents where meaningful parallelism between psychic and physical events takes place," and Tillich refers to the miraculous as "special constellations of elements of reality in correlation with special elements of the mind."

---

[51] Ibid., 107–8.

[52] Paul Tillich, *Systematic Theology*, (Chicago: University of Chicago Press, 1951), 1:117.

Parallel 2: Both the depth psychological definition of the synchronistic from Ulanov, and the theological definition of the miraculous from Tillich emphasize a meaningful parallelism between inner psychological states and outer objective physical realities which are unusual, induce wonder, and elicit interpretations related to their high levels of subjective significance to the experiencer. Tillich uses the terms 'astonishing' and 'ecstatic' to describe this amazing subjective quality of miracles; in the case of Ulanov she refers to the example of life events happening in the physical world after they have already "occurred," or been referred to, in a dream (i.e., in the subjective realm) – an amazing sort of experience if one reflects on it for a moment.

Parallel 3: If we keep these two parallels in mind we find a third parallel emphasis between synchronicity and the miraculous. Tillich emphasizes the New Testament link between the terms "sign" and "miraculous wonder," which resonates with Ulanov's implied association of synchronicity and wonder, an association which is present throughout her various works, where the understanding of the Self, the Center of the psyche, continues to be an important aspect of her texts, and is frequently present as a theme in the healing process of analysis.[53] For instance, commenting, by way of a metaphor, on the wondrous (or by implication, miraculous) changes that can manifest in those who progress further towards a connection with the Self, the Center of the psyche, in the process of individuation, Ulanov says:

---

[53] Ann Belford Ulanov, *The Wizard's Gate: Picturing Consciousness* (Einsiedeln, Switzerland: Daimon, 1994), provides a candid account of her countertransference experiences as a clinician, including synchronistic events related to a particularly exhausting case, 97-8.

Our conflicts do not cease but our capacity is greater not to get sweated up into a froth. Others can reach us because we are reached by the Center. So we look the same, perhaps even a little worse for wear. But we take heart from the story about the one who arrived at the Center. He is a rag-man who looks anything but unique or special or the saint he may be, but the cherry tree blossoms as he goes by.[54]

According to Tillich,

The New Testament often uses the Greek word semeion, 'sign,' pointing to the religious meaning of the miracles. But the word "sign" without a qualifying addition cannot express this religious meaning. It would be more accurate to add the word 'event' to 'sign' and to speak of sign-events. The original meaning of miracle, 'that which produces astonishment,' is quite adequate for describing the 'giving side' of a revelatory experience. But this connotation has been swallowed by the bad connotation of a supernatural interference which destroys the natural structure of events. The bad connotation is avoided in the word 'sign' and the phrase 'sign-event.'[55]

Tillich demonstrates a distinctive concern for the sign-interpreting role and the wholeness and integrity of the psyche in the experience of the miraculous, when he insists that we avoid the sense of the miraculous as "an interference which destroys the natural structure of events." It is fine for us to be amazed by the sign-event that reaches us from "the 'giving side'[56] of a revelatory

---

[54] Ann Belford Ulanov, "The Holding Self: Jung and the Desire for Being," *in The Fires of Desire: Erotic Energies and the Spiritual Quest*, ed. Fredrica Halligan and John J. Shea (New York: Crossroad, 1992), 163.

[55] Paul Tillich, "Revelation and Miracle," in *Miracles*, ed. Richard Swinburne (New York: Macmillan Publishing Company, 1989), 71.

[56] The immanent God.

experience", but not to assume that the sign-event is a disruption of reality.

The definitions of synchronicity and the miraculous from Ulanov and Tillich, both include allusions and references to these three significant parallels: a) inner subjective thoughts are reflected in outer physical reality in both synchronicities and miracles; b) as a result of the manner in which these inner and outer realities align, there *are subjective responses* of deep meaning in synchronicities, and *subjective experiences* of great amazement in miracles; and c) there is an essential role played by the Self (the Center of the psyche) in synchronicities, and by the "giving side of a revelatory experience" in the miraculous. In spite of these three significant parallels between synchronicity and the miraculous, richer and more frequent discourse about such parallels between them is relatively underdeveloped in the currently available literature either from depth psychology or from theology.

As we have seen in the preceding quotations, Jung, von Franz, and Aziz all emphasize the concept of acausality in relation to synchronicity. Jung says "I am therefore using the general concept of synchronicity in the special sense of a coincidence in time of **two or more causally unrelated events** which have the same or a similar meaning." Von Franz says "synchronicity is constituted by the coincidence or simultaneity of two psychic states, that is, a normal psychic state that can be adequately explained causally and another, not derivable from it, that is the critical experience which **is not causally connected** with the first." Aziz says, "Synchronicity, it will suffice to say...describes the meaningful paralleling of inner and outer events. These events, which by definition are **not causally related** to each other, are understood to be manifestations of a type of orderedness in nature itself – **an acausal orderedness**, to be sure, that transcends space and time...."

With the help of *The Interpreter's Dictionary of the Bible*'s definition of the miraculous, we see God's role in the miraculous, which is the parallel to the role of acausality in synchronicity, in the following: "Israel's confession of faith, as expressed in the ancient cultic credo, included the affirmation that **Yahweh** brought his people out of Egypt 'with signs and wonders'[miracles]...." Therefore in theology, Yahweh or God is the source of miracles, and can be viewed as a parallel to acausal orderedness as the source of synchronicity in depth psychology.[57]

The Fourth, Fifth, and Sixth Parallels Between Synchronicity and the Miraculous

Parallel 4: This parallel between synchronicity and the miraculous is hinted at in the earlier definitions of the miraculous from MacGregor and Tillich, where we encountered a debate about whether miracles are disruptive with regard to nature or not. We return to this debate once again with the aid of Easton[58] and F.

---

[57]Bold emphases are mine.

[58]"Matthew George Easton (1823-1894) was a Scottish Presbyterian preacher and scholar whose literary achievements included English translations of two of Franz Delitzsch's commentaries," see http://www.laridian.com/order/productpages/LBKEBD001.asp?order_platform=ce. Also see the following: "This bastion of knowledge, written by Matthew George Easton, was published in 1897, three years after his death. Using the most recent information in that day, Easton presented a concise volume that has aided both layman and scholar in their study of God's word," http://www.studylight.org/dic/ebd/). Although Easton, and his work are dated, his inclusion in this study has been made based on the following factors: a) As with many of my choices of material in this study, his work came to me serendipitously – this is in keeping with my approach to bricolage as an aspect of my method; b) Easton's work has enduring popular currency as resource in evangelical circles; c) when addressing the miraculous as a disruption of our understanding of how God works, he sounds remarkably like F. David Peat on how synchronicity is a rip in the fabric of our understanding about how nature works. This exploration of Easton is

David Peat[59] this time. According to *Easton's Bible Dictionary*, a miracle is

---

An event in the external world brought about by the immediate agency or the simple volition of God, operating without the use of means capable of being discerned by the senses, and designed to authenticate the divine commission of a religious teacher and the truth of his message (John 2:18; Matt. 12:38). It is an occurrence at once above nature and above man. It shows the intervention of a power that is not limited by the laws either of matter or of mind, a power interrupting the fixed laws which govern their movements, a supernatural power. "The suspension or violation of the laws of nature involved in miracles is nothing more than is constantly taking place around us. One force counteracts another: vital force keeps the chemical laws of matter in abeyance; and muscular force can control the action of physical force. When a man raises a weight from the ground, the law of gravity is neither suspended nor violated, but counteracted by a stronger force. The same is true as to the walking of Christ on the water and the swimming of iron at the command of the prophet. The simple and grand truth that the universe is not under the exclusive control of physical forces, but that everywhere and always there is above, separate from and superior to all else, an infinite personal will, not superseding, but directing and controlling all physical causes, acting with or without them." God ordinarily effects his purpose through the agency of second causes; but he has the power also of effecting his purpose immediately and without the intervention of second causes, i.e., of invading the fixed order, and thus of working

---

balanced by a use of *The Anchor Bible Commentaries, The Anchor Bible Dictionary, and The New Interpreter's Bible.*

[59] F. David Peat is a physicist and writer who "has worked actively as a theoretical physicist in England and Canada. But Peat's interests expanded to include psychology, particularly that of Carl Jung, art and general aspects of culture, including that of Native America. Peat is the author of many books including a biography of David Bohm, with whom Peat collaborated, books on quantum theory and chaos theory, as well as a study of Synchronicity" See http://www.fdavidpeat.com/biography/biography.htm. Also, see his *Synchronicity: The Bridge Between Matter and Mind* New York: Bantam Books, 1988.

miracles. Thus we affirm the possibility of miracles, the possibility of a higher hand intervening to control or reverse nature's ordinary movements.

Miracles are seals of a divine mission. The sacred writers appealed to them as proofs that they were messengers of God.[60] Our Lord also appealed to miracles as a conclusive proof of his divine mission (John 5:20, 36; 10:25, 38). *Thus, being out of*

---

[60]See these warnings about the need for discernment about false teachers who also work miracles, in themselves a sign of the end of the age: "When he was sitting on the Mount of Olives, the disciples came to him privately, saying, 'Tell us, when will this be, and what will be the sign of your coming and of the end of the age?' Jesus answered them, 'Beware that no one leads you astray. For many will come in my name, saying, 'I am the Messiah!' and they will lead many astray. And you will hear of wars and rumors of wars; see that you are not alarmed; for this must take place, but the end is not yet. For nation will rise against nation, and kingdom against kingdom, and there will be famines and earthquakes in various places: all this is but the beginning of the birth pangs. 'Then they will hand you over to be tortured and will put you to death, and you will be hated by all nations because of my name. Then many will fall away, and they will betray one another and hate one another. And many false prophets will arise and lead many astray. And because of the increase of lawlessness, the love of many will grow cold. But the one who endures to the end will be saved. And this good news of the kingdom will be proclaimed throughout the world, as a testimony to all the nations; and then the end will come. 'So when you see the desolating sacrilege standing in the holy place, as was spoken of by the prophet Daniel (let the reader understand), then those in Judea must flee to the mountains; the one on the housetop must not go down to take what is in the house; the one in the field must not turn back to get a coat. Woe to those who are pregnant and to those who are nursing infants in those days! Pray that your flight may not be in winter or on a sabbath. For at that time there will be great suffering, such as has not been from the beginning of the world until now, no, and never will be. And if those days had not been cut short, no one would be saved; but for the sake of the elect those days will be cut short. Then if anyone says to you, 'Look! Here is the Messiah!' or 'There he is!'—do not believe it. For false messiahs and false prophets will appear and produce great signs and omens, to lead astray, if possible, even the elect. Take note, I have told you beforehand. So, if they say to you, 'Look! He is in the wilderness,' do not go out. If they say, 'Look! He is in the inner rooms,' do not believe it. For as the lightning comes from the east and flashes as far as the west, so will be the coming of the Son of Man. Wherever the corpse is, there the vultures will gather," Matthew 24:3-28.

the common course of nature and beyond the power of man, they are fitted to convey the impression of the presence and power of God. Where miracles are there certainly God is. The man, therefore, who works a miracle affords thereby clear proof that he comes with the authority of God; they are his credentials that he is God's messenger. The teacher points to these credentials, and they are a proof that he speaks with the authority of God. He boldly says, "God bears me witness, both with signs and wonders, and with diverse miracles."[61]

We see here that there is a tension point between how Tillich views the miraculous and how Easton does. The proponents of existential theology, including Tillich, believe that "the course of nature cannot be broken into or interrupted by any powers beyond 'existence;' instead meaning comes to human beings as they authentically live in this immediate, conscious situation. They then discover the ground of their being."[62] If we return for a moment to a section quoted from Easton above we see that he has a point of view about the miraculous, totally opposite to Tillich's view that nature cannot be broken into by any powers beyond existence:

---

[61]Note also the similarity between this discussion of miracles and the earlier ones provided on miracles although they are produced roughly a century apart. According to Easton, "In the New Testament these four Greek words are principally used to designate miracles: (1.) *Semeion*, a 'sign', i.e., an evidence of a divine commission; an attestation of a divine message (Matt. 12:38, 39; 16:1, 4; Mark 8:11; Luke 11:16; 23:8; John 2:11, 18, 23; Acts 6:8, etc.); a token of the presence and working of God; the seal of a higher power. (2.) *Terata*, 'wonders;' wonder-causing events; portents; producing astonishment in the beholder (Acts 2:19). (3.) *Dunameis*, 'might works;' works of superhuman power (Acts 2:22; Rom. 15:19; 2 Thess. 2:9); of a new and higher power. (4.) *Erga*, 'works;' the works of Him who is 'wonderful in working' (John 5:20, 36)," *Easton's Bible Dictionary*.

[62]See Morton Kelsey's *Healing and Christianity*, Minneapolis: Augsburg, 1995, 22.

> The same is true as to the walking of Christ on the water and the swimming of iron at the command of the prophet. The simple and grand truth that the universe is not under the exclusive control of physical forces, but that everywhere and always there is above, separate from and superior to all else, an infinite personal will, not superseding, but directing and controlling all physical causes, acting with or without them. God ordinarily effects his purpose through the agency of second causes; but he has the power also of effecting his purpose immediately and without the intervention of second causes, i.e., of invading the fixed order, and thus of working miracles. Thus we affirm the possibility of miracles, the possibility of a higher hand intervening to control or reverse nature's ordinary movements.

While this is a very old debate about whether or not God can interfere with reality as it has already been created, and also while this debate cannot necessarily be resolved very far here, it is interesting to note what Peat says about synchronicity as disruption of our limited understandings, much of which would appear to pertain to the disruptive nature of the miraculous as well:

> A bridge can....be built between interior and exterior worlds and...synchronicity provides us with a starting point, for it represents a tiny flaw in the fabric of all that we have hitherto taken for reality. Synchronicities give us a glimpse beyond our conventional notions of time and causality into the immense patterns of nature, the underlying dance which connects all things and the mirror which is suspended between inner and outer universes. With synchronicity as our starting point, it becomes possible to begin the construction of a bridge that spans the worlds of mind and matter, physics and psyche.
>
> To view the world in terms of patterns and interconnections of individual events would not have appeared strange to inhabitants of the Middle Ages or, for that matter, ancient China. The Bayeaux Tapestry, which relates the Norman Conquest of England in 1066, heralds this dramatic invasion with the appearance of a new comet in the sky. And so the crowning of kings, outbreaks of war or disease[63], and

the birth of famous men was always accompanied by a variety of natural portents. According to such a worldview there are affinities between apparently different things and sympathies that act between body, soul, and the outer world. Indeed all of nature was considered to be a single, giant organism in which each person had his or her own place. To become part of this harmony of the universe was the key to right action and bred a form of knowledge which was never separate from subjective values and beliefs.[64]

Peat describes how the ruptures that we experience in synchronicity, are ruptures in our assumptions about how things work. This is very similar to Easton's description that miracles are ruptures in our understandings of how reality and God work. From these two perspectives then, the important thing to note is that in both synchronicity and the miraculous, it is not the way in which things work that is violated, but rather, it is our *limited understandings* (even with our best assumptions) about the way things work that get disrupted by synchronicities or the miraculous.

Furthermore, we see that while Easton emphasizes that in the miraculous "everywhere and always there is above, separate from and superior to all else, an infinite personal will, not superseding, but directing and controlling all physical causes," Peat says that synchronicities "give us a glimpse beyond our conventional notions of time and causality into the immense patterns of nature, the underlying dance which connects all things and the mirror which is suspended between inner and outer universes.... To become part of

[63]Note especially the references to the outbreak of disease and war in relation to these references to the synchronicity principle, a point very much at the center of this study whether on an individual or collective level. See sections in Chapter Three on the synchronicity principle in relation to curative factors on the intra and inter levels of depth psychology, where the case is made that inner curative transformations can have synchronistic effects whether or not such curative factors are understood as synchronistic by either the therapist or the client.

[64]Peat, 2-3.

this harmony of the universe was the key to right action and bred a form of knowledge which was never separate from subjective values and beliefs." Again, while Easton focuses on the transcendence of God in the miraculous, and Peat focuses more on the immanent aspects of synchronicity (in the psyche, the laws of nature), they both seem to be addressing two sides of the same coin regarding disruptions in the normal course of human experience that point us to our most important and urgent moral imperatives.

Parallel 5: This parallel between synchronicity and the miraculous can be identified by comparing definitions of synchronicity from Jung and von Franz on the one hand, to the definition of the miraculous from *The Interpreter's Dictionary of the Bible* on the other. This fifth parallel is between the role of the acausal level of reality in producing deeper transformations in us towards wholeness through synchronistic warnings, and of God's use of miraculous messages to transform us towards deeper wholeness.

For example, in the case of von Franz's illustration about the lady and the three tigers described earlier, the analyst tries to warn the patient about her need to adjust, her need to transform her inner power drive, to no avail. The analyst's warning is confirmed by the acausal synchronistic appearance of the real tigers which then manage to get her attention. Based on *The Interpreter's Dictionary* definition of the miraculous we can see the miraculous with regard to God's transformative power as follows: "The frequent association of biblical words for 'wonder' with signs suggests another characteristic of biblical miracles. Not only do they witness to the wonderful character of God's actions, **but they also have the effect of confirming the word of God, spoken in threat or promise, disfavor or favor.**" God's word warns people to adjust in a variety of ways; God's miracles confirm what God has warned people to change in their lives. In other words, God smiles or frowns through the miraculous to get people to transform for the better, just as synchronistic occurrences are produced by the acausal orderedness of reality which may get people to transform themselves for the better.

Scripture highlights how every time one is obedient to God's laws, principles, and direction, the fullness of life opens up miraculously; every time one is disobedient to God's direction the world of security and opportunity in life closes down, life becomes difficult, and people enter into uncanny forms suffering.[65]

Then the glory of the Lord appeared at the tent of meeting to all the Israelites. And the Lord said to Moses, "How long will this people despise me? And how long will they refuse to believe in me, in spite of all the signs that I have done among

---

[65]This is a very tricky area having to do with faith in relation to failed healing, as well as to the understanding of various other types of suffering and victimization. It is unwise to conclude that every bad thing that happens to anyone is the result of their disobedience to God, or their lack of faith in God's power. This is because in my understanding, the Christian faith encourages us to recognize that there is a transcendent level to evil in human experience. The reality of this transcendent dimension of evil is described in Ephesians 6:10-12: "Finally, be strong in the Lord and in the strength of his power. Put on the whole armor of God, so that you may be able to stand against the wiles of the devil. For our struggle is not against enemies of blood and flesh, but against the rulers, against the authorities, against the cosmic powers of this present darkness, against the spiritual forces of evil in the heavenly places." As a result of "spiritual forces of evil in the heavenly places," quite often one can be deeply in tune with God's ways, and yet at the same time can experience suffering (as in the case of Job), and even death which seems to be without just cause. In such cases, the mystery of God's justice in the face of seemingly inexplicable suffering can be found in the assurance of other dimensions of existence, namely the afterlife, in which faith asserts all such injustice is resolved by God. Miracles, synchronicity, suffering, and evil are the phenomena that point to such other dimensions of existence, the fuller realities of which we cannot grasp while we reside in this existence.

them? I will strike them with pestilence and disinherit them, and I will make of you a nation greater and mightier than they," Numbers 14: 10-12.

Elsewhere, scripture says the following:

Then the Lord said, "I do forgive, just as you have asked; nevertheless − as I live, and as all the earth shall be filled with the glory of the Lord − none of the people who have seen my glory and the signs that I did in Egypt and in the wilderness, and yet have tested me these ten times and have not obeyed my voice, shall see the land that I swore to give to their ancestors; none of those who despised me shall see it," Numbers 14: 20-23

Deut 28:1-14; 15-28.

Parallel 6: The Ego-Self Framework as a Parallel to the Soul-God Framework

The sixth parallel between synchronicity and the miraculous is based on a parallel I am drawing between the ego-Self framework and the soul-God framework that was first described in the introduction. Jung's ego-Self framework is a powerful tool for analyzing the ego's resistance to synchronicity. This is the case because synchronicity can be seen as a reflection of the ego's surrender to the Self or of the Self's access to the ego. Furthermore, because synchronicity demonstrates parallels to the miraculous, it seems plausible to go further and say that where we discern ego resistance to the Self, not only will we see neglect or rejection of synchronicity, but perhaps, we might see rejection of the miraculous as well.

Furthermore, this study has found that where there appears to be a predominant focus on the psychodynamics within and around an individual's ego (i.e. what we referred to in the introduction as the intra level of depth psychology), such as in the work of Freud, and where therefore there is no real acceptance of the Self or God beyond their roles in the defenses, the rejection of synchronicity and the miraculous is near total.

There is a theological parallel to the intra level in depth psychology when we consider Feuerbach's views of the miraculous.[66] For instance, he declares that the miraculous is the result of deep inner yearnings which emerge from within people as a result of delusional fantasies. Using the method of integration in this study, we can then build bridges between the intra level in depth psychology which ordinarily rejects synchronicity and the miraculous, and its intra parallel in theology where the miraculous is rejected based on suspicions about human delusion.[67] Similarly, this study has found that where there is a major focus on the psychodynamics at the inter level of depth psychology, there is again, quite often, an indifference to, or rejection of, synchronicity and the miraculous (as we shall see in Chapters Three, Four, and Five). As with the intra level, this level of predominantly interpersonal focus in depth psychology has parallels in theology and other disciplines. This study has found that where there is a major focus on psychodynamics at the trans level, there is a significant embrace of synchronicity and the miraculous. This level

---

[66]The intra level has parallels in other disciplines besides theology and depth psychology, such as African American social cultural formation which will be addressed more fully in Chapter Five.

[67]It appears to be the case that quite often, when a psychological or theological theory can be identified as being of the intra type as in the manner established in this study, the theory rejects the notion that synchronicity and the miraculous are real. However, this rejection need not be inevitable. In other words, we can use intra level ways of thinking to be appropriately suspicious of reports about synchronicity and the miraculous without automatically having to reject such reports as being only defensive or delusional.

of predominantly transpersonal focus also has parallels in other disciplines besides psychoanalysis and theology.

Also, what this study has found is that even in trans approaches in depth psychology which embrace synchronicity and the miraculous, or in trans approaches in theology which embrace synchronicity and the miraculous, there is no thorough-going integrated simultaneous embrace of synchronicity and miraculous using the intra, inter, and trans levels in both depth psychology and theology. Thus this study seeks to integrate synchronicity in depth psychology and the miraculous in theology using the intra, inter, and trans levels in both depth psychology and theology, in such a way that this integration is strengthened by a rich exploration and understanding of the parallels between the ego-Self framework and the soul-God framework. More specifically, this study has found that a given event, be it a synchronicity or a miracle, can be interpreted from the perspective of the ego-Self framework alone, or from the perspective of the soul-God framework alone. However, as will be demonstrated throughout this study, there is great value in integrating interpretations based on both the ego-Self and soul-God frameworks without collapsing them, when we are examining synchronicity or the miraculous.

We now turn more fully to how this sixth parallel between the ego-Self framework and the soul-God framework allows us to demonstrate the intra, inter, and trans levels at work, and serves as a basis for the thesis of this study that there is enormous value in addressing synchronicity and the miraculous simultaneously. Explorations of synchronicity in depth psychology are useful to our understandings of the miraculous in theology, and explorations of the miraculous in theology are useful to our understandings of synchronicity in depth psychology. Focusing on the contributions of synchronicity to the miraculous alone is quite beneficial in that synchronicity makes the miraculous more accessible to us in normal everyday actual lived experience.

SUBJECTIVE EXPERIENCE

My Subjective Experience of Synchronicity as this Enriches the Miraculous

THE PRECEDING SECTIONS of this chapter have looked at the ways in which theoretical definitions of synchronicity and the miraculous reveal six main parallels between them. Now the study turns to a brief discussion of my subjective experience of the ways in which synchronicity enriches the miraculous, and the miraculous enriches synchronicity.

Synchronicities often feel like the miraculous to me, and this type of feeling suggests to me that synchronicities can help us as stepping stones to greater acceptance of the miraculous. In other words, it is my belief that synchronicities can prepare us to experience the more powerfully transcendent, healing, and liberating dimensions of life, which biblical miracles (such as someone being raised from the dead) so brilliantly and powerfully display. In deepening the exploration of the manner in which synchronicities can assist us towards a deeper embrace of the miraculous, we must always keep in mind, however, that we are not to reduce them to each other.

These then are some of the gently miraculous effects of synchronicities I have felt in my own life.[68] 1. Synchronicities

---

[68]Although I believe my experiences of synchronicity to be authentic, and take care to ensure that they are not manufactured or fake, there is always the danger that I can slip into misinterpreting certain experiences as synchronistic when they are not. In addition, even with the

usually catch my attention in amazing and surprising ways that make them feel like the miraculous. 2. Synchronicities feel miraculous as well, because they seem to appear like signs from beyond normal everyday ways of experience. They seem to confirm that the entire universe is fully interconnected and works in wondrous ways; that there is something very powerful, loving, and wise which is capable of communicating with us in profoundly helpful and redemptive ways from "the beyond." The main way in which synchronicities demonstrate the attribute of some divine presence relating to me is through their *acausal* nature; in the fact that even though I have not actually caused the synchronicity, it has tremendous depth of meaning for me.

The depth of personal meaning which attends my experiences of synchronicity leads me to describe this special way of knowing as an intuitive-affective way of knowing. Jung describes it as absolute knowledge. By calling this way of knowing intuitive-affective, I intend it to refer to knowledge gained, on the trans level of the system developed throughout this study, through synchronicity in relation to the ego-Self framework, as well as to knowledge associated with the miraculous in relation to the soul-God framework.

Jung describes the immediacy of this type of knowledge in the following context:

The unconscious also contains subliminal perceptions (as well as forgotten memory-images that cannot be reproduced at the moment, and perhaps not at all). Among the subliminal contents we must distinguish perceptions from what I would call an inexplicable "knowledge," or an "immediacy" of psychic images. Whereas the sense-perceptions can be related to probable or possible sensory stimuli below the threshold of consciousness, this "knowledge," or the "immediacy" of unconscious images, either has no recognizable foundation, or else we find that there are recognizable causal connections with certain already existing, and often archetypal, contents. But these images, whether rooted in an already existing basis or not, stand in analogous or equivalent (i.e., meaningful) relationship to objective occurrences which have no recognizable or even conceivable causal relationship with them. How could an event remote in space and time produce a corresponding psychic image when the transmission of energy necessary for this is not even thinkable? However incomprehensible it may appear, we are finally compelled to assume that there is in the unconscious something like an a priori knowledge or an "immediacy" of events which lacks any causal basis. At any rate our conception of causality is incapable of explaining the facts.[69]

Jung also ties this way of synchronistic knowing, which he calls absolute knowledge, to the psychoid factor in the collective unconscious as follows:

By far the greatest number of spontaneous synchronistic phenomena that I have had occasion to observe and analyse can easily be shown to have a direct connection with an archetype. This, in itself, is an irrepresentable, psychoid factor of the collective unconscious. The latter cannot be localized, since either it is complete in principle in every individual or is to be found to be the same everywhere. You can never say with certainty whether what appears to be going on in the collective unconscious of a single individual is not also happening in other individuals or organisms or things or situations. When, for instance, the vision arose in Swedenborg's mind of a fire in Stockholm, there was a real fire raging there at the same time, without there being any demonstrable or even thinkable connection between the two. I certainly would not like to undertake to prove the archetypal connection in this case. I would only point to the fact that in Swedenborg's biography there are certain things which throw a remarkable light on his psychic state. We must assume that there was a lowering of the threshold of consciousness which gave him access to "absolute knowledge." The fire in Stockholm was, in a sense, burning in him too. For the unconscious psyche space and time seem to be

---

[69]Jung, *Synchronicity: An Acausal Connecting Principle*, 30–1.

relative; that is to say, knowledge finds itself in a space-time continuum in which space is no longer space, nor time time. If therefore, the unconscious should develop or maintain a potential in the direction of consciousness, it is then possible for parallel events to be perceived or "known."[70]

Jung also describes this special knowledge as an inborn knowledge which is not connected with the ego's normal ways of knowing:

Whether we like it or not, we find ourselves in this embarrassing position as soon as we begin seriously to reflect on the teleological processes in biology or to investigate the compensatory function of the unconscious, not to speak of trying to explain the phenomenon of synchronicity. Final causes, twist them how we will, postulate a foreknowledge of some kind. It is certainly not a knowledge that can be connected with the ego, and hence not a conscious knowledge as we know it, but rather a self-subsistent "unconscious" knowledge which I would prefer to call "absolute knowledge." It is not cognition but, as Leibniz so excellently calls it, a "perceiving" which consists – or to be more cautious, seems to consist – of images, of subjectless "simulacra." These postulated images are presumably the same as my archetypes, which can be shown to be formal factors in spontaneous fantasy production. Expressed in modern language, the microcosm which contains "the images of all creation" would be the collective unconscious.[71]

Also, Jung discusses the concept of absolute knowledge in relation to the body-soul problem:

The synchronicity principle possesses properties that may help to clear up the body-soul problem. Above all it is the fact of causeless order, or rather, of meaningful orderedness, that may throw light on psychophysical parallelism. The

---

[70]Ibid., 65.
[71]Ibid., 77–8.

"absolute knowledge" which is characteristic of synchronistic phenomena, a knowledge not mediated by the sense organs, supports the hypothesis of a self-subsistent meaning, or even expresses its existence. Such a form of existence can only be transcendental, since, as the knowledge of future or spatially distant events shows, it is contained in a psychically relative space and time, that is to say in an irrepresentable space-time continuum.[72]

In light of Jung's concept of absolute knowledge in relation to the ego-Self framework, synchronicities bring with them special knowledge in relation to the soul-God framework as well. Therefore synchronicities often can get me to pause and make deeper interpretations about my direction in life, just as certain miracles often seem to do for various characters in the Bible (e.g., the miracles of Moses in Pharaoh's court which are intended as signs to Pharaoh to change his mind and let the children of Israel free). 3. Synchronicities can come not only as communications from the beyond, but also in ways that actually ease the pressures of terrible burdens and struggles in surprising, joyful, economical, and seemingly miraculous ways. Synchronicities usually create for me a sense of power, elegance, efficiency, and effectiveness about the way life can sometimes work, that goes far beyond my normal everyday experiences. I experience synchronicities as gracious, loving, rescuing divine providential interventions in my life.[73]

---

[72]Ibid., 90.

[73]In terms of the soul-God framework, this intuitive-affective way of knowing can be said to be mediated by the Holy Spirit. For instance see Matthew 10:19-20: "When they hand you over, do not worry about how you are to speak or what you are to say; for what you are to say will be given to you at that time; for it is not you who speak, but the Spirit of your Father speaking through you." Although I believe my experiences of synchronicity to be authentic, and take care to ensure that they are not manufactured or fake, there is always the danger that I can slip into misinterpreting certain experiences as synchronistic when they are not. In addition, even with the exceptional intuitive-affective guidance I frequently receive through

Perhaps, more widespread dissemination of these understandings about synchronicity can stimulate and prepare people to make a transition from an awareness merely of luck, good fortune, or coincidence that has no significant meaning to them, towards a fuller embrace of the transcendent and numinous which leads ultimately to a deeper embrace of the miraculous.

However, none of this is to ignore the fact that actual miraculous events such as those told in the Bible are seemingly infrequent in the daily lived realities that most of us experience. Nor is it to ignore the fact that such miracles are well nigh impossible for many people in our day and age to accept in any serious manner, except as relatively non-literal, symbolic, or ignorant tales from the past. In view of such blocks to the miraculous per se then, synchronistic events may be thought of as gentler, more frequent, accessible, and believable pointers to miracles of biblical dimensions.

My Subjective Experience of the Miraculous as this Enriches Synchronicity

For me as a Christian, I am inspired to interpret synchronicity in the light of biblical miracles, most of which are outside of normal actual everyday lived experience. These miracles include the most amazing one of them all, the ultimate miracle of the Christian faith, the resurrection of Jesus from the dead. The miracle tradition in Christianity declares that the resurrection did happen. Secondly, the Christian tradition declares that this miracle must be taken seriously; that this miracle is the ultimate of all the miracles; that without this miracle there is no redemption and the Christian faith is in vain. If the tradition says all of this about the resurrection, and

synchronicities, both in terms of the ego-Self framework and the soul-God framework, keen discernment of such experiences is essential, as serious mistakes in judgment are still possible nevertheless.

if synchronicity helps to make the miraculous more accessible to us, then it stands to reason, that synchronicity can indeed make many other Christian claims more accessible to us as well.

Jung himself was in many ways reorganizing a set of religious traditions, the old wine he had inherited, into the new wine-skins of his depth psychology. These new wineskins were necessary if he and his contemporaries were to make sense of their lived experience in relation to the religious doctrines of the past. In a similar manner, we are using synchronicity to bring new life to the concepts of the miraculous, while using the miraculous to bring new understanding to our approach to synchronicity.

When I say that I interpret synchronicity in terms of biblical miracles, or that the miraculous enriches our understanding of synchronicity, what I mean is that first of all, I understand synchronicity to be a part of God's redemptive work through Jesus. This is something I accept by faith, in much the same way as I accept that Jesus redeems us through our faith in him and his saving death and resurrection. Thus, I frequently think of synchronicity as somehow being both implicated in God's creative design, as well as in God's plan of redemption through the death and resurrection of Jesus. So, when I experience a synchronicity, I am able by faith to say to myself that this is a small piece of what a fuller more dramatic miracle must be like. My faith helps me to trust that while I may not yet be able to have biblical miracles on demand, that God has created an existence in which we are promised that such things are possible, and indeed are to be expected. In this existence, synchronicities then become a promise of so much more of what is to come us miraculously.

The final move in these associations of synchronicity with the resurrection of Jesus, is one in which I am able to fantasize that with the right ego-Self orientation regarding my various psychodynamics, together with the right soul-God dynamics in relation to the problem of sin and my various mistakes, I might be able to experience such a magnificent synchronicity that it would actually manifest in some way that is reflective of the resurrection of Jesus.

In other words, with faith in the resurrection of Jesus as a constant focus of my soul-God journey, and with on-going attention to synchronicity as I work on my ego-Self dynamics, it seems plausible to suggest that the resurrected Lord Jesus, as he presides over my deepening maturity in the faith, would stimulate an evolution in my life from the milder types of synchronicity that are an almost everyday occurrence for me now, until these eventually become more and more dramatic, and then actually flow into the kind of miracles evidenced in the Bible such as with the resurrections of Lazarus, the rich man's daughter, and the like.

The biblical miracles always cause me to ask for more faith to believe and understand and accept them as described. These miracles get me to challenge my assumptions when my assumptions contradict the biblical miracles, rather than causing me to challenge the miracles themselves.

Of course this simultaneous exploration of synchronicity and the miraculous, and of the similarities between them has to involve both depth psychology and theology since these are the theoretical contexts within which these two phenomena are typically observed and examined. Synchronicity from the perspective of depth psychology provides us with plausible and accessible ways to understand ourselves in relation to the transcendent through the dynamics of the unconscious and identity. By themselves however, synchronicity and depth psychology might not take us into the heart of the matter regarding such miracles as the resurrection. The miraculous from the perspective of theology challenges us to wrestle continuously with how the seemingly impossible miracles and signs and wonders told of in the Bible could be. By themselves, the theological assumptions involved in the miraculous might be relatively easy to dismiss as implausible. When we view synchronicity in depth psychology and the miraculous in theology simultaneously, we avail ourselves of plausible explanations for the even deeper reality and significance of synchronicities and the miraculous, and at the same time neither is reduced to the other.

PARTNERSHIP

IT IS OF THE UTMOST importance for us to learn and teach more about synchronicity and the miraculous simultaneously, because this simultaneous engagement of synchronicity and the miraculous can provide people without a meaningful awareness of these phenomena with ways to embrace them more fully in order to lead richer and more powerful lives. Given that this type of sustained simultaneous exploration of synchronicity in depth psychology and the miraculous in theology has never been done before, and yet clearly promises significant benefits, this type of study warrants further exploration.

Focusing on the contributions of synchronicity to a greater understanding of the miraculous alone is quite beneficial, and focusing on the contributions of the miraculous to a deeper appreciation of synchronicity alone is also quite beneficial. Again, this study advances the thesis that the benefits to therapists and clients as well religious leaders and their communities, are even greater when the contributions of synchronicity to the miraculous and of the miraculous to synchronicity are both held together simultaneously.[74] Depth psychology helps us to understand

---

[74]Because the nuances involved here are easy to miss, let us put it more starkly: A (synchronicity) is helpful to B (the miraculous); B is helpful to A; focusing on how A is helpful to B is very beneficial just by itself; focusing on how B is helpful to A is also beneficial just by itself; the thesis of this study is that a simultaneous embrace

synchronicity as a manifestation of the causal dynamics between the ego and the Self, while theology amplifies for us that these psychological dynamics actually partake in the relationship between the finite human and the infinite divine.

While Jung's focus on subjective experience with regard to synchronicity is helpful, Jung's use of the term "acausal connecting principle" can, ironically, make the causal link between the Self and the ego in the manifestation of synchronicities seem somewhat ambiguous. This ambiguity is based on Jung's claim that he cannot really say very much about this acausal connecting principle. Theology can provide clearer principles that highlight the causal nature of the relationship between the infinitely divine and the finitely human with regard to synchronicities. In other words, theology can help to reduce the ambiguity that Jung presents.

In the following story, provided by von Franz, we see psychological dynamics at work between the ego and the Self which yield synchronistic results. At the same time, the story allows us to show how theology parallels and enriches depth psychology:

Once when I was giving a lecture at the Jung Institute on synchronicity and causality, a Japanese man came up to me and said, "Now I understand what causality is! When I was reading about Western physics, I always thought it was all synchronistic. And now that you have taken so much trouble to show the differences, I am able to understand for the first time what causality is!" In the East people think so differently that they cannot even understand what we mean by causality. Many Oriental peoples seem to understand physical happenings as a synchronistic reflection of the psychic realm. There is a beautiful story about this from the annals of the Tang period. Once a volcano erupted. First a crater lake formed and then in middle of it a volcanic cone arose. The empress of the time was a very domineering woman who had entirely deprived her husband of power.[75] This empress visited the

of A's help to B and B's help to A is all the greater.

mountain and called it Fortunate Mountain. A servitor wrote her a polite letter. "Your Majesty, I have learned that the world is destroyed when the breath of Heaven is destroyed. When the breath of earth is destroyed, the human soul is destroyed. Your Majesty has set herself in the masculine fashion above the feminine. I would advise Your Majesty to take the path of remorse and repentance, so that no misfortune falls upon the empire." The empress had a fit of anger and banished the outspoken citizen from the court. Now, ken, a mountain in Chinese, is a masculine principle. "Lake" is called tui and is a feminine principle. A mountain having formed over the lake, synchronistically reflected the psychic state of the empress or of the royal court. Thus the external occurrence was seen as a representation of a psychic situation.[76]

This story illustrates the powerful way in which natural environmental phenomena can play a synchronistic part in psychological phenomena. The synchronistic manifestation of a volcano on top of a lake may be seen to reflect the psychic condition of an empress whose ego (parallel to the finite self from a theological perspective) is out of harmony with the Self (parallel to God from a theological perspective). Such a disharmony can be said to be further reflected in a disharmony between her male and female sides (the intra level), and in her domineering attitude toward her husband (the inter level), all of which portends ill for the earthly empire according to the servitor unless she repents because the "breath of Heaven is destroyed" (the trans level).

If we set this story up in a theological parallel to von Franz's depth psychological formulation, it can be seen that such a synchronistic story deepens our understanding of the causal

[75]The use of this story is not to make the chauvinistic implication that a woman should not be a ruler in a way that outshines her husband. The story states that an unhealthy and extreme imbalance had arisen because the empress had "entirely deprived her husband of power." Such an imbalance of power would be in need of correction if the roles of the empress and her husband described here were reversed.

[76]Marie-Louise von Franz, *Psyche and Matter* (Boston: Shambhala, 1992), 18-9.

manner in which an infinite transcendent principle (God) – represented by the phrase "breath of Heaven" in this story - relates to finite humans in their obedience or disobedience towards divine laws, principles, and commandments. In this story, for example, the principle that domestic harmony should be pursued to strengthen a marriage was being ignored by the empress with disastrous synchronistic environmental consequences for the realm.

Of course, the divine principles of causality in this story appear mostly as light traces which could be easily brushed aside or ignored without the aid of a theological lens. With a theological lens, the story begins to look quite similar to the many biblical stories in which an Israelite prophet admonishes a king of Israel to repent from evil or suffer the consequences of God's wrath not only personally, but with regard to the fortunes of the nation of Israel as a whole.[77]

---

[77]For example see 2 Chronicles 34: 22-33 - "So Hilkiah and those whom the king had sent went to the prophet Huldah, the wife of Shallum son of Tokhath son of Hasrah, keeper of the wardrobe (who lived in Jerusalem in the Second Quarter) and spoke to her to that effect. She declared to them, 'Thus says the LORD, the God of Israel: Tell the man who sent you to me, Thus says the LORD: I will indeed bring disaster upon this place and upon its inhabitants, all the curses that are written in the book that was read before the king of Judah. Because they have forsaken me and have made offerings to other gods, so that they have provoked me to anger with all the works of their hands, my wrath will be poured out on this place and will not be quenched. But as to the king of Judah, who sent you to inquire of the LORD, thus shall you say to him: Thus says the LORD, the God of Israel: Regarding the words that you have heard, because your heart was penitent and you humbled yourself before God when you heard his words against this place and its inhabitants, and you have humbled yourself before me, and have torn your clothes and wept before me, I also have heard you, says the LORD. I will gather you to your ancestors and you shall be gathered to your grave in peace; your eyes shall not see all the disaster that I will bring on this place and its inhabitants.' They took the message back to the king. Then the king sent word and gathered together all the elders of Judah and Jerusalem. The king went up to the house of the LORD, with all the people of Judah, the inhabitants of Jerusalem, the priests and the Levites, all the people both great and

The empress in the story above is parallel to a king of Israel; the servitor is parallel to an Israelite prophet and speaks with clarity and authority about the causal link between the empress's psychological distortions and the dire fate of her empire, and also calls her to repent and turn from her distortions. The essential point being advanced here is that in a story such as the one just outlined, theology helps us to introduce the causal links between the behavior of finite human beings and an infinite God, a causal theological link which would be absent otherwise, if our only concern were the manner in which depth psychology highlights the psychological experiences involved in such synchronistic occurrences.

Thus theology helps us to understand the miraculous as a manifestation of the causal dynamics between finite humans and an infinite God, while depth psychology amplifies for us that these theological dynamics are parallel to, and indeed, actually partake in the subjective richness of the causal and synchronistic relationship between the ego and the Self.

In Leviticus 26:1–20, for example, we can observe a causal link between the keeping of the commandments and the bestowal of God's providential benevolence through naturalistic phenomena, in a manner akin to the synchronicity in the story of the empress and the volcano:

small; he read in their hearing all the words of the book of the covenant that had been found in the house of the LORD. The king stood in his place and made a covenant before the LORD, to follow the LORD, keeping his commandments, his decrees, and his statutes, with all his heart and all his soul, to perform the words of the covenant that were written in this book. Then he made all who were present in Jerusalem and in Benjamin pledge themselves to it. And the inhabitants of Jerusalem acted according to the covenant of God, the God of their ancestors. Josiah took away all the abominations from all the territory that belonged to the people of Israel, and made all who were in Israel worship the LORD their God. All his days they did not turn away from following the LORD the God of their ancestors."

You shall make for yourselves no idols and erect no carved images or pillars, and you shall not place figured stones in your land, to worship at them; for I am the LORD your God. You shall keep my sabbaths and reverence my sanctuary: I am the LORD. If you follow my statutes and keep my commandments and observe them faithfully, I will give you your rains in their season, and the land shall yield its produce, and the trees of the field shall yield their fruit. Your threshing shall overtake the vintage, and the vintage shall overtake the sowing; you shall eat your bread to the full, and live securely in your land. And I will grant peace in the land, and you shall lie down, and no one shall make you afraid; I will remove dangerous animals from the land, and no sword shall go through your land. You shall give chase to your enemies, and they shall fall before you by the sword. Five of you shall give chase to a hundred, and a hundred of you shall give chase to ten thousand; your enemies shall fall before you by the sword. I will look with favor upon you and make you fruitful and multiply you; and I will maintain my covenant with you. You shall eat old grain long stored, and you shall have to clear out the old to make way for the new. I will place my dwelling in your midst, and I shall not abhor you. And I will walk among you, and will be your God, and you shall be my people. I am the LORD your God who brought you out of the land of Egypt, to be their slaves no more; I have broken the bars of your yoke and made you walk erect. But if you will not obey me, and do not observe all these commandments, if you spurn my statutes, and abhor my ordinances, so that you will not observe all my commandments, and you break my covenant, I in turn will do this to you: I will bring terror on you; consumption and fever that waste the eyes and cause life to pine away. You shall sow your seed in vain, for your enemies shall eat it. I will set my face against you, and you shall be struck down by your enemies; your foes shall rule over you, and you shall flee though no one pursues you. And if in spite of this you will not obey me, I will continue to punish you sevenfold for your sins. I will break your proud glory, and I will make your sky like iron and your earth like copper. Your strength shall be spent to no purpose: your land shall not yield its produce, and the trees of the land shall not yield their fruit.

The commandment from an infinite all-powerful God of signs and wonders to a finite and error-prone people is that they eschew idolatry; that they have no other gods except the one true God – if they do this they will be amply protected by God miraculously; if they are disobedient they will suffer.[78]

Depth psychology enriches our understanding of these theological dynamics first of all by getting us to take seriously the synchronistic and naturalistic link between human behavior in relation to the acausal connecting principle (parallel to God - God does actually cause the environment to support or undermine us based on our obedience or lack thereof regarding divine law). Depth psychology also gets us to enrich our understanding of the intrapersonal and subjective dynamics involved in the relationship between humans and God. With the aid of depth psychology we can enrich our understanding of the developmental and defensive factors that need to be addressed in order for the causal links of obedience and faithfulness between humans and God to be enhanced. Perhaps the children of Israel could have been supported to be more obedient to God immediately after the exodus from Egypt if each person had been supported to understand his or her own unique developmental and defensive issues in relation to ego-Self dynamics (e.g., depth psychology could help us to explore and understand their residual slave mentality inclining them to emulate

---

[78]Further examples of the causal link between the obedience (or lack thereof) of finite human beings and the commandments of the infinite God in relation to signs and wonders are to be found in the following passages: Deuteronomy 6.22-25: "The LORD displayed before our eyes great and awesome signs and wonders against Egypt, against Pharaoh and all his household. He brought us out from there in order to bring us in, to give us the land that he promised on oath to our ancestors. Then the LORD commanded us to observe all these statutes, to fear the LORD our God, for our lasting good, so as to keep us alive, as is now the case. If we diligently observe this entire commandment before the LORD our God, as he has commanded us, we will be in the right." See also, Deuteronomy 7.19-26; Deuteronomy 26.8-19; and Deuteronomy 34.11-12: "He was unequaled for all the signs and wonders that the LORD sent him to perform in the land of Egypt, against Pharaoh and all his servants and his entire land, and for all the mighty deeds and all the terrifying displays of power that Moses performed in the sight of all Israel."

their former masters and even hanker for a return to the place of their bondage)

The causal links between obedience to God's commandments and the miraculous ("signs and wonders" in the following text) are sounded explicitly in Deuteronomy 4.34–40:

> Or has any god ever attempted to go and take a nation for himself from the midst of another nation, by trials, by signs and wonders, by war, by a mighty hand and an outstretched arm, and by terrifying displays of power, as the LORD your God did for you in Egypt before your very eyes? To you it was shown so that you would acknowledge that the LORD is God; there is no other besides him. From heaven he made you hear his voice to discipline you. On earth he showed you his great fire, while you heard his words coming out of the fire. And because he loved your ancestors, he chose their descendants after them. He brought you out of Egypt with his own presence, by his great power, driving out before you nations greater and mightier than yourselves, to bring you in, giving you their land for a possession, as it is still today. So acknowledge today and take to heart that the LORD is God in heaven above and on the earth beneath; there is no other. Keep his statutes and his commandments, which I am commanding you today for your own well-being and that of your descendants after you, so that you may long remain in the land that the LORD your God is giving you for all time.

If we shift back to depth psychological concerns regarding causality we can discern (as noted earlier) an ambiguity about causal links in the thinking of Jung that is not a part of the thinking in the biblical texts just cited. According to von Franz:

> Jung noted that in nature there is also something that he called acausal orderedness, for instance all a priori facts in physics, such as half-lives and the speed of light. These cannot be causally explained; they can only be observed, but we can give no cause for them. In the psychic sphere, an acausal orderedness can be found in the properties of the natural integers. The natural integers are a psychic content

that just simply is the way it is. Five, for example, is a prime number. That is just the way it is. We cannot ask why five is a prime number. It is one, and everyone can see that it is. In other words, our psychic, intellectual processes are ordered in such a way that this strikes us as evident. We are so structured that we must see it this way. Perhaps on other stars there is another psychic structure for which this is not the case. But for us it is, though we cannot account for this causally. The question "Why?" or "Where does that come from?" or "What makes it that way?" appears to be meaningless.[79] *The properties of the natural integers are thus a psychic orderedness, as half-lives are a physical orderedness. Both are phenomena that Jung characterized by the concept "acausal orderedness," by which he meant an a priori "just so" order that we cannot account for in terms of cause and effect or probability.*

Thus we have two phenomena: on the one hand, something like an acausal orderedness seems to exist in the domain of both psychic and material reality; and on the other hand, sporadic, irregular synchronistic events occur. The acausal orderedness is regular, generally determinable, universally valid, and observable at all times. By contrast, none of this is true for the sporadic cases of synchronicity. They are primarily characterized by their unexpected, irregular, unpredictable occurrence. But they also manifest acausal orderedness. In this regard, Jung considered a hypothesis according to which synchronistic events, being sporadic "miracles," were only a special case of the more general principle of acausal orderedness. In fact, they are those special cases in which the observer is in a position to know the tertium comparationis, the meaning in the simultaneity of the psychic and physical events. It may well be the case however, that we are often not in a position to recognize a meaning in what happened and therefore cannot understand it as a psychophysical synchronistic event.[80]

---

[79]While it is true, as Jung says here, that the "given-ness" of reality due to acausal orderedness (a parallel to God) cannot be made more accessible by questions about why things are the way things are, the manifestation of miracles (parallel to synchronicity) based on the relationship between humans and God presented in this study from the Bible, does not view miracles as "unexpected, irregular, or unpredictable occurrences;" rather, they are normally the predictable result of utter surrender and obedience to God.

[80]Von Franz 28-9.

According to von Franz, in Jung's depth psychology "synchronistic events, being sporadic 'miracles,' were only a special case of the more general principle of acausal orderedness. In fact, they are those special cases in which the observer is in a position to know the meaning in the simultaneity of the psychic and physical events." Here we see the role of depth psychology in providing us with an integrated approach to the relationship between synchronicity and the miraculous. A principle of acausal orderedness (the trans level), gives rise to synchronistic events ("sporadic miracles"), in which the observer is able to know the meaning in the simultaneity of the psychic (the intra level) and the physical events (the inter level).

This depth psychological Jungian approach to the link between synchronicity and the miraculous through the intra, inter, and trans levels can greatly enrich our subjective comprehension of the interconnections of the various levels in our lives. One deficit of this depth psychological system on its own is that it conveys a sense of lowered expectations in which synchronicities (and miracles) are unpredictable and irregular.[81] This study encourages us towards a

---

[81]As an example of the relationship of mutual support and criticism between depth psychology and theology, Ulanov explains that "Theologians can support psychologists by probing the ontological assumptions and the implicit doctrine of man in a psychological system and can encourage psychologists to consider such wider ramifications of their empirical work. Theologians can correlate the psychologist's empirical picture of man with the contents of the Christian faith. This keeps lively and relevant the interchange between the timeless truths contained in Christian symbols and the fluctuating human situation. Psychological investigation can furnish empirical data to flesh out theological categories which otherwise are often empty abstractions. Psychologists can press the theologians to shape the message of Christianity in more concrete language," Ulanov, *The Feminine*, 7-8. As another example of the mutual support and criticism between depth psychology and theology, Ulanov describes how depth psychology underscores Tillich's emphasis on human existence between the finite and infinite, through its empirical methods related to the enormous realms of the unconscious which are not available to the

more decisive embrace and understanding of the acausal and causal principles underlying both synchronicity in depth psychology and the miraculous in theology.

From a theological perspective, and as laid out in numerous biblical texts, Jung's "acausal orderedness [which] is regular, generally determinable, universally valid, and observable at all times," appears to be none other than a parallel to God's law. The biblical message is clear about the causal link between a deep human love for and adherence to God's law, and a lived human experience of God's blessings of deliverance – in miracles (a parallel to synchronicity) - as a consequence. The biblical message is also clear about the causal link between a human rejection of God's law and a consequent lived human experience of suffering due to God's judgement and wrath.

Von Franz assists us to understand that Jung, in this context (of acausality, synchronicities, and the miraculous), is not overtly given to the view that God is the prime mover or cause for all the universal laws for which we have no explanations. As we saw in the previous quotation from von Franz, for Jung, with regard to these givens of life, "the question 'Why?' or 'Where does that come from?' or 'What makes it that way?' all appear to be meaningless.

more limited ego. Furthermore, "The exploration of compelling unconscious motives concretizes the theological doctrine of 'bondage of the will' which asserts that all our actions are perforated by ambiguity and a mixture of good and evil intentions. Studies of the shattering effects of parents' unresolved problems on their children give fresh poignancy to the saying, 'The sins of the forefathers are visited upon the children.' Empirical descriptions of states of 'omnipotence,' 'inflation,' 'oral fixation,' 'projection,' etc., make palpable our ancient sins of pride, anger, greed, envy, etc," Ulanov, *The Feminine*, 7-8. As another example of the mutual support between theology and depth psychology, Ulanov describes how psychoanalysis relies on nonverbal approaches to healing, which is akin to theology in its reliance on sacraments and symbols. Furthermore, analysis is somewhat religious or theological in that the analysand must accept some degree of belief in the healing power of the process before transformation is actually possible," Ulanov, *The Feminine*, 7-8.

The properties of the natural integers are thus a psychic orderedness, as half-lives are a physical orderedness. Both are phenomena that Jung characterized by the concept 'acausal orderedness,' by which he meant an *a priori* 'just so' order that we cannot account for in terms of cause and effect or probability."

The apparent meaninglessness of the givens and *a prioris* of life for Jung, and of our inability to account for them in terms of cause and effect[82] is addressed much less ambivalently or ambiguously by biblical writers. They tell us unequivocally again and again that God is the cause of all the laws of life. They tell us that miracles of

---

[82]Von Franz underscores how insight about our inner world influences synchronicities in the outer world, and at the same time, she summarizes many of the elements of this study when she says the following: "A synchronistic event can, for example, consist either of something being foreseen in a dream, i.e., inner, psychically perceived scenes that in the external world take place somewhat later (only rarely precisely simultaneously); or of several external-world and inner-world events that are connected through their meaning or are coincident in some improbable fashion; as, for example, when through a salesgirl's error, someone receives a black dress rather than the colored one ordered, just on the day of the death of a close relative....Before continuing our consideration of synchronicity, we must have a closer look at its complementary opposite, the causality principle. We know today through the results of modern nuclear physics that strict causality is only an interpretive mode of our intellect, that in nature there are only probabilities (in the sense of the probability calculus), and that therefore, logically, accidents or chance occurrences must also exist. Among these countless accidents, which we tend to characterize as 'blind' chance, we are struck by those meaningful coincidences that seem to the experiencer not to be 'mere chance,' but rather 'meaningful,' 'marvelous,' or 'as though ordained by Providence.' In this category belong all 'signs and wonders,' all numina (divine signs), and all oracular occurrences, which have been observed in all times and places, in primitive as well as higher cultures. Naturally such coincidental events all have their own causal connections; only the coincidence itself is to be understood acausally" *Psyche and Matter*, 204-5). While von Franz suggests that synchronicities are both causal and acausal, here, she appears to collapse synchronicity and the miraculous. See Chapter Three on Richo, and more generally throughout, regarding the benefits of not collapsing synchronicity and the miraculous, but rather of integrating them.

deliverance are predictable and regular aspects of life when it is lived through adherence and devotion to God's law. In this way theology serves as a corrective to depth psychology when depth psychology becomes unsure of itself with regard to the nature of cause and effect regarding synchronicity and the miraculous. On the other hand, depth psychology encourages an enriched subjective apprehension of our experiences of synchronicity and the miraculous which theology by itself might not be able to foster due to its heavy investment in tradition and law.

From a New Testament perspective, Paul says in 1Corinthians15:13-14: "If there is no resurrection of the dead, then Christ has not been raised; and if Christ has not been raised, then our proclamation has been in vain and your faith has been in vain." In Romans 10: 8 – 13 Paul says,

"But what does it say? 'The word is near you, on your lips and in your heart' (that is, the word of faith that we proclaim); because if you confess with your lips that Jesus is Lord and believe in your heart that God raised him from the dead, you will be saved. For one believes with the heart and so is justified, and one confesses with the mouth and so is saved. The scripture says, 'No one who believes in him will be put to shame.' For there is no distinction between Jew and Greek; the same Lord is Lord of all and is generous to all who call on him. For, 'Everyone who calls on the name of the Lord shall be saved.'"

And also in 1 Corinthians 2: 4-5, Paul says,

When I came to you, brothers and sisters, I did not come proclaiming the mystery of God to you in lofty words or wisdom. For I decided to know nothing among you except Jesus Christ, and him crucified. And I came to you in weakness and in fear and in much trembling. My speech and my proclamation were not with plausible words of wisdom, but with a demonstration of the Spirit and of power, so that your faith might rest not on human wisdom but on the power of God.

In contrast to the depth psychological approach to miracles described above, from a theological perspective, each text above describes a very predictable approach to the miraculous. We are to believe in the resurrection; we are to believe specifically in Jesus' resurrection as the cornerstone of our faith; and we are to depend on the "demonstration of the Spirit and of power," in order that [our] faith "rest not on human wisdom but on the power of God" (1 Corinthians 2: 5).

Summary

In summary then, the six parallels between synchronicity and the miraculous we have derived from the definitions of synchronicity and the miraculous are as follows: 1) in both, inner subjective and outer objective realities correlate; 2) in both cases there are subjective experiences of amazement and meaning; 3) acausality in synchronicity parallels God in the miraculous; 4) both produce significant disruptions in our limitations of understanding; 5) both can produce positive transformations; and 6) the ego–Self framework in synchronicity is parallel to the soul–God framework in the miraculous. Furthermore, these parallels can be approached through references to the intra, inter, and trans levels which serve as a simple bridging language for providing us with a simultaneous grasp of the many parallels between synchronicity in depth psychology and the miraculous in theology.

2. AUTOBIOGRAPHICAL BACKGROUND

IN ORDER TO ACCOUNT for my fascination with synchronicity and the miraculous and now culminates in the form it does, I outline a few of the relevant aspects of my intellectual and spiritual journey. Walter Wink's sentiments reflect mine when he says the following, in reference to his explorations of the Powers in various Gnostic texts:

> I have not attempted to disguise my own convictions in this study, though I have tried to keep them from violating the data. As Heisenberg taught us, the viewer is a part of the field being viewed. We cannot know something as it is in itself, but only as that with which we are in dynamic interaction. There are no such things as objective facts....Understanding is always a hermeneutical enterprise, that is, it is a quest for the meaning of texts. And that meaning cannot simply be read off the texts, but is the result of a conversation between two worlds, ours and theirs. We can only render texts meaningfully if we interpret them in terms intelligible to ourselves. This requires the use of analogies from our own experience. Consequently, understanding...[texts]...becomes also a way of understanding more about ourselves and our world today. Why else would we bother to read them?[83]

[83]Walter Wink, *Cracking the Gnostic Code*, Society of Biblical Literature, (Atlanta, GA: Scholars Press, 1993), viii.

In this chapter then, I use three conversion experiences of mine to demonstrate various traces of synchronicity and the miraculous in my personal evolution. I do this in an integrated way through the further use of the ego–Self and soul–God frameworks; the intra, inter, and trans levels; and also through a focus on African social cultural formation by way of the story of Ananse the Spider from my African cultural background, and a focus on African American social cultural formation through The African Americans and the Bible Research Project.

In my first conversion I accepted Jesus as my savior in order to overcome a gripping fear of eternal torment. In my second conversion, I experienced a tremendous spiritual and psychological awakening in which I perceived a seamless integration of psychology and spirituality. In my third conversion, I began to deepen my commitment to an integrated approach to synchronicity and the miraculous. This study now elaborates on each of these conversion experiences.

ANANSE

AS A CHILD growing up in Ghana, West Africa, I was terrified and traumatized by the numerous tales from the local culture about gruesome head-hunting rituals. The tales were bad enough in themselves, but life was made even more traumatic as a result of actual headhunting scares. These were occasions on which, during the celebration of the death of one or another of the significant tribal chiefs, human sacrifices were conducted to replenish the supply of royal servants for these departed chiefs in the after-life. During these anniversaries school children around the country would be warned by the various school systems to be on guard getting to and from school as there were royal executioners afoot searching for victims to send into the service of the departed chiefs in the afterlife. As a result, as a child, I had many sleepless nights.

Even when I would turn to the common Western children's tales I was familiar with, such as Hansel and Gretel, Snow White, Cinderella, Puss in Boots, Rumpelstiltskin, Rapunzel, Snow White and the Seven Dwarves, and Blue Beard, I was terrified. Each story had an evil figure with dangerous powers. Even Santa's crimson red outfit was terrifying in its closeness to the color of blood. God, as taught to me in elementary school, (I was exposed to no formal religious system by my parents), was constantly threatening and killing people, and Jesus was killed by his loving father, as Isaac almost was by his father. The Devil seemed a particularly nasty creature from the drawings I remember, and then there was the business about heaven and hell and eternal damnation.[84]

I can see now, that as I child and teenager, I was slowly developing a thirst for anything that might explain sinister figures in life or stories by considering the afterlife, specifically anything pertaining to heaven, paradise, and the Garden of Eden. Anything else to neutralize the terrors of life, and my fear that living things had to die had to be considered. I can also see more clearly now the fortifying presence in my psyche, as a child, of the local Ananse stories.

Also, as a way of gaining a broader perspective on the ways in which the African culture I grew in might have influenced me in a

---

[84]It appears that my own unique intrapersonal traumas while growing up, when joined with the inter and trans influences of the culture and the stories I was exposed to in Ghana, led me to interpret what, for many other Western children, might have been merely entertaining bed-time stories, as exposes on belief systems which include a strong respect for, and knowledge about the supernatural. However, no doubt, for many Western children, Harry Potter and various other super-heroes probably function the same way as Ananse did for me: i.e., to educate one about superhuman powers for overcoming evil.

protective psychological way through the Ananse stories told to us as children, this study now takes a brief detour away from my own personal story regarding synchronicity and the miraculous, and addresses a few select aspects of Akan social cultural formation in relation to the trickster figure, Ananse, and the supernatural. This exploration also addresses, in part, a question posed earlier in this study about whether or not there are African and African-derived systems of thought and practice that resonate with Western-derived depth psychological and theological approaches to synchronicity and the miraculous. By including this exploration of Ananse here, this study integrates a positive example of an African parallel to the European systems of thought and practice.[85]

In Ghana the trickster figure par excellence of the Akan people is Ananse the Spider. It is impossible in telling Ananse stories in English to convey the various subtleties by which Akan listeners would be moved, for indeed the fullest impact is experienced when the story, the story-teller, and audience all belong to the same world view.

---

[85]See also Yvonne Chireau, "The Bible and African American Folklore," in *African Americans and the Bible: Sacred Texts and Social Textures*, (Continuum: New York, 2000), on the link between African and African American folklore, the supernatural and miraculous, and the Bible: "Many of these folklore traditions convery African American's preoccupation with the supernatural, making reference to the invisible realm, the world that parallels the material world and is manifest in dreams, visions, and miracles. While some of these accounts, such as witchcraft tales, haunts and ghost stories, share much with their European folklore counterparts, others possess distinctively African styles that raise the possibility of independent cultural origins. Take for example, black American hoodoo traditions, which figure thematically in a variety of folktales from the early nineteenth century onward. Hoodoo practices, magical techniques of healing and harming, are appropriated in the retelling of the Old Testament story of Moses, a favorite theme in black American folklore. This particular version of the classic tale, in which Moses successfully challenges the Egyptian priests in Pharaoh's court in a test of power, depicts one of the most revered biblical figures in African American culture. As in most folkloric retellings of biblical tales, the characters and events are described using a vernacular that is readily familiar to the hearers," 678.

Furthermore, it is quite fascinating to note how delightful the stories are when delivered orally even by a child, in Akan, as compared to the clumsiness and weakness with which the stories appear when rendered in written or spoken English. In order for us to appreciate more fully the Ananse story below, I now outline a few of the elements of the Ashanti (the predominant group within the Akan) view of psychospiritual development which are embedded in the story. However, what may be gleaned even from the briefest of treatments in English, is how reliant an Akan child might be on such a figure as Ananse, as a threshold introduction to an Akan's acceptance of the supernatural and the ability of same to have a major impact on an Akan's life.

The Ashanti nation which produced the Ananse stories arose in the 18th century when a number of Akan-speaking groups united. Today the so-called traditional or indigenous religious world view of these Ashanti peoples consists of a supreme heavenly creator, *Nyame*, and 2 groups of lower agencies, one of which includes *Asaase Yaa* who is also described as the spirit of the domesticated land. This group also includes the *samanfo*, or ancestors.[86] [87]

Asaase Yaa rewards harmony among the people with good harvests, and punishes disarray with poor harvests. The second group of lower agencies contains the *abosom*, who are the spirits connected with the rivers and lakes, and they reward the people for their appropriate attentions in the various cults dedicated to them. Also in this group are the *mmoatia* (who are also known as fairies, dwarves, or "little folk"); they inhabit the forests and are considered to be the messengers of the *abosom* of the waters, and also are considered to be catalysts of individual human strivings which may point in positive or

---

[86]This paragraph relates to the trans level which will be addressed more fully in Chapters Three, Four, and Five.

[87]See Meyer Fortes and Robin Horton, *Oedipus and Job in West African Religion* (New York: Cambridge University Press, 1959), 64-71.

negative directions - red dwarves are considered to be especially dangerous for their ability to aid humans in creating deadly anti-social spells.

Horton further distinguishes these two groups of powers by naming *Asaase Yaa* and the *samanfo* as the "forces of society" and the *abosom* and the *mmoatia* as the "forces of nature." This further distinction will be of some importance later on. When it comes to the development of the individual as such, the term *mogya* refers to the mother's blood which is essential for the growth of the fetus, and which is also connected to the term *saman*, which refers to a spiritual force from the ancestral stock which enters the individual at conception and leaves at death to return to the original stock in the spirit plane. *Mogya* (or blood) and *saman* (ancestral stock) produce the individual's outward social mask and compliance.

Sunsum and *ntoro* refer to forces which enter the individual with the father's semen at conception, and are linked to the *abosom* (or "forces of nature" noted above); they color a person's unique qualities apart from the collective such as weaknesses, deviations from social norms, strengths, creativity, strivings, and achievements. Finally there is the *kra*, which is understood to mediate the intrapsychic development of both *mogya* (representative of the mother's blood or the forces of society) and the *sunsum* (representative of the father's semen or the forces of nature). This *kra* originates in heaven, where before its owner is born, it comes before *Nyame* and declares its *nkrabea*, or those words which will direct the life-path of its owner from start to finish on earth. During life on earth, the kra is the guardian of the *nkrabea* and so monitors the fortunes of the individual. Sometimes the *kra* is even sought out by an individual and asked to withdraw negative words declared in the original audience with *Nyame* and substitute new more positive ones. At death the *kra* returns to *Nyame*.[88]

Next a brief glance at an individual Ashanti male's psychosocial development rounds out the picture of several other elements which are woven into our Ananse story. As Horton points out, due to the matrilineal nature of the Ashanti kinship system, at the start, a male child who is brought up by a mother and father witnesses the mother's loyalties being torn between her husband and her brothers, "as are the husband's between his wives and his sisters, between his own children and his sister's children. The growing child is aware of these divided loyalties and experiences quite a bit of insecurity as a result. As such a child moves into adulthood, he becomes more and more aware that the balance of his rights and obligations is going to lie not with his father who brought him up and cherished him, but with his mother's brothers. He increasingly finds himself expected to subordinate his individuality to a matrilineage whose demands, lacking strong roots in early upbringing are seen as artificial, coercive and basically irksome."[89]

To recap the above briefly before going on: the Ashanti believe in a supreme God, *Nyame*, whose lower agents are *Asaase Yaa* and the *saman* (the forces of society), and the *abosom* and *mmoatia* (or forces of nature); the intrapsychic correlates of these agencies can be viewed as the *mogya*, the maternal principle in the psyche which governs an individual's conformity to society, and the *sunsum*, the paternal principle which governs one's individuality. The *kra* appears to be a more direct transpersonal representative of God's in the psyche which mediates between the opposing intrapersonal forces, and those interpersonal forces of society and nature.

And now a story about Ananse the Trickster. I have adapted this Ananse story from a number of cruder texts which were collected and translated by Captain R. S. Rattray in the 1930s. His labors were part

[88]See Fortes and Horton, 64–71. This paragraph relates to the intra level which will be addressed more fully in subsequent chapters.

[89]See Fortes and Horton, 66.

of the imperial effort to understand and thereby dominate the Ashanti for the Gold Coast Colony of the British Crown. The story is about the origins of the Anansesem - those stories which actually involve Ananse. The Anansesem are usually told within certain formal structures, so that a story-teller would begin by greeting the audience with the phrase "Ago!!!" which symbolizes a knocking at the door of a home one is attempting to visit; the ritual response from the audience being "Ame!!!" - or "enter," the signal that there is a readiness and anticipation in the audience to receive and digest the story. The raconteur then proceeds with a phrase such as "Enye Kwaku Ananse na naa owo ho ena.....," the English equivalent being "Once upon a time there existed Kwaku Ananse...." A story usually ends with a standard statement approximating this meaning: "If my story was good or even if it was not, let it spread outward and let other stories spread inward towards me."

In the story entitled "How it Happened that the Sky-God's Stories Became Known as Ananse-Stories," Kwaku Ananse, the Spider, once went to Nyankonpon also known as Nyame, the Sky-God, in order to buy the Sky-God's stories. The Sky-God said, "Great and powerful cities from all around have come, and they were unable to purchase them, and how are you, a mere masterless person going to buy them?" Then Ananse said, "What is the price of the stories?" The Sky-God said, they cannot be bought for anything except an Onini (a python); some Mmoboro (or hornets); and an Mmoatia (a fairy). Ananse said, "I will bring all of these things, and what is more, I'll add my mother to the lot." The Sky-God said, "Go and bring them then." Ananse went and told his mother all about it, saying, "I wish to buy the stories of the Sky-God, and the Sky-God says I must bring a python, some hornets, a fairy, and I said I would add you to the lot. Next, Ananse consulted his wife Aso, saying "How are we to capture a python?" And Aso said to him, "Go and get yourself a branch of a palm-tree, and get some string from a creeper as well, and walk alongside the stream where python resides shouting the words I will give you.[90]

So Ananse did as he was told and as he walked by the stream he shouted "It's longer than he is, it's not as long as he is; you're a liar, it's longer than he! And the python hearing this imaginary conversation inquired, "What's all this noise about?" And Ananse said, it's all my wife's fault; she's arguing with me that this palm-branch is longer than you, and I say she is a liar. And the python said, "Bring the palm-branch and let's measure to see who is right. Then Ananse took the palm-branch and laid it along the python's body, and said, "Stretch yourself out;" and then he took out the string from the creeper and wound it tightly along the entire length of the python. When he had finished he shouted at the python, "You fool, now I shall take you to the Sky-God and receive the Sky-God's tales in exchange. Then Ananse took the python off to the Sky-God who said, "I receive this, but there remains what still remains." So Ananse returned to his wife, recounted what had happened and said, "There remain the hornets." And his wife said, "Obtain a gourd, fill it with water, and go off and do with it as I tell you.

And Ananse went off into the bush as he had been instructed, and eventually he came to a swarm of hornets hanging on a bush, and from a hidden position he sprayed them with some of the water from his gourd. Ananse then poured the rest of the water on himself, and held a banana frond over his head as though it were an umbrella, and came out and addressed the hornets: "As the rain has come, had you not better enter my gourd, so that the rain will not soak you completely; for as you can see I am protecting myself from the rain with this banana frond and yet I am still wet?" Then the hornets said "We thank you, we thank you," and they all flew,

---

[90]We could say that Aso represents the medium for the transmission of intuitive-affective knowledge, on the trans level in relation to synchronicity and the ego-Self framework, as well as in relation to the miraculous and the soul-God framework.

disappearing into the gourd with a loud buzzing. Ananse plugged up the gourd saying, "Fools, now I have got you, and I am taking you to the Sky-God in exchange for the Sky-God's tales.

And he took the hornets to the Sky-God who said, "I receive this, but there remains what still remains." So Ananse returned to his wife, recounted what had happened and said, "There remains the fairy." And Ananse carved a black flat-faced wooden doll, smeared some sticky gum from the rubber tree onto the doll's body, put some delicious mashed yam in the doll's hand, tied a string to the doll's head, and went and placed the doll at the foot of an Odum tree where the fairies liked to play. And a fairy came along, saw the doll and said "Hey there, may I have some of your mashed yam?" At which point Ananse tugged at the string, and the doll nodded her head. The fairy told one of her sisters standing beside her, "She says I may eat some of her mashed yam." Her sister replied, "Go ahead and eat some of it then." And after the fairy had finished eating some of the mashed yam, she thanked her (that is the doll). But when the fairy thanked her, the doll did not respond, and the fairy said to her sister, "When I thank her, she does not reply." The fairy's sister replied "Slap her in the face," and the fairy slapped the doll in the face and there was a loud noise (Pa!), and her hand stuck to the doll. And the fairy said to her sister, "My hand is stuck." And her sister said, "Slap her again with your other hand," and she did again with a loud noise and this hand too stuck fast. Then her sister said "Give her a shove with your stomach." And the fairy did and her stomach got stuck to the doll too.

And Ananse came out from his hiding place and tied up the fairy saying, "Fool, now I have got you, and I shall take you to the Sky-God in exchange for the Sky-God's stories." And Ananse went off home with the fairy, and when he got home he told his mother, "Rise up, let us go, for I am taking you along with this fairy to the Sky-God in exchange for Sky-God's tales." So he lifted them both

94

onto his shoulders and took them to the Sky-God. And when he arrived he said, "Sky-God here is a fairy, as well as my mother whom I promised to you." Then the Sky-God called all the elders, the leaders of the army and put the matter before them saying, "Very great kings have come and they were not able to buy Sky-God's stories, but Kwaku Ananse, the Spider, has been able to pay the price; I have received from him the python, the hornets, and a fairy, and of his own accord he added his mother to the lot. And Sky-God said, "Everyone, sing Ananse's praises, for from this day on and forever, I hand my tales over to you with my deepest blessings. No more shall we call them the stories of the Sky-God, but we shall call them Ananse stories." "If my story was good or even if it was not, let it spread outward and let other stories spread inward towards me." ("This my story which I have related, if it be sweet, if it be not sweet, take some of it elsewhere, and let some of it come back to me").[91]

It is possible to recognize in the story several of the key elements found in the Ashanti psychospiritual and social developmental worldview outlined earlier such as: the supreme heavenly creator – Nyankopon (or Nyame); the various forces of nature – the python, the hornets, and the mmoatia; and the forces of society – represented by Ananse's wife and mother.[92] Ananse himself, as the kra would do, declares his nkrabea or prenatal destiny in an audience before Nyame; and also Ananse again much like the kra, shuttles between the forces of nature, the forces of society, and the supreme God; we may also be seeing in the story, some hints of the Ashanti ambivalence towards the matrilineal system, which may be the reason Ananse offers up his mother to Nyame unbid, while at the same time he relies on his wife to help him pull off his tricks and accomplish his social goals.

---

[91]See R. S. Rattray, Akan-Ashanti Folk Tales (New York: AMS Press, 1983).

[92]From a Jungian perspective Ananse's wife and mother represent anima figures.

Furthermore, the story anthropomorphizes the various animals in it, and Ananse even as a spider, is addressed by Nyame as a person, which serves to highlight Ananse's liminal function as a link between the divine, the human, and the animal realms. In this vein, Pelton suggests that "Indeed, it is this very ambiguity of the trickster-figure that the Ashanti story stresses and that Ananse demonstrates in all the stories about him. He is both fooler and fool, maker and unmade, wily and stupid, subtle and gross, the High God's accomplice and his rival."[93]

Now this study turns to the depth psychological implications of Ananse and the Ashanti culture which produced Ananse. First of all, from the earlier account of Ashanti psychospiritual and social development, (leaving aside the more metaphysical categories of that scheme for the moment), we can discern if we choose to, in a manner loosely analogous to the Freudian system, the elements involved in intra-psychic conflict for the Ashanti. This can be see in the way the instinctual forces of nature (the sunsum or id forces) clash with the forces of society (the moyga or superego forces) within an individual, and in turn, how the individual tussles with society at large, while the kra, (loosely analogous to the ego), engages in mediation between the various countervailing forces.

Although we can make out some connections between Freud's structural model of the psyche (which refers to the id, the superego, and the ego) and the Ashanti model, Freud does not provide us with direct treatments of the trickster in general, let alone of Ananse. Nonetheless we are aware of Freud's interest in humor, riddles, accidents and parapraxes (or slips of the tongue), and of his view of their importance in psychoanalysis, and so can perhaps track the spirit of the trickster in his work implicitly through these avenues. At

---

[93]See Robert D. Pelton, *The Trickster in West Africa: A Study of Mythic Irony and Sacred Delight* (Los Angeles: University of California Press, 1980), 27-8.

the very least it seems safe to say that Freud would see in this and other Ananse stories, significant projections of the intrapsychic conflicts of the Ashanti.

Jung on the other hand does consider trickster figures in his work, although in a somewhat contradictory manner, because from one perspective he seems to discount them as useless vestiges of the distant and infantile past of the human race when he says of the trickster figure: "In his clearest manifestations he is a faithful copy of an absolutely undifferentiated human consciousness, corresponding to a psyche that has hardly left the animal level....When, therefore, a primitive or barbarous consciousness forms a picture of itself on a much earlier level of development and continues to do so for hundreds or even thousands of years, undeterred by the contamination of its archaic qualities with differentiated, highly developed mental products, then the causal explanation is that the older the archaic qualities are, the more conservative and pertinacious is their behavior. One simply cannot shake off the memory image of things as they were, and drags it along like a senseless appendage."[94] However, Jung also views trickster figures as important representations of the shadow archetype (and transformational agents i.e., Hermes/Mercury), representations which must be differentiated out from unconsciousness and be consciously integrated into the psyche in every person who is to individuate or develop fully.[95]

Even more to the point with regard to supernatural, healing, and even salvific themes Jung has this to say about the trickster figure:

---

[94]See Jung's commentary in Paul Radin, *The Trickster: A Study in American Indian Mythology* (New York: Shocken Books, 1972), 200.

[95]See Radin, 211.

"*Since all mythical figures correspond to inner psychic experiences and originally sprang from them, it is not surprising to find certain phenomena in the field of parapsychology which remind us of the trickster. These are the phenomena connected with poltergeists, and they occur at all times and places in the ambience of pre-adolescent children. The malicious tricks played by the poltergeist are as well known as the low level of his intelligence and the fatuity of his 'communications'. Ability to change his shape seems also to be one of his characteristics, as there are not a few reports of his appearance in animal form. Since he has on occasion described himself as a soul in hell, the motif of subjective suffering would seem not to be lacking either. His universality is co-extensive, so to speak, with that of shamanism, to which, as we know, the whole phenomenology of spiritualism belongs. There is something of the trickster in the character of the shaman and medicine-man, for he, too, often plays malicious jokes on people, only to fall victim in his turn to the vengeance of those whom he has injured. For this reason his profession sometimes puts him in peril of his life. Besides that, the shamanistic techniques in themselves often cause the medicine-man a good deal of discomfort, if not actual pain. At all events the 'making of a medicine-man' involves, in many parts of the world, so much agony of body and soul that permanent psychic injuries may result. His 'approximation to the saviour' is an obvious consequence of this, in confirmation of the mythological truth that the wounded wounder is the agent of healing, and that the sufferer takes away suffering.*"[96]

The final move presented here suggests a number of ways in which the trickster manifests in actual therapeutic encounters in the intra, inter, and trans categories. These are through paradoxical directives to the patient on the part of the therapist, dream interpretation, reading for latent content in connection with experiencing a host of synchronistic phenomena, and what Freud preferred to refer to as thought-transferences. Pelton brings all three categories into clear focus with regard to the trickster in connection with therapy when he says: "The trickster's association

---

[96]Ibid, 195–6.

with divination already suggests some of the possibilities of these patterns as creative forms of imagination. If Chinese divination is a marvelous type of linguistic iconography, West African divination discloses both a passion for sociotherapy and a conviction that such therapy is the creation of that mode of social [inter], personal [intra], and cosmic [trans] composition which [is] the work of the ironic imagination...."[97] (brackets added).

Even more to the point regarding the trickster and synchronicity, Pelton says the following:

"...it is as the master of language – possessor of all stories, linguist of the gods...embodiment of the 'word of the world,' metaphor of social conversation – that the trickster reveals the human world itself to be language. Thus as 'image, fiction, model, metaphor,' or, more abstractly, as active reciprocal of the human capacity to converse with every other mode of being, the trickster reveals man in his inmost and most daily reality. He is a composition of the human juggling and flip-flopping needed to hold in balance the words arising from all the conversations in which man is engaged. As the trickster's myths are told, his dances danced, his twisted word unraveled, and his hidden presence discerned, his multiformity insists that the words of all dimensions meet in man. His synchronicity discloses that life as it is and as it ought to be are ironically joined in the present - a now which is never finally imagined."[98]

As Akans, our assumptive world includes the almost unconscious belief that such cultural heroes in sports, religion, and ancient and contemporary political leadership, derive their immense powers of genius, mastery, and achievement from God, the ancestors, or other spirits. However, for me as a youngster my good feelings about the positive supernatural characteristics of my heroes seemed to be largely and frequently overshadowed by my more fearful thoughts,

---

[97]Ibid, 274.
[98]Ibid, 271.

feelings, and experiences. As a result of my childhood experiences of trauma and hope I was led early on to be deeply interested in the supernatural, which in turn predisposed me to be open to experiences of synchronicity and the miraculous later in life.

FIRST CONVERSION

IN WHAT WAS TO BE the next set of traumas in my life, I left home at the age of ten for Accra Academy, a seven-year secondary and boarding school for boys in Ghana. For the next seven years, I spent nine months of each year away from home. Initially, I was totally disoriented and in shock about the squalor, oppression, and hazing experiences of this new life. Also for the first time I had to start grappling with religious anxieties about the fate of my soul in a more conscious manner, because almost as soon as arrived at the school I was pressured by the older boys to accept the gospel of Jesus Christ. I was inducted into the small group of "believers" on campus known as the Scripture Union. As a result of the evangelical goals of this group, missionaries from that far away, mysterious and captivating land flowing with milk and honey, America, would come to the campus with their stirring Christian plays, music, glamour, and messages of salvation. This was a welcome relief from the squalid and oppressive conditions of the entire boarding school system. I accepted Jesus as my savior because I was pounced on by the older proselytizing devout Christian boys who warned me that I would go straight to hell if I got involved with those boys on the campus who went to dances and fooled around with girls and smoked and drank. The anxiety in this situation was unbearable, and I decided to follow their advice and accept Jesus as my personal savior to avoid all the putative horrors of eternity in hell. Several of the questions I asked back then, and that have continued to plague me about this predicament are as follows: Why are we here? Where do we come from? Where is God? Why do such horrible things happen to us? Why so much death and punishment and horror everywhere? Where are the putative magical and heroic responses of the supernatural realm in our lives?

I accepted Jesus as my savior partly as insurance against the possibility of the reality of a condition called hell, and partly because of a deep yearning for emotional and esthetic fulfillment, a yearning triggered in me by my encounters with visiting American missionaries. A seed of redemption had been sown in my soul which was gradually to bear fruitful answers to the many questions which have simmered in my psyche over the years, answers that help me to be more effective at addressing my own fundamental anxieties, and increasingly those of the people I work with clinically.

During my teenage years, while on vacation from boarding school, I enjoyed the classics of Western literature, while I struggled with the usual concerns of adolescence: parents, siblings, peers, romance, sexual experimentation, and acne. I would spend my time engaged in the youthful pursuits of two very separate, yet coexisting cultures. I would fish and hunt, and trap small birds, reptiles, and mammals to keep as pets. This I did with one set of friends, most of whose families lacked the basic amenities of Western culture such as clean homes, clothes, and shoes, not to mention television sets, radios, telephones, cameras, bicycles, cars, and magazine subscriptions. With another set of more westernized friends, I concerned myself with the latest fashions in clothes, and popular music and dance, as well as factors (i.e., academic work, U.S. college application procedures, and sources of financial aid) that we understood to be important for getting to the Promised Land of America. Memorable experiences of this period included my passing the excruciating General Certificate Examinations with distinction, being elected Chapel Prefect of the student governing board, and being admitted to the Medical School of the University of Ghana.

I experienced cultural heterogeneity in a deeper way due to the fact that my father is a black African, and my mother is a white American. They both educated me about their cultures by direct verbal instruction, and also through visits to their hometowns. My mother made a pilgrimage back to the U.S. in 1976 for the bicentennial celebrations of America's independence, and also to visit her family and friends after almost ten years of not having been to the U.S. My two sisters and I came along with my mother, and after six weeks of American television, fast food, and summer fun, I had no other goal than to return to the United Sates independently, and as soon as possible, to continue exploring this amazing culture to which I had been all too briefly and tantalizingly exposed.

SECOND CONVERSION

I CAME TO YALE in September 1977, thinking that I had finally escaped from the backward and oppressive meritocracy and squalid conditions I had experienced in the Ghanaian educational system due to the frequent corporeal punishment and the relative lack of material and technological resources. At Yale, I thought I would be sitting and studying at the feet of the various reincarnations of Socrates, Plato, and Aristotle, while learning more about, and espousing and practicing with respectability, a blend of Epicurean hedonism, and a 60s and 70s style of hippie-like antipathy to various systems of oppressive authority. In a contradictory manner, I also initially believed that I had won a gentleman's sinecure – that I was now guaranteed a successful career in medicine, and that a life of wealth and ease would eventually present themselves to me as I serenely pursued the nobler aims of the mind and spirit.

Instead I found intense academic competition and stringent requirements all over again, and even more so than before in Ghana. In addition, I experienced unrequited love, bitterly cold winters, large bursar's bills, racism, and a whole host of my own terrible ineptitudes. I was puzzled and in agony, but all the while refused to admit to myself and to others that I might be experiencing culture and future shock. I did what I needed to in order to keep my head above water, and then spent a lot of the rest of my time and energy in self-pity.

I experienced occasional release from my gloom, my bad "luck," such as when one semester, in particular, I was very successful in my economics, English, and history classes. In all three of these courses I felt engaged by the material, could see how the underlying themes in all three courses related to economic and political success, and I was well-liked and supported and encouraged by each of my professors. To my mind here at a last was some good "luck." This should have been a sign to me that I was better suited for the humanities than the sciences in this new, yet difficult life I was living.

It was not too long after this meaningful convergence in my course work that I experienced my second conversion, which was in itself, as I have looked back on it, saturated with synchronicity. When this second conversion - this peak experience - occurred, I was exhausted after the first semester of my senior year at college from a variety of stresses and strains related to my school work and relationship difficulties. My mother, my two sisters, and I traveled, at Christmas time, from Ohio to Kentucky to visit some Canadian friends we had known when we lived in Ghana. During our stay with them, I came upon the books, *I'm O.K, You're O.K.*, and *Games People Play*, explications of transactional analysis. I remember seeing these books on my parents' bookshelves when I was growing up in Ghana, although they did not make much sense to me at the time. However, it was because I recognized them from Ghana that I asked to borrow them from our friends in Kentucky. They said I could keep them and, upon our return to Ohio, I started to plow through them. I remember how easy both books were to read, especially because they made so much sense to me, and were able to provide me with great comfort regarding my academic and romantic miseries.

My second conversion happened on one particular day, while I was lying on the sofa in the living room of my mother's three bedroom apartment in Columbus, Ohio. I was reading through *I'm O.K., You're O.K.*, my mother was in the kitchen preparing lunch, and my two younger sisters were in their room reading. Although it was a bitterly cold day in the dead of winter, the sun was shining very brightly through the living room windows. I was feeling relaxed and excited all at once about the connections and insights that were piling up on top of one another as I was reading.

The above collection of synchronicities – my various courses converging in a meaningful way; being together in Kentucky with our friends from Ghana; and also rediscovering books of my parents which I remembered from Ghana, all seemed to integrate into a powerful state of awareness that triggered my second major conversion. At one very clear and definable moment during my reading, I realized for the first time that the Christian categories of Father, Son, and Holy Spirit, and the psychological categories of Parent, Child, and Adult, from Transactional Analysis that I was reading about on the sofa, and Freud's Superego, Ego, and Id were parallel conceptions from different fields. In the moment that this realization occurred to me, my consciousness began to expand, time seemed suspended, my vision seemed to be directed down the corridors of eternity, and I was in a completely exhilarated state; a state of utter joy, vitality, and insight.

I arose from the sofa and rushed to my mother in the kitchen where I tried to explain all at once what was happening to me. My sisters hurried out of their room to find out what all the commotion was about. Although I could not fully explain what I had realized to my mother or my sisters that day, I was determined from that day to make sense to them eventually as well as to others and to myself out of this the most amazing experience of my life to that point in time.

That day of realizing in my bones the connection between medical/psychiatric, psychological, spiritual, and supernatural structures, (a realization I today call my unitive and transformative crisis), was followed by a long ten-year period of second-guessing the powerful simplicity of my own experience because of various scientific and religious scruples about "the quest for truth," and positivism. In other words, I did not want to mislabel, misunderstand, or misinterpret my conversion through subjective delusions about mere physical and biochemical epiphenomena in the brain, and so I started assessing it from many different objective perspectives. But it was precisely this process of assessing parallels from different disciplines that started me seriously toward seeing the interconnectedness of such a thing as a synchronicity (from a depth psychological viewpoint) and the miraculous (from a theological perspective).

My desire to verify my experience as rigorously as possible eventually moved me away from being a biology major, to being a theology student, and then to being a student of psychology. This second conversion experience compelled me to see all of life as interconnected and what I was struggling to do in a seemingly restless journey from field to field, was clear to me as an effort to unify my fragmented understanding about the relationships between body, mind, and spirit, in a way that took both science and religion seriously.

My initial commitment to combine these fields through a medical specialty I described as "theological neuropsychiatry," eventually became modified away from a positivistic scientific approach,[99] in favor of an eclectic and more symbolic approach, which in turn, eventually led me to the Psychiatry and Religion program at Union.

It was the unifying impact of my second conversion which motivated me to begin to scrutinize my experiences for more and more meaningful interconnections, and which caused me to be gratefully amazed by a chance meeting with a Ghanaian cousin of mine, Adwoa, in the summer of 1981, just after I had graduated from college. This coincidence provided me with powerful intuitive-affective knowledge, on the trans level in relation to synchronicity and the ego-Self framework, as well as in relation to the miraculous and the soul-God framework because it made me mindful of healing taking place in my life with regard to my experience of cultural dislocation in coming to the United States from Ghana. I had not seen Adwoa for several years, since a summer vacation I spent with my Ghanaian aunt and uncle who lived, at the time, together with Adwoa, in Westbury, Long Island.

[99]Writing this reminds me of one of the great humiliations of my life. It was when as a freshman in college, I eagerly if somewhat naively and cockily assumed that I would take the freshman course in quantum mechanics. I flunked the placement test for this course and was required to go back into General Chemistry which I had already had in high school. This experience shattered my confidence and soured me about the education I was about to embark on. Later on, I gained some perspective about my inadequate preparation for that course, and have never lost the feeling of being attracted to the New Physics, and also the connections of the New Physics to the synchronistic dream involving Professor Wimbush as a wisdom figure referred to further on in this chapter. In other words, it is worth noting that this wisdom figure's great powers of mind-reading, materializing and dematerializing at will, and being in several different places at once, all point to a state of existence completely unbounded by the ordinary laws of physics as we know them. It is also important to note the connections between this theme of the New Physics as it appears in regard to shamanism in Fred A. Wolf's *The Eagle's Quest: A Physicist's Search for Truth in the Heart of the Shamanic World*, New York: Summit Books, 1991; with regard to holography in Miachel Talbot's *The Holographic Universe*, New York: HarperPerennial, 1991; and with regard to synchronicity in F. David Peat's, *Synchronicity: The Bridge Between Matter and Mind*, New York: Bantam Books, 1987.

Our coincidental meeting in 1981 happened at LaGuardia Airport. I ran into Adwoa there while I was waiting for a flight. But I had no idea she would be there when I was and she had no idea I would be there when she was. What was so amazing to me was the way in which we almost did not connect with each other. Slightly different decisions on either of our parts would have led to completely different pathways, which in a crowded and busy airport would surely have meant that we would not have run into each other.

Adwoa's experience on arriving in America had left her frozen for several years, but under much worse circumstances than my own and yet she had landed on her feet, a fact she recounted to me with much delight during our meeting at LaGuardia Airport. Adwoa's early difficulties in America were because she had been brought here from Ghana by my Ghanaian Aunt and Uncle who reduced her to the role of a servant. During her four year stay with them she did not know what to do to extricate herself from those demeaning circumstances and had remained frozen in them. Yet she had now gotten her own apartment, a good job she enjoyed and she was happily and successfully independent.

I realize that Adwoa may have been a model for me, someone who like myself had arrived in America from Ghana and had eventually landed on her own two feet, after experiencing difficult initial circumstances in this new land. (Before this meeting with Adwoa, I did not know that her earlier difficult life circumstances had changed so significantly for the better).

In the summer of 1981, when I ran into Adwoa, I was just beyond my overwhelming college experience (my first years in America); I was somewhat uncertain of what to do next; in college I had felt frozen, and now I had a number of positive options to consider for my future, including medical school, business school, divinity school, and graduate school.

In New Haven, when I first came to America, I was overwhelmed by culture shock and internal divisions in my emotional life. Through our meeting, my discovery of the resonance between Adwoa's emergence from her difficulties and my graduation from my difficult years in college offered a wonderful and timely reassurance to me. At that moment in the airport that I discovered Adwoa had come out of her difficult circumstances so successfully, I felt my own condition of having been frozen melting even more.

This was yet another experience of synchronicity for me but now I was beginning to understand how I could learn from such experiences if I considered them reflectively. Here, of course, the meeting with Adwoa was an opportunity for a synchronicity to bolster my faith in my own future at a time of uncertainty, which indeed it did.

Therefore, upon reflection about Adwoa's appearance in my life at LaGuardia Airport, I understood more from this experience in terms of what Jung, von Franz, Aziz and others mean when they refer to synchronicity as "the simultaneous occurrence of a certain psychic state [my wondering if I could get past "being frozen in New Haven"] with one or more external events [my meeting with Adwoa] which appear as meaningful parallels to the momentary subjective state [her deliverance encouraging mine]."[100]

Similarly, I understood from the theological definitions of miracles as events that can evoke a deeper commitment to God's plan of redemption (due to their extraordinary manifestations of God's guiding presence, power, providence, and deliverance), that my meeting with Adwoa was a sign of God's redemptive presence in my life as it related to my Ghanaian culture, family, and career.

---

[100]See definitions of synchronicity from Jung, *Synchronicity: An Acausal Connecting Principle*, 25, as well as from the citations from von Franz and Aziz in Chapter One.

In a more startling experience of synchronicity a year later, I had a dream about a frail and emaciated black woman whose head was lifted towards heaven as she blindly and inconsolably wailed her deep lament to the universe. This dream brought me special intuitive-affective knowledge on the trans level in relation to synchronicity and the ego-Self framework, as well as in relation to the miraculous and the soul-God framework. This is because within a week of my having had this dream, a Ghanaian woman by the name of Sarah whom I had met several years earlier through friends, but had not seen for quite some time, showed up at my door with a woeful story of her homelessness and destitution, a personification of the woman in my dream.

My church at the time attempted to respond to Sarah with a place to stay, companionship, and somewhat incompetent counseling. After a few weeks of concerted responses to Sarah, it became clearer to us that she was deeply wounded at a level that we could not even remotely begin to understand. She would describe to us how she spent night after night wailing and crying out to God about how miserable her circumstances were. None of our ministrations appeared to be of any use, and the whole experience seemed to be a real-life enactment of the suffering of Job.

It was quite a surprise to me when I realized several weeks later that my dream about the wailing woman was about Sarah, and that the dream had occurred about a week before she showed up at my house. Aside from noting the connection between my dream about this friend, and her subsequent re-entry into my life, I had no scheme with which to order this experience but became yet again more determined to be attentive to the supernatural, synchronistic, and miraculous events in my daily life and to find better ways of responding to such events. In fact, today I can see that at the time I was still suffering through my disorientation with life in a new country and culture and wondering how much my charismatic church could genuinely respond to suffering of such an abstract order when the dream and then Sarah herself appeared to test the waters for me.

Again, in retrospect, Sarah's appearance in my life reflected the understandings of Jung, von Franz, Aziz and others when they refer to synchronicity as "the simultaneous occurrence of a certain psychic state [the dream about a suffering woman so similar to Sarah] with one or more external events [Sarah then showing up at my door and subsequently seeking aid from my church] which appear as meaningful parallels to the momentary subjective state [the experience of suffering and questioning my community's abilities to respond to same]."[101]

Also the definitions of the signs and wonders as events that can evoke a deeper commitment to God's plan of redemption due to their extraordinary manifestations of God's guiding presence and power, were reflected in my amazing meeting with Sarah after my dream about someone similar, and could be taken as yet another sign of God's redemptive presence in my life as it related to my Ghanaian culture.[102] In this particular case, God's redemptive presence in my life was manifested as a call to minister to Sarah, someone from Ghana who served as an initial divine prompt for me to deepen my pastoral counseling competence in a way that would be relevant to Ghanaians as well as all others who came from a state of deprivation feeling dislocated but seeking more. By dedicating myself to this path of ministry and working for the healing of others, I began to deepen my own healing and my interest in both synchronicity and the miraculous, which took me beyond an isolation in only one perspective, such as was advocated by my church at the time.

---

[101]See definitions of synchronicity from Jung, *Synchronicity: An Acausal Connecting Principle*, 25, as well as from the citations from von Franz and Aziz in Chapter One

[102]See definitions of signs and wonders in Chapter One

My church at this time was a non-denominational charismatic Christian church. I participated in this church for five years (1981 to 1986) as a devout member, and thereby absorbed the very strong belief this community had in the New Testament worldview, which includes beliefs in the supernatural realm in both its positive and negative aspects. In this group, we were constantly admonished to engage in valiant spiritual warfare against the Devil and other evil forces through deep and sustained worship, prayer, and Bible study. Also, while we were encouraged by the leadership of the church to fight against supernatural evil, we were also encouraged to pray and seek miraculous results in all areas of our lives. Frequently, for example, we sought out and testified about miraculous deliverances from all types of problems, which included minor physical ailments, such as colds and headaches, as well as more serious and life-threatening illnesses, such as cancer and heart disease.

At the time, as I reflected on our community's fascination with the supernatural and the miraculous, it was clear to me that we were fervent in our beliefs and practices to prove to ourselves that the word of God as expressed in scripture is all true, even the seemingly impossible parts about miracles. It seemed important for us to experience miracles such that our treasured faith would not be reduced to a faith that was not very special in relation to other human systems of belief and practice. What would make our system truly divine and compel others to embrace it, would be the amazing evidence of God's infinite love expressed as God's unlimited ability to overcome the bitter consequences and sufferings of an evil and wayward world through displays of miracles for us today, like those from the past recounted in scripture. In this way, evidence of miracles in our lives could help to win converts and to defend against detractors from the Christian message as we understood it.

Over time, however, I became concerned about the lack of what seemed like an intellectually plausible basis for our view of the miraculous, not to mention the general lack for me in this community of demonstrable and incontrovertible miracles. It seemed to me at times that the leadership of this group frequently insisted that miracles had occurred when and where in fact they might not have. This caused me to think and feel that in this group we were caught up in pretense - a participation mystique in which members of the church became good at telling stories of miraculous deliverance from one problem or another, but where it was always difficult to gauge whether the stories had been fabricated to bolster the credibility of the faith, or whether they had actually happened as recounted.

In the end, I left that charismatic community to seek a more learned approach to the Christian faith. But I never left my interest in the miraculous. However, in the academic communities I joined over time, (such as Hartford Seminary and the Yale Divinity School), there was very little serious belief about the supernatural or the miraculous in most of the programs. Instead, I found that the miracles in the Bible were not considered by most students and teachers to be historically accurate events, although they were considered true representations of belief systems and traditions of the distant past. It seemed as though I was ridiculed or given an amused and indulgent look every time I tried to raise a serious question about the supernatural or the miraculous. This was going too far to the other extreme for me.

As a result of my church experience and my academic experience, I encountered two extremely different views concerning the existence of miracles. Under the first view, my main worshipping community at one time, the charismatic church, over-emphasized the miraculous in inappropriate ways, and under the second view, my liberal mainline Protestant academic community de-emphasized and implicitly rejected the miraculous.

From the disparity of these divergent views my quest began in earnest. Initially, it was a quest to find a means to harness the power of the miraculous in a way that is reverent to God (the trans level), and yet was also credible and useful within community (the inter level), even a skeptical community, and was able to support coherence and efficacy of healing in the individual soul (the intra level). The ideal then was to locate and make accessible to others a view of the miraculous that could work on both fronts, i.e., for the charismatic church as well as the mainline academic and church community. Over time this initial quest has evolved into the simultaneous embrace of the synchronicity and the miraculous through the ego–Self and soul–God frameworks detailed in this study.[103]

---

[103]Many of the difficulties of polarization I encountered in my spiritual journey, from my charismatic church experience to my liberal academic theological experience, were revisited in my formation as a psychotherapist. In a program that purported to be committed to pastoral psychotherapy there was often very little real effort applied by my Freudian or other psychodynamic teachers to engage fully, the theological dimensions of psychotherapy, while some of the more conservative Christian participants in parts of the program found the psychoanalytic notion of the unconscious irrelevant in the healing process, and instead were committed to approaching healing only in terms of the power of the Holy Spirit. Also, within the psychoanalytic side of the community there existed numerous psychological camps seemingly pitted against one another. In view of this fragmentation within the psychological camp of my training community, and also between the psychological and theological camps, my goal became to evolve a coherent perspective which, once again, could include the most significant of the psychodynamic models into one system and which would be theology-friendly as well. In other words, when it comes to synchronicity and the miraculous, we do not have to consign ourselves simply to overheated fakery on the one hand or smug intellectual dismissiveness or reductionism on the other. Having offered these critiques, I am mindful that my perceptions are not perfect either, and that at any point along the way in which I critique others, the limitations and errors of my own ego and soul are ever at work producing distortions in my perceptions, observations, insights, and conclusions.

Four Dreams

Over the next several years, starting in 1984, I had four dreams about snakes which involved intuitive-affective knowledge, on the trans level in relation to synchronicity and the ego-Self framework, as well as in relation to the miraculous and the soul-God framework. These dreams were very powerful for me in that they were harbingers of a healing process for me and my family, and they also furthered my interest in synchronicity and the miraculous. I experienced the first three dreams during normal periods of sleep over several weeks in 1984 before I returned to Ghana to visit my father. The fourth "dream" occurred seven years later while I was fully awake and in the presence of other people.

In 1984, after I had the first three dreams, I went from the United States to Ghana, West Africa where my father lived, to sort out my unfinished emotional business with him. This was a compelling need for me because I had seen first-hand the pain my father had gone through as a result of his own father having died at a young age. It seemed that my father was left with a heavy burden of parent-hunger, through which he was often immersed in poignant wonderings about the early loss of his father.

His father was a paramount chief of the Akim Kotoku traditional area in the Eastern Region of Ghana, and my father tells the story (perhaps apocryphal?) of how his father was poisoned by rivals who managed to get their treacherous scheme past the royal food-tasters. In any case, whether this account is accurate or not, the fact is that his father died mysteriously at the age of forty-six, and this early loss caused my father much pain, which in turn made me quite anxious to deal with as much of our unfinished emotional business as possible so I would not have to go through the same agony (if he should die before me).

My difficulties with my father, and the complications of family and ancestral connections, are significant for the synchronistic view of the dreams I had before I went to see my father in Ghana. The first dream had me peering into a cage that contained a vicious and huge anaconda-sized snake that clearly wanted to kill me. I was terrorized by it, and yet managed to stay just beyond its venomous fangs and crushing reach by standing about a foot away from the bars of the cage.

Several days later I had another dream about a snake. In the dream, I knew it was the same snake as before, although it was smaller and spotted unlike the first one. In this dream, the snake presented itself as a dangerous trickster (it kept appearing and disappearing like the Cheshire cat in *Alice in Wonderland*, in and around a huge woodpile). But my father was in the dream with me this time, and we were both trying to kill this elusive snake with big sticks. The key feature of this dream that I remember is that although the snake was still as dangerous as the one in the first dream, my father and I together had it on the defensive.

About a week after this dream, I had a third dream about this same snake. This time, I was standing on the dam of a water reservoir. At a distance of about half a mile, I could see the snake slithering across the floor of the reservoir, the water being clear, and thereby allowing this sort of clarity of vision. The snake communicated to me that it was retreating for a time, was offering a truce in our battle for now, but had every intention of returning some day. In this dream, the snake had stripes, and appeared to be smiling in a rather sly manner, again reminding me of both Alice's Cheshire cat and a trickster.

A few weeks later, I was in Ghana with my father. During our time together in Ghana, it was clear to me that my father did not have the appetite for what I was trying to accomplish. He was much more concerned that I get my career back on track and resolve to go to medical school and leave my "ludicrous religious speculations" behind. Unbeknownst to my mother (from whom he was separated, and estranged, though not yet legally divorced) and my two sisters, my father had remarried and started a new family.

During this trip, we paid a visit to the current paramount chief of my father's traditional area. In the main reception area of the chief's "palace," the various pictures of past chiefs, including my grandfather's were in view. The current chief made several references to our ancestral links, and promised during the annual festival of tribute to the ancestors, to summon them to meet and support me on my path back in the United States. At the time I was highly skeptical of the world-view pertaining to ancestors and their influence on the living that the chief was alluding to, and remember asking him whether, as a lawyer trained in the U.K., he really believed all this or not. He clearly did. [104]

Given that I had been away from my home in Ghana for seven years, without the benefit of close nurturing from my father, or opportunities to learn from my father, I wanted to put some things in our family that were out of joint in order. I had planned on staying in Ghana with my father for the next two years but he seemed more concerned that I return and follow through on my education in the United States than that I stay with him. Thus, it was with some degree of frustration that I heeded my father's exhortations that I return to the United States to resume my education. And so I returned to the United States after only six weeks in Ghana even though I had originally planned to stay for two years. At the time I felt, nevertheless, that I had done my best to deal with my unfinished emotional business with my father, and

---

[104]Another Uncle has told me stories about his deceased father (my grandfather the poisoned chief), appearing to him as a spirit in a variety of places and ways related to episodes of major illness in this uncle's life, always with healing and other beneficial results.

that I would not have to live the rest of my life wondering painfully about him if he predeceased me.

Seven years after my visit with my father in Ghana, my two younger sisters (who lived in Manhattan at the time) and I were finalizing plans for a family reunion in the United States which was scheduled for July, 1992. My father had requested that we try to arrange for him to meet with our mother because he had some "unfinished business" he wanted to try to take care of between them. The whole process of getting all of us together, after fifteen years of various forms of estrangement, was rather delicate. Nonetheless, we all finally came together for several weeks in July, and unbelievably, had the most astounding sense of family togetherness we have ever known. We visited the family who gave me their copy of *I'm O.K., You're O.K* (the book so instrumental in my second conversion back in 1980), the couple my parents had known during their married years in Ghana; we ate together; played together; and even fought together some; my parents even got into the habit of holding hands from time to time.

One sunny day during this reunion, my father, my youngest sister, and I were standing and talking very comfortably in a small circle on the little porch outside my apartment in Middletown, Connecticut. Suddenly a little garter snake slithered out of the grass on one side of the porch, headed straight for my sister, went directly over her bare feet, and slithered into the grass on the other side of the porch, all before any of us could even react. For a couple of moments afterwards we were all very excited, and lamented that we had not been able to get a picture of this weird snake coming out of nowhere, and for no apparent reason, crossing over my sister's feet. It was in those very moments that it suddenly dawned on me that this was the snake of my three previous dreams: the snake had returned as it had promised, and I had been expecting it these eight years, and I recognized it the moment it appeared.

There was something very different about this snake though: it had lost all its malicious and venomous intent towards me and my family, as its embodiment in the form of the harmless garter snake demonstrated. This was in general accord with the tapering off of the snake's viciousness in my dream sequence, although after that sequence I had always remained apprehensive that the snake would return with its original viciousness. My interpretation of the manifestation of this real and harmless snake in the presence of a joyful family reunion, was that the destructive forces afflicting my family system (and that I began to recognize and take on in 1984, through my visit to my father in Ghana) were finally depotentiated - there was nothing more to fear because a dangerous and life-threatening venom had been removed from our lives.

Over the years, I interpreted these four dreams as synchronistic reflections of my increasingly victorious integration of my shadow – those unacceptable aspects of my psyche that I had repressed into my unconscious or of which I was otherwise unaware[105] - and also of recurring struggles against certain forces of evil, separation, and destruction present in, and threatening my family in a way which involves our lineage in terms of the past, present, and future.

In the seven years before this fourth snake appeared, and after I returned to the United States from visiting my father, I continued to

---

[105]In an experience of Clinical Pastoral Education (CPE) at Hartford Hospital in 1992 I was characterized by my supervisor partly as follows: "David...[sought]...to move away from his reliance on his adaptive, highly polished self in his group work. He sought to express his more aggressive energy directly rather than letting it go underground. For David this work focussed specifically on accessing his erotic feelings, his anger, his own power, and his identity as a Black man. He thought of himself as the 'trickster' or the jazz soloist who actively 'plays' and gyrates himself and others towards new levels of experience and understanding. These were transitional figures for David which allowed him to express more of his dark side in a manner acceptable to the program and controlled by himself," in Joan E. Hemenway, "Clinical Pastoral Education at Hartford Hospital, Hartford, CT: Supervisor's Final Evaluation," 1992.

explore the boundaries between religion and mental health by working, consecutively, over four years in an immunology lab (for one year), in a school for the autistic and neurologically impaired (for one year), and in a school for severely emotionally disturbed adolescents (for two years), while exploring various meditation practices. I was looking for an environment where my scientific training as a biology major could be seriously synthesized with my religious conversion experience, and my growing interest in synchronicity and the miraculous, and where I could explore the questions that had been raised for me about time, death, the supernatural, and the nature of consciousness and mental health.

I had talked with several people in the Yale community and could not find anyone who seemed interested in the questions of synthesis I was trying to raise. In all of this I felt that if I did go to medical school to pursue psychiatry it would be because it was an appropriate vehicle for me to explore my deepest interests, and not merely to satisfy my father's ambitions for me. In many ways I was trying to make use of the best that my father had given me through his scientific background as a plant physiologist, and at the same time I was trying to fill in the religious and spiritual gaps I sensed were there because of his completely secular worldview and values.

As I worked assiduously to discern and pursue my vocation, I continued to tend to the germinal issues about my father and family background that were raised for me when I visited him in Ghana back in 1984. The summer of 1992 continued as an unprecedented period of synchronistic convergence in my life that tied many themes together, including the dream sequence about the snakes, and brought me much personal relief and emotional healing.

The summer started in the satisfying glow of my knowledge that I would be coming to Union in the fall, and this opportunity to study in the Psychiatry and Religion department represented the best solution to my needs to synthesize religion, science, and psychology. At the same time, I enrolled in the clinical residency program at the Blanton–Peale Graduate Institute to be trained as a pastoral psychotherapist, and continued to participate in the process leading towards ordination as a priest in the Episcopal church. In the midst of these convergences, I received a totally unsolicited and unexpected call from the director of CPE at Hartford Hospital in which he invited me to return there for another unit of CPE and to serve as a stipended chaplain in the hospital's geriatric center for the summer. I quickly accepted the offer, expressing my amazement to the director at how "kairotic" his call was to me.

As I worked that summer at the hospital in Hartford, at the same time, I was reading Anthony Stevens' book, *On Jung*, and quickly discovered that the intimate connection between, if not unity of, psyche and matter (what is known as the psychoid)[106], is related to Jung's idea of synchronicity. As Stevens puts it, synchronicity is

---

the 'acausal connecting principle' that creates meaningful relationships between events occurring at the same time. Since all life is pattern, it follows that time functions as an aspect of that pattern. Anything that happens is related to everything else that happens through the time at which the happening occurs. The Chinese attempted to determine empirically how patterns of meaning unfold in the universe through time. The I Ching used this empiricism to provide a meaningful context for events occurring at any particular moment. Jung was sympathetic to this approach because it corresponds to how we experience meaningful coincidences and also to how we experience time....The Western mentality dismisses such coincidences as meaningless, but life reaches beyond the significance of mere causality.[107]

---

[106]My reading of Monick's *Phallos* had introduced me to the concept of the psychoid just a few weeks before my discovery of Stevens' *On Jung*.

[107]Anthony Stevens, *On Jung*, New York: Routledge, 1990, 266.

Before I made these discoveries about the psychoid unconscious and synchronicity, I accepted the fourth snake's appearance described above as a synchronistic waking dream in a relatively unschooled fashion.[108] Through my initial explorations of Jung's approach to synchronicity (as described above) it became much easier for me to understand the importance of my dream sequence about the snakes with regard to my family and my own growth as an individual and a young man.

Again, upon reflection, the appearance of the snake in my life reflected the conceptions of Jung, von Franz, Aziz and others when they refer to synchronicity as "the simultaneous occurrence of a certain psychic state [wrestling with and overcoming fears related to filial harmony and becoming actualized as an adult myself] with one or more external events [a harmless snake going over my sister's foot] which appear as meaningful parallels to the momentary subjective state [my then sudden state of calm despite my three previous dreams about sinister snakes]."[109]

In a similar manner the definitions of signs and wonders, as events that can stimulate deeper commitment to God's plan of redemption due to their extraordinary manifestations of God's guiding presence and power, are reflected in my amazing sighting of the snake passing over my sister's foot after my three dreams about snakes, and could be taken as yet another sign of God's redemptive presence in my life as it relates to my family and Ghanaian culture.[110] This redemptive experience felt undeniable

---

[108]The appearance of the snake in our midst was really an astounding event for me, because prior to that time (and since my arrival in the U.S. in 1977 to attend college) I cannot recall ever having seen a snake in the U.S., except on television and at the zoo. And so for my first natural sighting of a snake in the U.S. to entail all the details of family cohesion and physical proximity may make it a bit clearer why the event had so much meaning for me.

[109]See definitions of synchronicity from Jung, *Synchronicity: An Acausal Connecting Principle*, 25, as well as from the citations from von Franz and Aziz in Chapter One.

because there we were – my sister, my Dad (on a rare visit to the U.S. from Ghana), and me – standing together in a picture of family unity and harmony, after so many years of separation and alienation between Ghana and the U.S. At the same time, instead of the huge anaconda-sized elusive snake with venomous fangs like the two other sinister snakes from my earlier dreams, a harmless garter snake enters into our midst signaling that the evil forces afflicting us had been routed.

THIRD CONVERSION

MY THIRD CONVERSION is about my gradual embrace of an integrated and simultaneous approach to synchronicity and the miraculous. For centuries, prior to the Enlightenment and the later emergence of psychoanalysis and depth psychology, occurrences of unexpected fortune and misfortune were often attributed to divine intervention. In the last century, since the emergence of psychoanalysis and depth psychology, an enormous number of unexpected events in the lives of individuals in the secular mainstream that were either fortunate or unfortunate for them were regarded primarily for their psychological implications, exclusive of any theological considerations. This study has found that a simultaneous appreciation for what has been previously attributed to divine intervention alone, and what has been more recently regarded for psychological implications alone, can lead to a fuller appreciation of the human experience.

Based on the preceding modes, individuals who might otherwise be dubious regarding either the threshold question of the existence of God or, the more subtle question, regarding how actively God may or may not intervene in our day-to-day existence, start to

[110]See definitions of signs and wonders in Chapter One.

entertain the latter. That is, after observing enough synchronicities with meaning and harboring enough curiosity about what lies beyond synchronicity, an individual may proceed to have an interest in miraculous possibilities.

Here a person may be actively open to and seeking divine miraculous relief from an oppressive condition of some kind already or they may merely be open to the possibility of same. Such a person usually possesses a well developed belief in God, in miraculous phenomena, and in God's relationship to miraculous phenomena, and often also has a belief in such other things as the efficacy of prayer for experiencing miracles but none of these are imperative. As a threshold matter though, based on earlier curiosity springing from an appreciation of synchronicity, here a person may have an avid interest in discovering authentic accounts of miraculous healings and other miraculous events.

The following example is actually of yet another synchronicity, but one that, in its content, pertained to miracles and so opened me up to the miraculous more fully, and thereby motivated and led me to be more interested in miraculous possibilities. In other words, in this next example, I experienced an inspiring multi-layered synchronicity about the topic of the miraculous itself.

I was several years into my doctoral studies at Union, and deeply immersed in preparing for one of my comprehensive exams on the topic of the miraculous. One day during this preparation period, I took a break from my studying and happened to tune in to a documentary on T.V. about miraculous healings at the shrine at Lourdes. Later in that same week I took my comprehensive exam which had a question on it about healing shrines. I was able to use some of the material I had seen in the documentary in writing the exam, and while writing I had an overwhelming sense of a divine presence guiding me. In fact, the meaning of this synchronicity about the miraculous was so profound for me that I burst into tears of unspeakable joy at my desk for several minutes.

In this example, I was becoming more immersed in my interest in synchronicity and the miraculous through my studies. I was paying attention to the subject in the media, and in a moment during which much pent up tension was being released as I was writing the exam, I could feel a deep and inexpressible kinship with the Self or God. This powerful sense of guidance, support, and protection even, was available to me because of my particularly charged up state of mind in which the ego became more surrendered to the Self.

Again, the ego's system of resistance is not to be underestimated, for it requires daily renewal and discipline to prevent the ego from going back into a state of cloudiness about its need for a deep, abiding, and conscious relationship with the Self. The ego has a tendency to want to avoid this relationship with the Self, and therefore it can use the mere surface amazement of such coincidences to lull itself into an avoidance of a truer and ever-deepening relationship with the Self.

One point which needs to be stressed again and again is that the manifestation of synchronicities requires that the ego be surrendered deliberately, consistently, and consciously to the Self in order for the true value of synchronicities to be grasped for further benefit. This process of surrendering the ego to the Self is an arduous and draining one, which requires systems of education and support to enable as many people as possible to engage in and benefit from it. At the same time, this study has found that an approach to the miraculous through the soul–God connection can also benefit from systems of education and support about synchronicity and the ego–Self framework. By systems of education and support, we are referring to opportunities for people to tell their stories of synchronicity in terms of their ego–Self dynamics, and at the same time to integrate such understandings of synchronicity with biblical miracles.

Also, this study has found that a beginning appreciation for experiences of synchronicity and the miraculous can inspire one to deepen living in a mode of awareness that is more consistently sensitive to both synchronicity and the miraculous, such that this mode of awareness can be taught to and learned by others. This study has also found that there are tremendous benefits to doing so, and that the alternatives to this are not simply exaggerated enthusiasm about miracles on the one hand, or smug intellectual defensiveness against miracles on the other. Synchronicities encourage comparisons with what might be considered a middle-of-the-road approach to even more amazing types of miracles.

To deepen our on-going capacity to make deliberate and habitual connections between synchronistic and miraculous phenomena, to correlate them with each other, and to regard them simultaneously helps us to become more open to understandings and practices of how we may believe in and achieve the seemingly impossible. In order to understand this more fully, let us now turn our attention to a number of examples in which teaching and learning about synchronicity and the miraculous in a simultaneous manner are addressed.

What follows now is a dream of mine which is an example of the synchronistic and miraculous manner in which such experiences can provide us with guidance into a fuller existence. As a result of this dream, I was alert to and, therefore, capitalized on an opportunity when it came, to participate in The African Americans and the Bible Research Project.[111] As a part of my involvement in the

---

[111] The African Americans and the Bible Research Project "seeks to fathom the complex historical and perduring interaction between African Americans and the Bible. It is less about the meaning(s) of the Bible than about the Bible and meanings(s), less about the world(s) of the Bible than about how (post-biblical)

project, I initiated discourse on whether or not, and how African Americans engage synchronicity and the miraculous in the context of psychotherapy, especially in relation to biblical themes.

A sequence of significant synchronicities had been initiated for me about three years earlier, when, before I knew anything about The African Americans and the Bible Research Project and Professor

worlds and Bible interrelate. Participants in the project are exploring as deeply and as broadly as possible the long and continuing history of engagements between the people that have come to be known as African Americans and that complex of rhetorics, visions, and ideologies that have come to be referred to as the Bible. With its promise of moving inquiry beyond either traditional biblical studies or traditional African American studies, this project involves serious interdisciplinary collaboration. Funded by the Lilly Endowment for a period of three years (1997-99), the project brings together scholars and other experts from a wide range of academic and cultural-artistic disciplines.

While the overarching perspective is historical, the research examines the dynamics and stages of the history of different types of African American cultural representations that are understood as engagements of the Bible: music, oratory, folklore, ritual, visual art, literature, and so forth, focusing primarily, but not exclusively, on the United States. The project also examines phenomenological and comparative perspectives on the uses and functions of sacred texts in culture in general, but especially those that have been most influential in the construction of African American culture. This includes multi-disciplinary, multi-field perspectives on the implications and ramifications of past and contemporary African American interactions with the Bible that may provoke different thoughts about the effects of the past and possibilities and challenges for the future.

An international conference, at which parts of the multi-year structured discussions were presented, was convened April 8-11, 1999 at Union Theological Seminary in New York City. Scholars of different disciplines and fields, artists, clergy, and lay persons were invited to the conference. The advisory group anticipates publication of some of the material presented at the conference. This material will provide, through the African American exemplum, a broader challenge to academy and culture, especially regarding the politics of the construal of the academic study of the Bible in particular, religious and theological studies and interpretation of the arts in general. The results are expected to advance more nuanced and 'text'-ured understandings of how identities and cultures are formed and indicate the consequences and possibilities," http://www.uts.columbia.edu/projects/AFAMBIBL/.

Wimbush's leadership of it, I had had a dream in which a wisdom figure I clearly recognized at the time as Professor Wimbush[112], was seated opposite me in a small room. As we conversed, he promised to open up the wisdom of Africa, the motherland, to me in a nurturing healing way. This dream provided me with powerful intuitive-affective knowledge on the trans level in relation to synchronicity and the ego-Self framework, as well as in relation to the miraculous and the soul-God framework.

This is a dream I had about what would later prove to be Professor Wimbush's deep African and African American-inflected influence on me through my eventual involvement in the actual project itself. One of the amazing and miraculous aspects of this synchronistic experience is that I had the dream three years before I really began to get to know Professor Wimbush that well, and three years before I knew about or became involved in The African Americans and the Bible Research Project.

There are several additional facts which amplify the amazing miraculous and synchronistic elements of this dream for me. First, a year after the dream I started working as a psychotherapist in the Riverside Church counseling department. The 17th floor tower office in which I started to see clients was clearly the room featured in my dream with Professor Wimbush a year earlier. Second, in the dream, Professor Wimbush was seated in a rocking chair. The room at Riverside in which I started seeing clients subsequent to the dream also has a rocking chair in it which I sat in when in sessions with clients. Third, prior to my joining the Riverside staff, I had never been on the 17th floor of the church, or in any of the offices on that floor.

---

[112]Up to this point in my stay at Union Theological Seminary, I had often seen Professor Wimbush, and knew of his prominence as Professor of Christian Origins at Union but had never had occasion to interact with him in any way.

Additionally, it is worth noting that the wisdom figure in my dream displayed enormous powers, such as being able to read my mind, to materialize and dematerialize at will, to be in several different places at once, and to be completely unbound by the ordinary laws of physics. In spite of this, there was nothing distorted about the rest of the reality we shared in the dream space. In other words, I functioned as a normal person while this wisdom figure offered to bestow on me, and teach me about whatever supernatural gifts I had the presence of mind to ask for, and was interested in learning about.

While the unusual connections between my dream and the office I had a year later, (e.g., both having to do with small rooms containing a rocking chair), caught my attention, I did not remain significantly aware the wisdom figure from the dream who had promised to open up the wisdom of Africa and the miraculous to me. However, I did not have to wait long to encounter the synchronistic manifestation of the wisdom figure from my dream in waking reality.

Subsequent to starting my work at Riverside Church, I heard about The African Americans and the Bible Research Project, and was encouraged to participate in it by a friend who was aware that the psychology division of the project was under-represented, and who therefore believed I would be a valuable contributor to that particular division and to the project as a whole.

However, as with many of my past academic and career decisions, I was anxious and uncertain about this one. I was under serious time pressures with regard to my doctoral work, and felt out of my depth at the prospect of collaborating with experienced and much-published scholars while being a mere doctoral student myself, and one constantly struggling to complete my program at that. Eventually, though, when I had my initial interview with Professor Wimbush about participating in the project, he was warm, friendly, and very encouraging about the value he believed I could bring to the project, and I recognized him as the synchronistic manifestation of the wisdom figure from my dream, and began my active participation in the project. Under the guidance of Professor Wimbush, and in connection with the project, I used my psychotherapy practice as a "research site" for exploring how my African American clients make use of the Bible in relation to synchronicity and the miraculous.

As a result I obtained a miraculous story from an African American couple with whom I was working as their marriage therapist. Among other relationship concerns, this couple was having difficulty starting a family, ostensibly because of fertility problems. They had not pursued the full range of various available medical alternatives for enhancing their fertility yet, the wife still eventually became pregnant during our course of psychotherapy, and both husband and wife were ecstatic about this development, and both viewed the conception as a miracle, given their earlier sustained difficulty to start a family. We discussed and celebrated this event in their lives at some length when it first came to light.

Several months later, as a participant in the social sciences division of The African Americans and the Bible Research Project, I prepared and distributed to ten couples I was working with in 1998 (including the particular couple I have described above), a survey instrument[113] containing several questions about synchronicity and the miraculous, and which Bible passages these couples found most healing and appealing. I discovered that both the husband and wife I described above were fond of Psalm 23.[114] In addition to this they

---

[113]See Appendix.

[114]Psalm 23:

"The Lord is my shepherd, I shall not want.

He makes me lie down in green pastures;

he leads me beside still waters; he restores my soul.

responded, in the affirmative to a survey question inquiring whether they had ever experienced a miracle, citing their unexpectedly and delightedly becoming pregnant after many years of difficulty in trying to do so.

One of the most dramatic results of the survey I employed was that there is much more biblical knowledge and understanding on the part of my clients than normally surfaces in our sessions. In other words, without a survey instrument to surface clients' relationship to the Bible, much of their knowledge remains hidden.

Also, I noticed that during therapy sessions, I tend to make more references to the Bible than do my clients when the focus is couples work; when there is a shift to individual or family work, there are more client references to thoughts, principles, prayers, dreams, and visions that are biblical.

The following is a range of presenting treatment issues and problems I encountered with clients: extended family conflicts; career, work, and money; addictions and chemical dependency; upward class and social mobility; education; love and sexuality: orientation, fidelity, roles, performance and fulfillment, gender roles, parenting; religion and spirituality (affiliations and attendance); race, ethnicity, culture, and color; class issues; motivation; trust; emotions; anger; fear; anxiety; depression; psychosis; violence; and abuse.

He leads me in right paths for his name's sake.
Even though I walk through the darkest valley,
I fear no evil; for you are with me;
your rod and your staff – they comfort me.
You prepare a table before me in the presence of my enemies;
you anoint my head with oil; my cup overflows.
Surely goodness and mercy shall follow me
All the days of my life, and I shall dwell in the house of
the Lord my whole life long."

In each of these presenting problems with clients, I imagine that as I pursued therapeutic breakthroughs with them, my clients probably had a wealth of synchronistic and miraculous experiences to recount, or could have, if they had been encouraged to pay attention to these categories. The lack of such attention on the part of both psychotherapists and their clients leads to inattention to synchronicity and the miraculous, which in turn leads to reduced efficacy in the healing process because these all-important dynamics (i.e., dynamics pertaining to synchronicity and the miraculous), remain unharnessed. Therefore, it is crucial that teaching and learning about synchronicity and the miraculous be included as part of the psychotherapy process.

My dream about Professor Wimbush, and the rich sequence of subsequent synchronistic experiences and miracles around it led me into a richer and fuller life with my family and friends, with mentors and elders, and with this topic. The abundant and enriched interconnections I experienced within myself (the intra category), between myself and several significant individuals and communities (the inter category), and also between myself and the source of miracles – God (the trans category), is akin to the miracle of the unexpected catch made by the disciples when Jesus directed them where to drop their nets after they had toiled fruitlessly all night and caught nothing.[115]

---

[115]Luke 5:1-11. Verses 4-7 say the following: "When he had finished speaking, he said to Simon, 'Put out into the deep water and let down your nets for a catch.' Simon answered, 'Master, we have worked all night long but have caught nothing. Yet if you say so, I will let down the nets.' When they had done this, they caught so many fish that the nets were beginning to break. So they signaled their partners in the other boat to come and help them. And they came and filled both boats, so that they began to sink." This sinking of the disciples' boat seems akin to the sinking feeling the ego can feel when synchronicities and miracles multiply at the behest of the Self, the Master, faster than they can be fully processed and interpreted (or appropriately landed).

In other words, as I toiled with my experiential and methodological nets trying, with limited success initially, to catch something of use beyond my experiences and intuitions about them regarding the connection between synchronicity and the miraculous, gradually, I was directed by God and the Self into more fruitful engagement with the topic. In fact, the feeling frequently became that I had so much that the nets were bursting and could not contain the catch, as was the case with the disciples and their unexpected catch. As I evolved towards making this abundant catch which seemed to have sprung from my dream about Professor Wimbush, my various transformations involved increasingly simultaneous awakenings in all three of the intra, inter, and trans categories of my life (which are explained in greater detail below).

The extraordinary combination of synchronicities and minor miracles which started with my dream about Professor Wimbush underscored the benefit of keeping a focus on teaching and learning about both synchronicity and the miraculous simultaneously because of the wealth of interconnections that emerged from this focus that helped me both as a student and teacher. As a result, I was led into membership in a community of over one hundred African and African American scholars where I could further develop and hone my teaching and learning, not only about synchronicity and the miraculous, but about African and African American social cultural formation in relation to synchronicity, the miraculous, and healing. I was promised that I would be empowered to do these things in the dream with the wisdom figure, and this was further evidence to me the abundance of life involved in teaching and learning about synchronicity and the miraculous simultaneously can deliver.

If I had been focused only on the miraculous and theology, I might have then missed various synchronicities along the way, together with the psychological implications about addressing issues of identity with regard to my cultural heritage, and overcoming my various ego-centric manifestations of uncertainty and anxiety with regard to my academic and career investments in connection with the project. Because I was attentive to synchronicity, I was able to follow, to indeed press on with regard to their psychological implications.

On the other hand, if I had only been attending to synchronicity and not the miraculous in this series of events, I might have missed the connections between such synchronicities and the sweep of the miraculous which the biblical tradition bears witness to. This biblical tradition assures us over and over again that God delivers us from affliction with mighty signs and wonders, the purpose of which are to draw us and those we bear witness to, ever-closer to God and God's unsurpassable providence. Once again it was clear to me that it is through a simultaneous appreciation of both synchronicity and the miraculous that I could continue to teach and learn most efficaciously about healing the psyche and soul.

In Summary

The method of this study based on integrating the three levels of intra, inter, and trans, and also the ego-Self framework and the soul-God framework, posits that it should be possible to identify the three levels, in depth psychology with regard to synchronicity, in theology with regard to the miraculous, and also with regard to both synchronicity and the miraculous in African American social cultural formation when this is focused on biblical psychotherapy. Usually, when we can identify a predominance of the intra or inter levels in a particular discourse, there will also be a rejection or neglect of synchronicity and the miraculous. When we can identify a predominance of the trans level I a given discourse we will often see an embrace of either synchronicity or the miraculous, or in some cases of both of these.

The need for practice at identifying the intra, inter, and trans levels and their relationship to synchronicity and the miraculous, has been demonstrated repeatedly in my own experiences as well as with clients, students, friends, and family. Often I hear a story which points to the trans level in that the story has synchronistic and miraculous implications. However, the person narrating the story often opts for an explanation of these implications as being some form of luck, or coincidence, or may even go so far as to say "nothing happens by coincidence." In such a case, the phrase "nothing happens by coincidence" usually means that there is a deeper Self-directed and God-ordained purpose behind the seeming coincidence. Nonetheless, even in such cases where a narrator of a story with synchronistic and miraculous implications does intuit a deeper psychological or God-ordained purpose behind a seeming coincidence, such a narrator often does not see the fuller synchronistic and miraculous implications of the experience they are recounting mostly because they are not practiced in making such connections. This study attempts to lay a foundation for supporting people to strengthen their practice of seeing the fuller synchronistic and miraculous implications of their experiences of luck and coincidence.

Furthermore, this study has found that in depth psychology and theology, as well as in African American social cultural formation with regard to the Bible and psychotherapy, various aspects of the intra, inter, and trans system are often missing. This absence of a practiced approach to the entire three-level system can hinder the richer expressions to be found in the simultaneous approach to synchronicity and the miraculous, an approach which leads people into stronger psychological wholeness as well as stronger faith in the living and breathing God of all creation who still speaks to us today in miracles for our complete redemption.

3. DEPTH PSYCHOLOGY

THIS BOOK NOW initiates a fuller investigation into the relationship between synchronicity and the miraculous from the side of depth psychology. The basic purpose of this chapter is to demonstrate significant aspects of the different developmental and healing or curative factors in the intra, inter, and trans levels of the psyche, and to begin to show how an integrated approach to these levels can aid us with regard to our simultaneous understanding of synchronicity and the miraculous.[116]

On the intra level, the aspects of Freud this study focuses on are the inner instinctual forces and the mechanisms of repression, as well as on the rejection of synchronicity and the miraculous . On the inter level, the aspects of Klein this study focuses on are the effects of internalized objects; the focus in Winnicott is on the restoration of a real self, as it is in Kohut through the therapist's proper attunement to the client; in Stern, while there are important similarities to Klein, Winnicott, and Kohut regarding the role of the inner and outer psychological environment of the client, the focus is not on object relations as such, but rather on the intersubjective

---

[116]In this study, I am focusing on the intra aspects of the Freudian system, on the inter aspects of the object relations schools, and on the trans aspects of the Jungians – this is not intended to reduce these three theoretical orientations to an overly general or rigid classification system, or to ignore that there are many overlapping areas between these various theoretical orientations and their practitioners.

(inter) experience of the client in relation to the therapist. On the trans level, using the work of Jung and Ulanov, the focus is on the integration of the ego and the objective, transcendent Center of the psyche, the Self, often with attendant synchronistic results.

One of the basic premises of the method of integration presented here, is that none of the curative factors from any one theory level (intra, inter, or trans) of depth psychology is necessarily incompatible with curative factors from any other level, and that they can indeed all be integrated into a more holistic approach. This can be crucial for healing. Another area of concern in this method is that overemphasis on a particular level at the expense of another may be the result of mechanisms of psychological repression regarding theory levels outside the ones being emphasized. A further area of concern for this method is that the occurrence of synchronicities is a well documented aspect of the trans level, and yet is absent, or is explained away in those theories emphasizing the intra and inter levels. This lack of integrated emphasis on all three levels may be attributable to forces of psychological repression, through which certain individual levels become almost exclusively favored and emphasized. A major thrust of this method is that the various hermeneutical dispositions (for, against, indifferent towards, or seemingly ignorant of synchronistic and miraculous phenomena) need to be examined level by level. Therefore, the method of integration presented here is intended to provide a way to organize and evaluate various hermeneutical systems with regard to the three levels of depth psychological theory being addressed, as well as with regard to the simultaneous relationship between synchronicity and miraculous in these systems.

The relative paucity in the Freudian (intra), and object relations (inter) arenas, of positive conceptions of synchronicity and also of miraculous phenomena in particular, and therefore also of any sustained investigation of the relationship between them, have reasons that, ironically, can be found in the positive contributions of the Freudian and object-relations schools to a whole host of religious questions.

In both the Freudian and object-relations schools, God representations (and by implication, the religious phenomena associated with them such as miracles), are addressed largely as neurotic manifestations from very early in life. This approach is tremendously helpful when it comes to dealing with many types of psychopathology in religious experience. However, the disadvantage of these two approaches alone, is that human experience is replete with well-documented synchronicities which are not reducible merely to the neurotic explanations of the Freudian and object-relations schools. In fact, Jung, von Franz, and Ulanov among others (representing the trans level), describe for us positive conceptions of the ego-Self framework, which parallels the soul-God framework as described in Chapter One. In terms of the ego-Self framework, the objective psyche, while it can be colored by our neuroses, demands of us that ultimately we strive to shed these neurotic overlays onto the objective psyche not to eliminate the numinous impulse within us, but to purify and strengthen our relationship to it, or suffer dire consequences. This objective psyche is not accounted for in a satisfactory manner in the Freudian and object-relations schools – indeed, they reject it. Also, in so far as the ego-Self framework parallels the soul-God framework as laid out in Chapter One, and given that the trans levels in depth psychology embraces, rather than rejects the ego-Self framework, then this implies that the trans level, in depth psychology, embraces the soul-God framework as being more than merely a manifestation of neurosis.

However, although the objective psyche and synchronicity are embraced in a positive manner in Jungian schools, and this serves as a positive reinforcement of the numinous impulse in humans – an impulse which is not reducible to neurosis alone - these Jungian schools have not typically correlated synchronicity and the miraculous with each other in an extensive manner.

As has been indicated in the introduction, synchronicity and the miraculous need each other. Conceptions and experiences of synchronicity can make the miraculous, for the Christian concerned about the significance and ultimacy of the resurrection, more accessible in normal everyday lived experiences, while conceptions about the miraculous can guide approaches to synchronicity towards the embrace of the ultimate miracle of the resurrection, which is for certain Christians, including myself, crucial to the whole belief system.

Theology also tells us that the miracle of the resurrection (and thus all the other miracles as well) is inherent in the biblical story of redemption as evidenced by the following confessional formula in Romans 10: 9 – "because if you confess with your lips that Jesus is Lord and believe in your heart that God raised him from the dead, you will be saved."

I am aware that this confession, which represents my particular theological stance, is not one with which everyone might agree. This confession tells us that in order to be rescued in an ultimate sense from evil, our entire beings must be surrendered to Jesus ("Jesus is Lord"), and that we have to arrive at the point at which we understand and trust - by faith - in the miracle of his resurrection from the dead as part of his saving work for us ("believe in your heart that God raised him from the dead"). What does it mean that Jesus was raised from the dead? How does our believing that Jesus was raised from the dead save us? It is my belief that an important aspect of the power of this confession lies in our ability to perceive, accept, and rely on the synchronistic effects of tunneling into the worlds suggested, represented, and claimed by the confession. In other words, this confession is the key that unlocks a doorway leading into a synchronistic and miraculous domain in which the resurrection of Jesus can make more sense to us. We take this confession up again more fully in Chapter Four.

We cannot truly grow towards a deepening understanding of the realities and possibilities suggested by the confession if we cannot embrace the confession. Nonetheless, people may still experience synchronicities which can eventually ready us for the ultimate embrace of the confession, even if they do not embrace this confession at all to begin. Jung tells us in psychological terms that there is an objective psyche beyond our neuroses, and that this objective psyche signals to us in important ways through synchronicities. Theology on the other hand tells us that there exists a God of ultimate and utter salvation from evil, sin, and death, who signals to us through miracles the ultimate one being the resurrection of Jesus from the dead.

A sustained investigation of how to integrate the best insights of the intra aspects of the Freudians, the inter aspects of the object-relations and self-psychology schools, and the trans aspects of those Jungians who understand the relationship between the objective psyche and synchronicity, can lead to the development of ever more powerful and comprehensive psychoanalytic psychotherapeutic strategies. For the Christian, such psychotherapeutic strategies can be (indeed need to be) harmonized with fully salvific strategies which hold on to the core confession and experience of God's saving and miraculous power as manifest in the life, death, and resurrection of Jesus. This study seeks to demonstrate such integration.

As an example of why the approach in this study to integrating synchronicity and the miraculous on the one hand, without collapsing them into each other on the other hand, is so important, let us examine David Richo's approach to synchronicity and the miraculous, in his book *Unexpected Miracles: The Gift of Synchronicity and How to Open It.* Richo makes the connection between synchronicity and the miraculous both in the title of the book, and elsewhere within the book itself as follows:

> St. Thomas Aquinas says that a miracle is unusual, like a healing, not routine like a sunrise. It has to be unexpected, a surprise, the result of a power beyond human making. It is an amazing grace! Synchronicities are unusual, unexpected, not constructed by the human ego. In this sense they are miracles of conjunction between ourselves and the events of the world. When we reconcile ourselves to the conditions of our existence, when reconcile the opposing forces in our psyche, when we reconcile ourselves to those who have hurt us, many stunning marvels begin to happen. We cannot cause miracles, but we can greet them and grant them hospitality in the yet unopened rooms of our souls. Then the unexpected, unsuspected miracles are respected![117]

When we look at Richo's approach to synchronicity and the miraculous using the method of this study, and the parallels between them based on the ego-Self framework and the soul-God framework, as developed in Chapter One, we observe the following: Richo presents an awareness of the relationship between synchronicity and the miraculous as involving parallels between inner and outer realities; subjective experiences of amazement; transformation; and acausality. However, he tends to collapse synchronicity and the miraculous into one another, rather than embracing them simultaneously as parallel systems from depth psychology and theology as this study attempts to do. The benefits of this integrating and paralleling rather than collapsing approach,

---

[117]David Richo, *Unexpected Miracles: The Gift of Synchronicity and How to Open It*, New York: Crossroad Publishing Company, 1999, xx.

are that we can focus on how the concept of miracle enriches that of synchronicity, and how the concept of synchronicity enriches that of miracle. As mentioned above, synchronicity and the miraculous strengthen each other because synchronicity helps to make the miraculous more palpable to us on a daily basis, while the miraculous confronts us with the challenge of the resurrection of Jesus. If we collapse synchronicity and the miraculous in the manner Richo does, we are more apt to miss the reciprocal benefits they provide to each other.

In spite of the many interesting links that can be made between synchronicity and the miraculous, such connections have not been developed in a sustained manner. In many significant works on Jung's concept of synchronicity, for instance, such as Marie-Louise Von Franz's *On Divination and Synchroncity: The Psychology of Meaningful Chance*; Jean Shinoda Bolen's *The Tao of Psychology: Synchronicity and the Self*; F. David Peat's *Synchronicity: The Bridge Between Matter and Mind*; Allan Combs' and Mark Holland's *Synchronicity: Science, Myth, and the Trickster*; and Robert H. Hopcke's *There Are No Accidents: Synchronicity and the Stories of Our Lives*, there is indeed no significant reference to a relationship between synchronicity and the miraculous as such.[118] However, the absence of such a consideration of the relationship between synchronicity and the miraculous (and even more specifically the absence of a simultaneous consideration of synchronicity and the miraculous), is precisely what this study has found most fascinating to address. Just how and why this relationship has not considered more closely for so long, can only be explained by a review of the development of the background ideas in depth psychology and theology which have hindered the fuller association of synchronicity and the miraculous.

---

[118]The absence of such references may be the result of mechanisms of psychological repression regarding theory levels outside the ones being emphasized.

The Intra, Inter, and Trans Levels in Depth Psychology in Relation to Synchronicity and the Miraculous

This section of the study now highlights aspects of three different major theory levels in depth psychology (the intra, the inter, and the trans levels of theory) that shed light on the psyche's development, and how healing, in turn, also occurs in the psyche in relation to synchronicity and the miraculous. More specifically, this part of the study highlights how the intra, the inter, and the trans levels, each in their own distinct ways, help us to deepen and enrich our approach to a simultaneous embrace of both synchronicity and the miraculous. In each of these levels, then, we explore both synchronicity and the miraculous in a manner made helpful by that level.

This summary is part of the process towards exploring how the intra, the inter, and the trans levels of the psyche can be understood in an integrated or unified way,[119] and also how this

---

[119]G. W. F. Hegel, *Phenomenology of Spirit*, trans. A. V. Miller (New York: Oxford University Press, 1977). The dialectical approach in this method of identifying these levels of the psyche and of the theory related to them, sequentially, and so separately, and yet also synoptically and as a unity, is similar to Hegel's comments in the section of the *Phenomenology*, on "Independence and Dependence of Self-Consciousness: Lordship and Bondage," in which he says, "Self-consciousness exists in and for itself when, and by the fact that, it so exists for another; that is, it exists only in being acknowledged. *The Notion of this its unity in its duplication embraces many and varied meanings. Its moments, then, must on the one hand be held strictly apart, and on the other hand must in this differentiation at the same time also be taken and known as not distinct, or in their opposite significance,*" (emphasis mine) 111. In addition to his Lordship-Bondage (or master-slave) dialectic, Hegel believes that the African "has not yet reached an awareness of any substantial objectivity – for example, of God or the law – in which the will of man could participate and in which he could become aware of his own being....he is nothing more than a savage....For this reason, we cannot properly feel ourselves into his nature, no more than into that of a dog, or of

integrated approach can be explored analogically in Chapter Four from the side of theology, and in Chapter Five from the perspective of African American social cultural formation with regard to the Bible and psychotherapy.

FREUD

Synchronicity and the Miraculous - The Intra Level and Curative Factors

WHILE FREUD, AT first glance, appears largely opposed to religion as a useful and healthy human expression and experience, he is of use to us in this study about synchronicity and the miraculous, in that he assists us to be appropriately suspicious of our neurotic dependencies and affinities for synchronicity and the miraculous.

In Freud's classical psychoanalytic system the basic curative factor is insight, through which unconscious conflicts are resolved. According to Freud "We try to restore the ego, to free it from its restrictions, and to give it back its command over the id which it lost owing to its early repressions."[120] Insight works through coordinated and carefully graded interpretations of a client's transference reactions such that a client gains deeper self-understanding, and according to Laplanche and Pontalis, "lifts

a Greek as he kneels before the statue of Zeus," from excerpts of his *Lectures on the Philosophy of World History (1822-8)* in Emmanuel Chuwudi Eze, ed. *Race and the Enlightenment: A Reader* (Cambridge, MA: Blackwell Publishers, 1997), 127-8. Hegel's reflections on Africans are included here as an example of the liberation praxis aspect of my method. Here the focus on this part of the method involves embracing useful concepts from a theoretical system, while staying informed and critical of those aspects that are antipathic to the liberative imperatives of one's identity.

[120]Frank Auld and Marvin Hyman, *The Resolution of Inner Conflict: An Introduction to Psychoanalytic Therapy*, Washington, DC: American Psychological Association, 1991, 201.

those repressions that rob them of gratifications that it would be safe, and socially acceptable, for them to have. At the same time, they do not want to be concerned that their impulses will cause them to lurch out of control....The lifting of repressions enhances patients' ability to think and plan and releases them from the domination of unconsciously determined, repetitive patterns of behavior."[121] In addition to increased self-understanding through growing insight into unconscious dynamics, a client also experiences abreaction which is an "Emotional discharge whereby the subject [is liberated] from the affect attached to the memory of a traumatic event in such a way that this affect is not able to become (or to remain) pathogenic."[122]

The basic curative factor in the Freudian system is insight on the part of the person in treatment, through which unconscious internal conflicts are resolved. As a result of these inner conflicts, according to Freud,

---

A neurotic is incapable of enjoyment and efficiency – the former because his libido is not directed on to any real object and the latter because he is obliged to employ a great deal of his available energy on keeping his libido under repression and on warding off its assaults. He would become healthy if the conflict between his ego and his libido came to an end and if his ego had his libido again at its disposal. The therapeutic task consists, therefore, in freeing the libido from its present attachments, which are withdrawn from the ego, and in making it once more serviceable to the ego.[123]

---

[121]J. Laplanche and J.-B. Pontalis, *The Language of Psychoanalysis*, trans. Donald Nicholson-Smith (New York: W. W. Norton & Company, 1973), 202.

[122]Ibid , 1.

[123]Sigmund Freud, *Introductory Lectures on Psychoanalysis*, ed. James Strachey, The Standard Edition (New York: W. W. Norton & Company, 1920), 564.

These instinctual conflicts involving the ego's attempts to repress the libido, are described here as going on largely within the client's psyche. The conflicts occur in this relatively closed structural, economic, and topographic system involving the embattled ego, which has very little libido for attachment to objects. As a result, the undoing of the impediments to greater enjoyment and effectiveness in life are also equally intrapsychic and intrapersonal, and

---

can be accomplished only in part in connection with the memory traces of the processes which led to repression. The decisive part of the work is achieved by creating in the patient's relation to the doctor – in the 'transference' – new editions of the old conflicts; in these the patient would like to behave in the same way as he did in the past, while we, by summoning up every available mental force [in the patient], compel him to come to a fresh decision. Thus the transference becomes the battlefield on which all the mutually struggling forces should meet one another.[124]

Thus, although the transference is the arena into which the battling forces of the psyche are projected during the healing process, the main victories are won in the reworking of the dynamics involving the client's internal conflicts and dynamics through insight.

Part of what this study seeks to emphasize as one of its findings is that whether a given system of healing, such as the Freudian one, is self-conscious aware of the simultaneous connection between synchronicity and the miraculous or not, this simultaneous connection is nevertheless at work. In other words, the ego-Self framework which supports synchronicity, and the soul-God

---

[124]Ibid., 565. Paul Ricoeur, *Freud and Philosophy: An Essay on Interpretation*, trans. Denis Savage (New Haven: Yale University Press, 1970), integrates interests in language, signs, and religion, to explore the polarity between "an 'innocent' analogical relationship or a 'cunning' distortion in psychoanalytic hermeneutics, 17.

framework which supports the miraculous, are always at work simultaneously in the sustaining, life-giving aspects of every human being whether people are consciously aware of them or not. Thus, "although the transference is the arena into which the battling forces of the psyche are projected during the healing process, the main victories are won in the reworking of the dynamics involving the client's internal conflicts and dynamics through insight." It is these psychodynamic victories of insight, given that they implicitly have an impact on the both the ego-Self and soul-God frameworks, which can accelerate, therefore, the occurrence of true positive synchronicities and miracles, or it is the lack of such psychodynamic victories of insight in analysis which can invite negative synchronicities and hinder miracles.

To say that psychological insight can accelerate synchronicities and miracles[125], or that the lack of such insight can hinder positive miracles and invite negative synchronicities can be illustrated by the biblical story of David and Bathsheba. David had committed the sin of adultery with Bathsheba (2 Samuel 11: 2-5), for which the penalty was death. Until the prophet Nathan uncovered the nature of David's sin to him, and provided him with shattering insight (2 Samuel 12: 1-15), about his guilt in taking Bathsheba from her husband Uriah and killing Uriah (2 Samuel 11: 6-27), David does not appear to have been that conscious of either his sin (2 Samuel 12: 1-8), nor of the inescapable consequences of such sin, which Nathan eventually makes clear to him (2 Samuel 12: 8-14).

God also announces that because of David' adultery, the child conceived by him and Bathsheba would not live. David tries to alter the course of events required by divine justice (the penalty for adultery being death), by fasting and praying (triggers for

---

[125]Throughout this and other illustrations in this study, synchronicity and the miraculous are used as parallel conceptions which enrich each other, rather than as conceptions that are simply interchangeable.

synchronistic and miraculous release) to no avail.[126] However, because of his repentance David is allowed to live even though the death of the child will be grievously painful to him. His insight allows him to avoid a worse fate than his sinful behavior would have led to if left unrecognized and unrepented from. Thus, insight helps us to avoid further errors in our own immediate spheres of influence, but also softens the punishing synchronistic hand of God upon us even when we deserve harsher consequences according to God's law and justice.

It is noteworthy that before David comes to the deep and shattering insight about his crimes of adultery and murder, Nathan's story about the man with one sheep dear to him which a wealthy man with many sheep steals from him, causes David to proclaim hot indignation at the crime of the greedy wealthy man. David's inner conflicts about his crime of adultery and murder are buried so deeply, and he is so defended against them that his spontaneous reaction to Nathan's story is to project his own unconscious guilt and condemnation onto the wealthy man in the story. Nathan grabs a hold of that teachable moment with his "You are the man." David falls to the ground with the shock of insight into his crimes. God loves him and seeks to save him if David will

---

[126]While it may be tempting for us to try and fully unravel this story, and have precise demarcations about what is synchronistic and what is miraculous in the unfolding of the consequences for David's actions with Bathsheba and Uriah, suffice it to say, that where we are dealing with issues of awareness or its lack (i..e., the story Nathan tells David about the rich man, and David's lack of insight that this was about him), we are more in the domain of synchronicity and depth psychology; and where we are dealing more with disobedience to God's law (i.e., David's adultery with Bathsheba, the murder of Uriah, and the consequences of all this), we are dealing more with the miraculous and theology). Overall, our point is that synchronicity and the miraculous operate simultaneously in such situations, and a simultaneous focus on both of them helps us to stay alert to both the dynamics of ego awareness before the Self, and the dynamics of soul consciousness before God.

repent and seek a cleansing redemption once again. Insight allows him to correct himself and get back on the path of right living. Negative consequences (synchronistic in nature) are not avoided entirely, but are reinterpreted so that his energies can be redirected to enhance his growth, learning, and intimacy with God.[127]

Here, we see the interplay of the benefit of what we would describe in our day as depth psychological insight into an unconscious defense on David's part. Just being aware of his wrong

---

[127]As this story points out, while psychological insight into our misdeeds is important, there are consequences for lack of insight and the crimes against God and others that this leads to, and that the relationship we have to God provides a context for understanding and capitalizing on the synchronistic signals we receive. Thus while we cannot in and of ourselves cause or manufacture synchronicities or miracles, we may be able to influence their emergence into our lives based on our level of insight – the more insight we have the less punishing the synchronistic signals we need; the less insight we have the more intense, demanding, and punishing the synchronicities. Von Franz is of additional help in keeping our focus on the proper source or cause of synchronicities (i.e., the Self and Providence) when she says the following: "Another tendency to reject the synchronicity hypothesis is found among many who attempt to postulate a psychological or neurological causal explanation without producing any proof for it based on facts. Barbara Honegger, for example, makes the supposition that synchronistic events arise from the same source as dreams, namely, a neurological substrate in the brain (the inferior parietal lobule). ...Moreover, precisely with synchronistic events, a causal relationship of this type seems completely absurd. If I foresee in a dream in Zurich the crash in Holland of a particular airplane identified as, let us say, XA3-137, and the next day in Holland a plane with just this identification really is smashed to bits, it would be rather absurd to suppose that my 'Neurological substrate' had arranged this crash (which according to the newspaper was caused by the weather).

Jule Eisenbud falls into a similar trap when he tries to rescue causality by supposing that synchronistic events are [caused] by the latent psi-powers of the observer. This completely contradicts the rest of our experience of the collective unconscious. According to the Jungian view, the collective unconscious is not at all an expression of personal wishes and goals, but is a neutral entity, psychic in nature, that exists in an absolutely transpersonal way. Ascribing the arrangement of synchronistic events to the observer's unconscious would thus be nothing other than a regression to primitive-magical thinking, in accordance with which it was earlier supposed that, for example, an eclipse could be "caused" by the malevolence of a sorcerer. Jung even explicitly warned against taking the archetypes (or the collective unconscious) or psi-powers to be the *causal agency* of synchronistic events."[231] In other words, God and the Self operate independently of either the soul or the ego; we do cause them to act, Nonetheless, our behavior affects the results we experience in the ego and soul.

behavior and the guilt for it, hidden from himself and expressed as a projection onto the figure of the rich man in the story, brings David a benefit – he can be more clear about himself – he can no longer fool himself. The Freudian hermeneutic of suspicion has benefits in bringing us to greater awareness and thus wholeness about our unconscious sides. By itself though, the Freudian intra approach does not suggest the synchronistic ramifications of either our lack of insight, or the gaining of insight. For this we need the Jungian trans level. Nor does the intra or even trans approach to curative factors in the psyche get at the redemptive aspect of Divine guidance and correction that is inherent in biblical miracles in terms of the soul–God framework.[128] For this we need the explicitly Christian dimension of faith in God's miraculous power.

Synchronicity and the Miraculous – The Intra Level and Developmental Factors

In Freud's work we discover repeated attempts on his part to reduce "trans" phenomena to the "intra' level of his preferred theoretical approach based on various mechanisms of defense, and especially based on our infantile, but impossible-to-meet, and wholly unrealistic, need for an omnipotent divine protector.[129] And even

---

[128]The discussion above, beyond addressing how insight as a curative factor on the intrapersonal level influences the occurrence of synchronicities, also serves as the basis on which interpersonal curative factors addressed further on in this study can be said to influence synchronicity and the miraculous.

[129]See "A Premonitory Dream Fulfilled;" "Premonitions and Chance (An Excerpt); "Psychoanalysis and Telepathy;" "Dreams and Telepathy;" "The Occult Significance of Dreams;" and "Dreams and the Occult," all essays of Freud's arguing, in one way or another, for the reduction of various "trans" phenomena into "intra" phenomena, and to be found in George Devereux, ed., *Psychoanalysis and the Occult*, New York: International Universities Press, Inc., 1953. Similar arguments on Freud's part, but of a more general nature, are to be found in *The Future of an Illusion* The Standard Edition, ed. James Strachey. New York: W. W. Norton & Company, 1961.

when, as Aziz recounts, there are clear indications that synchronicities happened to Freud, as for instance when Jung predicted to Freud at the end of one of their visits that they would hear a loud report coming from one of the bookcases in the room they were in , by all accounts Freud dismissed this interpretation of the event as nonsensical.[130]

As we continue with our overview of Freud in relation to synchronicity and the miraculous, it appears that the way a degree of order and systemization can be brought to the seemingly chaotic study of Western approaches to personality theory, is to think of them in terms of the four interrelated areas of the structures, the energy dynamics, and the developmental sequences which lead to the formulation of any particular personality. The fourth area usually encountered in most theories has to do with the differences in development between males and females. Theorists emphasize different aspects of these four interrelated areas, so that some hardly pay attention to anything but structure, while others focus predominantly on either development or dynamics. As with so much else in the field, this four-pronged approach to theoretical formulations about the psyche can be credited primarily to Freud.

Mitchell reminds us that although the wheel of psychoanalytic progress trundles on, Freud's legacy to us cannot be left behind:

It is difficult to think of another figure in the Western intellectual tradition who has had more impact than Freud on the way people have come to understand themselves. Only Darwin and Marx seem to have had comparable influence.

Also it is of use to note Freud's appreciation of the oceanic feeling in *Civilization and Its Discontents*, as well as his appreciation of the primary process in *Interpretation of Dreams*, although with here as well, it appears Freud was driven to interpret these trans phenomena as intra ones.

[130]See Aziz, 91-3 for a fuller account of this synchronistic story.

Further, Freud had much to say about many things. The twenty-three volumes (plus index) which contain his writings are breathtaking in their range, often scintillating in their argumentation, and lovely in their literary style. Therefore, the abandonment of Freud's drive theory creates an enormous conceptual vacuum. Most of the would-be successors to the architect of drive theory have attempted to fill this void by substituting new systems of their own design. None of these models, in itself, has been up to the task - each has been stretched too thin. There is not substance to fill the same space or attain the depth and scope of Freud's drive theory. The result has been a series of partial solutions, each important in its own right and perhaps closer to the clinical data than classical drive theory, but not as rich, comprehensive, or compelling to large numbers of practicing analysts.[131]

In fact not only can Freud's system not be left behind, it seems any attempt to grapple with his theory, immediately leads to an understanding of how extensive and complex a web he spun.

Based on the following assessment of Freud by David Wulff, synchronicity and the miraculous would both be akin to magical thinking, which is based on the delusions derived from the omnipotence of thoughts:

The thought patterns underlying all forms of neurosis bear a resemblance to the animistic and magical thinking found among totemic peoples. Neurotics demonstrate a delusion that Freud calls OMNIPOTENCE OF THOUGHTS, the conviction that the mere thinking of some eventuality is sufficient to bring it about. Thus the neurotic who unconsciously wishes for the death of some associate feeds a sense of guilt appropriate to actually having carried out these wishes. Omnipotence of thoughts may be traced through three stages in the evolution of human understanding of the universe, says Freud. In the animistic stage, which corresponds to the period of narcissism in the young child, human beings ascribe omnipotence to themselves. In the religious stage, which parallels the shifting of libido to external

[131]See Stephen A. Mitchell's, *Relational Concepts in Psychoanalysis: An Integration.* Cambridge, MA: Harvard University Press, 1988, 6.

objects, above all to the parents, the omnipotence is extended to the gods, though it is also retained as a means of influencing them. In the scientific stage, the counterpart of which is the individual's renunciation of the pleasure principle and the attainment of reality-oriented maturity, human omnipotence is largely abandoned, except for the lingering faith in the power of the human mind to understand the laws of reality.[132]

Furthermore, according to Wulff,

The pattern of similarities between the protoreligious concerns of totemic tribes and the ceremonials and thought patterns of obsessive neurotics led Freud to look for deeper connections. He was struck by the correspondence between the fundamental prohibitions of TOTEMISM – against killing the totem animal and against having sexual intercourse with members of the same totem group – and two aspects of the Oedipus complex: the desire to eliminate the father and the wish to possess the mother. That the totem does represent the father, argues Freud, is suggested by two findings. The tribe members themselves believe that they are descendents of the totem, and young children occasionally have a PHOBIA of a particular species of animal. Analysis has identified animal phobias as a displacement of the ambivalence toward the father. If the totem animal is indeed the father, the two core prohibitions of totemism correspond to childhood's forbidden Oedipal wishes.[133]

How did totemism actually come about according to Freud? Male and female adult moralities and differences of moral perception may be seen to reflect these early processes in that men typically develop a ritualized totemic set of rules, in which no one male can be allowed to possess all power, because this would lead to the possession by one dominant male of all the women. According to

---

[132]David M. Wulff, *Psychology of Religion: Classic and Contemporary Views,* (New York: John Wiley & Sons, 1991), 276.
[133]Ibid.

Freud, this is what happened in the primal horde with the murder of the father who possessed all the women. With his murder, the sons, motivated by their guilt, established a totem to both atone for and prevent similar deadly rivalries. Most of our major institutions have been arranged in some manner similar to this with many men recapitulating in their own individual oedipal resolution, the pattern that will allow them to participate in the collective totemic practices of the race, such as are found in religious, military, and educational institutions.[134]

Wulff reinforces this idea and provides us with a specific illustration by way of the Eucharist.

In Freud's view, the impress of the Oedipus complex remains on all later religious forms and practices, including those in our own day. Freud postulates that each succeeding generation down to the present has inherited the sense of guilt resulting from having killed and devoured the father – or, given the omnipotence of thoughts, from merely having entertained such acts in fantasy. Although Freud acknowledges the grave difficulties of so uncertain and bold a premise, he argues that such a hypothesis is necessary to account for the survival of these traditions over the centuries.

Freud maintains that the Christian doctrine of atonement represents a particularly undisguised acknowledgment of the "guilty primaeval deed." Because humankind was redeemed from its burden of original sin when Christ gave up his own life, we infer that the sin was murder. That the outcome of Christ's sacrifice was reconciliation with God the Father suggests that the crime to be expiated was

---

[134]According to this Freudian scheme women do not figure in a significant way in the structuring of the dominant morality, except as the prizes of the various competitive battles of men. While this Freudian explication may have appeared to be empirically supported for much of human history until recently, it seems like a dubious explanation, especially in view of the pejorative assessments it has made of women being morally weak, diffuse, and the like. There is ample evidence of female moral clarity and strength both currently and in the past, as well as cross-culturally to refute the social implication of male moral superiority in Freud's approach.

PATRICIDE. *The son's ambivalence toward the father also plays a role here, for through his offering of atonement Christ himself became God and now replaces the Father as the center of religious devotion. The revival of the ancient totemic meal in the form of the EUCHARIST, the symbolic consumption of the body and blood of Christ, serves both as a means of identifying with the son in his new role and as a [new removal of the father in which the guilty deed is repeated].[135]*

Freud helps us with his warnings about the omnipotence of thoughts: just because we wish for something will not make it so; such wishing is frequently associated with our oedipal guilt. Let us use the following illustration to make this clearer. It is based on a dream about my father, who in real life had died 3 months before the dream. In the dream, my father is lying face up and dead on a narrow table. A group of mourners, including me, encircle the table. It is night time and the light we experience is cast by kerosene lanterns. We, the mourners, are somberly contemplating the corpse when I notice it beginning to stir. My father opens his eyes and then slowly, and to my utter astonishment, begins to lift his chest up off of the table. Next he slowly moves his feet off the table and down to the ground and walks away. There are no exchanges of any kind between us. My dominant thought is that this astonishing

---

[135]Wulff, 278. Freud seems to engage in a neurotic rejection of God, Christ, the miraculous, and synchronicity as objective phenomena. Why? See H.L. Philp, *Freud and Religious Belief*, Salisbury Square, London: Rockliff Publishing Corporation, 1956, for a detailed analysis of the various ways in which Freud makes errors in his arguments about the neurotic basis of religion: According to Philp and in references to just one such error regarding Freud's use of projection, we have the following: "The idea of God is the result to some extent of projection, for there is no other way in which such an idea could be formed. It is, however, an unwarranted assumption to say that because the idea is projected there is no corresponding God. If God is real, man could only come into contact with His reality in his own experience, and it does not follow that because our idea of God must arise in this way, it must be an illusion," 85.

miracle isn't really what I think it is – in other words, it is not really happening, and at any moment it will be revealed as a trick. Nonetheless, at the same time I'm aware that I very much want it to be a true happening - I want to see my dead father raised back to life.

Freud helps us to interpret this dream in a number of ways quite useful to our focus on synchronicity and the miraculous. First he cautions us to look for my own internal dynamics of conflict about my father (the intra focus). With Freud's help, perhaps the dream is a cover for my guilty and hateful feelings towards him. Perhaps what I really wanted was for him to be dead; to be out of my way; out of my life with his seemingly constant disapproval of me. The dream then helps me to slow down into an analysis of how his resurrection in my dream is actually a cover for my guilt in wanting him dead. Understanding this can only help me to deal with my unresolved anger at him. From this perspective I am merely using, albeit unconsciously, the fact of his recent death as the nexus for the conflict between my desire to see him dead, and my yearning to undo the guilt caused within me by this unleashing of my aggression towards such a powerful totem as my father.

No matter what the neurotic aberrations we might be bringing into our interpretation, and which we must address and clear up, we can still ask ourselves the following bedrock questions about every situation or experience after we have screened it for neurotic and other dysfunctional ruses: How does our salvation flow in this situation or experience from a soul-God focus on the miracle of the crucified and risen Lord; and in the light of the miracle of the crucified and risen Lord, how does one's psyche move synchronistically towards the wholeness of ego-Self integration signaled in this situation or experience about which we are making psychoanalytic interpretations on the intra level?[136]

Thus, while keeping in mind the benefits of the Freudian approach (the intra level in depth psychology) to the resurrection dream about my father outlined above, we can, indeed we must, explore what the meanings of the dream might be on the inter and trans levels psychologically, and on the intra, inter, and trans levels theologically through a simultaneous appreciation of synchronicity and the miraculous if we are to do a thorough analysis. In other words, a basic Freudian analysis of my dream about my father, does not exhaust all the legitimate and appropriate synchronistic and miraculous meanings of the dream about death and resurrection – there is much more gold to be mined from the dream in this regard.[137]

---

[136]A partial answer is that salvation flows into such situations and experiences by faith. Faith in what? See 1 Peter 1: 3-12 – "Blessed be the God and Father of our Lord Jesus Christ! By his great mercy he has given us a new birth into a living hope through the resurrection of Jesus Christ from the dead, and into an inheritance that is imperishable, undefiled, and unfading, kept in heaven for you, who are being protected by the power of God through faith for a salvation ready to be revealed in the last time. In this you rejoice, even if now for a little while you have had to suffer various trials, so that the genuineness of your faith—being more precious than gold that, though perishable, is tested by fire—may be found to result in praise and glory and honor when Jesus Christ is revealed. Although you have not seen him, you love him; and even though you do not see him now, you believe in him and rejoice with an indescribable and glorious joy, for you are receiving the outcome of your faith, the salvation of your souls. Concerning this salvation, the prophets who prophesied of the grace that was to be yours made careful search and inquiry, inquiring about the person or time that the Spirit of Christ within them indicated when it testified in advance to the sufferings destined for Christ and the subsequent glory. It was revealed to them that they were serving not themselves but you, in regard to the things that have now been announced to you through those who brought you good news by the Holy Spirit sent from heaven—things into which angels long to look!"

[137]See the sections on the inter and trans levels in this chapter, as well as the intra, inter, and trans levels in Chapter Five for my further treatment of this dream about my father.

DAVID C. ASOMANING

Synchronicity and the Miraculous - The Inter Level:
Klein, Winnicott, Kohut, and Stern

If according to my organizing and integrating scheme, Freud's theory deals mainly with the intrapsychic, and so can be described as the intra level, then the object relations approaches of Klein and Winnicott, together with the self psychology of Kohut and the narrative approach of Stern, while building on Freud, move us into the inter realm. We will also explore how the inter level sheds light on our simultaneous appreciation of synchronicity and the miraculous.

KLEIN

Synchronicity and the Miraculous - The Inter Level and
Curative Factors

THE INTER LEVEL assists us to approach our dependencies and affinities for synchronicity and the miraculous through the lens of our relationships. As a stepping- stone for approaching how Klein[138] helps us in this respect, let us first create for ourselves a an overview of the relevant aspects of her work.

---

[138]Melanie Klein "(1882-1960), [was an] Austrian psychoanalyst, who devised therapeutic techniques for children that had great impact on present methods of child care and rearing. Born in Vienna and strongly influenced by Sigmund Freud's close associates Sándor Ferenczi (1873-1933) and Karl Abraham (1877-1925), Klein after World War I began to develop methods of play therapy, showing that how children play with toys reveals earlier infantile fantasies and anxieties. In The Psychoanalysis of Children (1932), she showed how these anxieties affected a child's developing ego, superego, and sexuality to bring about emotional disorders. Through her methods she attempted to relieve children of disabling guilt by having them direct toward the therapist the aggressive and Oedipal feelings they could not express to their parents,"http://www.heartfield.demon.co.uk/klein.htm.

In Klein's system, as in Freud's, the basic curative factor is insight, although here this insight is applied to internal parental objects. In this we can notice a significant shift. Although this theory system maintains some elements of the Freudian intrapsychic system, as for instance in the internal war between love and hate, and the life and death instinct in the mind of the infant, the conflicts are not mainly about gratification through release of instinct or its lack. On the contrary, for Klein the problems begin almost right away in the mind of the infant because of its attachment to objects, unlike with Freud for whom there is little libido for such attachments. In other words, conflicts, according to Klein's system, are in the context of actual, albeit internal, relationships, while for Freud they are in the absence of relationships:

> The baby, to whom his mother is primarily only an object which satisfies all his desires − a good breast, as it were − soon begins to respond to these gratifications and to her care by developing feelings of love towards her as a person. But this first love is already disturbed at its roots by destructive impulses. Love and hate are struggling together in the baby's mind; and this struggle to a certain extent persists throughout life and is liable to become a source of danger in human relationships.[139]

The remedy for this state of affairs also involves a correction with regard to objects already being related to.

> If, in our patients, analysis diminishes the anxieties of destructive and persecuting internal parents, it follows that hate and thus in turn anxieties decrease, and the patients are enabled to revise their relation to their parents − whether they

---

[139]Melanie Klein, "Love, Guilt, and Reparation," in *Love, Guilt and Reparation, and Other Works, 1921-1945* (New York: The Free Press, 1975), 307-8.

be dead or alive – and to rehabilitate them to some extent even if they have grounds for actual grievances. This greater tolerance makes it possible for them to set up 'good' parent-figures more securely in their minds, alongside the 'bad' internal objects, or rather to mitigate the fear of these 'bad' objects by the trust in the 'good' objects. This means enabling them to experience emotions – sorrow, guilt and grief, as well as love and trust.[140]

Klein's approach focuses on primitive pre-oedipal object relations, and brings insight to the mechanisms of introjection, projection, projective-identification, and splitting involved at these early stages of development.

In Klein's system, as in Freud's, the basic curative factor is insight as applied to the drives and their unconscious conflicts, in addition to which

Now, however, we know more about the complex structure of internal objects and about the growth of the ego, not only as a maturational process but also as promoted or hindered by the relationship it has with its internal objects. We know something of the distortions in ego-development due to anxiety-ridden internal object relations and defensive processes directly affecting the wholeness of the ego, such as, for instance, splitting, fragmentation, pathological projective identification. The analysis of these processes restores the ego's capacity for a more correct perception of objects and enables it to achieve a more constructive object relationship which in turn can play its part in growth.[141]

Klein's approach focuses on primitive pre-oedipal object relations, and bringing insight to the mechanisms of introjection, projection, projective-identification, and splitting involved at these earlier stages.

---

[140]Melanie Klein, "Mourning," in *Love, Guilt and Reparation, and Other Works, 1921-1945* (New York: The Free Press, 1975), 369.

[141] Segal, 123.

Thus in Kleinian terms, a focus "on primitive pre-oedipal object relations, and bringing insight to the mechanisms of introjection, projection, projective-identification, and splitting involved at these earlier stages," and such insight can scrape away hindering neurotic residues, the removal of which can then permit the occurrence of positive synchronicities and miracles, just as a lack of such insight can create negative synchronicities and hinder miracles.

Synchronicity and the Miraculous - The Inter Level and Developmental Factors

If we return to my resurrection dream about my father, Klein enables us to interpret this dream in a way that is helpful to our simultaneous focus on synchronicity and the miraculous. First Klein helps me to come to a deeper understanding of my ambivalence about my father. I idealized his positive attributes – his intelligence, his effectiveness as a leader, his resilience in the face of adversity - and so in the dream I see him rising from the dead.

In the dream, my own faults, foibles, and failures – especially as a long-term graduate student – are emphasized through my father's lack of acknowledgment of me when he is resurrected in the dream, even though my hope that he would rise from the dead in the dream was a fervent one because I anticipated our joy in being reunited. His lack of acknowledgment of me accentuates my guilt over my not meeting his expectations of me to have finished my course of study sooner. In real life, when I first heard of his death, in a sort of manic defense against this guilt, at first, I made light of his death by declaring that I would not go to his funeral, and then I landed on a preoccupation about what would happen to him in the afterlife – would he fare well or would he be in torment?

And so for me to engage his death in a healing and redemptive way, I needed to move away from my manic approach to reparation

161

(which fosters the split), to one in which I accept my ambivalence (which fosters integration) both towards my father and myself. In this way I retrace and repair some of my early developmental challenges which occurred in my infancy, and I move from the paranoid-schizoid position, and ego- and object-splitting stages to a greater state of integration with a greater and healthier ability to withstand ambiguity and ambivalence in my object relations.

The Kleinian approach to the resurrection dream about my father helps me identify and began to clear up my neurotic guilt and ambivalence towards him based on actual occurrences in our relationship. To my mind, this personal clearing up of neurotic guilt towards my father which is constellated around a resurrection motif in my dream, can be extrapolated to the resurrection of Jesus to aid in a strengthening of a clean soul-God faith in the saving work of Jesus of work, and can draw us closer to salvation as it enables us to examine and clear up our ambivalent feelings about the miracle of the crucified and risen Lord. For instance, as we clear up our guilt, our ambivalence (i.e., why does God make this process of salvation through Jesus' death and resurrection so complicated?), or our manic defenses with regard to the miracle of the crucified and risen Lord, our psyches move synchronistically towards the greater wholeness of ego-Self integration as well.

The emphasis here as throughout, is on the fact that reality and our interpretation of it are not just simply rational or mechanistic–they are synchronistic as well as miraculous. Every thought we think, every action, every behavior has simultaneous synchronistic and miraculous implications whether or not we are aware of these implications. As we saw in Chapter One, the behavior of an empress towards her husband affects the natural physical and environmental conditions of her realm synchronistically. Also, in Chapter One we saw how in biblical parallels to the empress story, natural and environmental conditions are frequently the results of miraculous divine intervention. The point of aligning the empress story about synchronicity alongside parallel biblical stories about the miraculous, was to highlight that the empress story is actually about both synchronicity and the miraculous, and also that the parallel biblical stories are also both synchronistic and miraculous. Thus, with all this in mind, it seems plausible to suggest that my Freudian or Kleinian analysis and insights affect me both synchronistically and miraculously; my confession of Jesus as Lord and Savior affects me both synchronistically and miraculously. By working into a deeper affinity for what these simultaneous synchronistic and miraculous implications are, we open the way for more and more integrated, comprehensive, and compelling ego-Self and soul-God healings in our lives.

Even as I come to understand the benefits of the Kleinian approach (the object pole of the inter level in depth psychology) for a deeper understanding of the resurrection dream about my father just outlined above, and of Christ's death and resurrection, I must explore the meanings of the dream in the two remaining inter levels ("the self" and "intersubjective space" dimensions), and the trans levels psychologically, and on the intra, inter, and trans levels theologically in Chapter Four through a simultaneous appreciation of synchronicity and the miraculous there as well.

WINNICOTT

Synchronicity and the Miraculous - The Inter Level and Curative Factors

AS A WAY TO LAUNCH into how Winnicott[142] helps us to deepen our appreciation for synchronicity and the miraculous through the lens

---

[142]Donald. W. Winnicott (1896-1971) "was convinced by his own clinical

of our relationships we will now review the relevant aspects of his work. Winnicott's understanding of the curative factors in the therapeutic process is also relational, although here, there is a shift away from Klein's focus on internal objects, as well as Freud's focus on issues of libidinal repression and cathexis, to a focus on the "individual characteristics" of the patient. These curative factors involve the similarity of the therapist to the nurturing and good enough mother, who fosters a strong ego in the client, which in turn leads to experimentation from an authentic self, and then to ego-integration.

...we see ourselves affecting the patient's ego in....the early stages of an analysis, because of the ego-support that we give simply by doing standard analysis and by doing it well. This corresponds to the ego-support of the mother which (in my theorizing) makes the infant ego strong if and only if the mother is able to play her special part at this time....[then] the patient's confidence in the analytic process brings about all kinds of experimenting (on the part of the patient) in terms of ego independence....the patient begins to show and to assert its own individual characteristics, and the patient begins to take for granted a feeling of existing in his or her own right.[143]

---

experience, first as a pediatrician and later as a child analyst, of the importance of the first months of infancy. He is often quoted as saying that there is no such thing as a baby but, instead, the mother-child interaction....Winnicott worked successfully with children and the severely disturbed and was able to tolerate considerable regression in his patients. His work is groundbreaking and even revolutionary in spite of the fact that he never founded a school. Born in Devon, England he completed his medical training at Cambridge, worked first as a pediatrician and later completed his psychoanalytic training at the British Psychoanalytical Association where he served as president" http://www.apsa-co.org/ctf/pubinfo/bios/winnicott.html.

[143]D. W. Winnicott, "The Aims of Psycho-Analytical Treatment," in *The Maturational Processes and the Facilitating Environment: Studies in the Theory of Emotional Development* (Madison, CT: International Universities Press, INC., 1965), 168.

For Winnicott curative factors have to do with the therapist being like the nurturing and good enough mother. Like the good enough mother, the therapist supports the development of a robust ego in the client, and this then supports the clients to explore life from an authentic self, which then leads to ego-integration, and these benefits – a therapist who simulates a good enough mother; a robust ego in the client; exploring through an authentic self; and ego-integration - can catalyze positive synchronicities and miracles, or their lack can generate negative synchronicities and inhibit miracles.

Synchronicities and the Miraculous - The Inter Level and Developmental Factors

Winnicott appreciates and uses Kleinian understandings of the importance of objects, and yet is clear that he claims as his fundamental inheritance, the classical system with its rather simpler understanding of unconscious or deeply buried instinctual conflict, transference dynamics, as well as the role of insight. In Winnicott's own words,

Although psycho-analysis may be infinitely complex, a few simple things may be said about the work I do, and one is that I expect to find a tendency towards ambivalence in the transference and away from more primitive mechanisms of splitting, introjection and projection, object retaliation, disintegration, etc. I know that these primitive mechanisms are universal and that they have positive value, but they are defenses in so far as they weaken the direct tie to the object through instinct, and through love and hate. At the end of endless ramifications in terms of hypochondriachal fantasy and persecutory delusion a patient has a dream which says: I eat you. Here is stark simplicity like that of the Oedipus complex.

Stark simplicity is only possible as a bonus on top of the ego-strengthening that analysis brings about. I would like to make special reference to this but must refer to the fact that in many cases the analyst displaces environmental influences that are

pathological, and we gain insight of the kind that enables us to know when we have become modern representatives of the parent figures of the patient's childhood and infancy, and when by contrast we are displacing such figures.[144]

In addition to applying the standards of insight and transference, when it comes to his unique contributions to the curative factors in the therapeutic process Winnicott emphasizes the similarity of the therapist to the nurturing and good enough mother, which fosters a strong ego in the client, which in turn leads to experimentation from an authentic self, and then to ego-integration. About these factors Winnicott says the following:

It is this ego-integration that particularly concerns me, and gives me pleasure (though it must not be for my pleasure that it takes place.) It is very satisfactory to watch the patient's growing ability to gather all things into the area of personal omnipotence, even including the genuine traumata. Ego-strength results in a clinical change in the direction of a loosening up of the defenses which become more economically employed and deployed, with the result that the individual feels no longer trapped in an illness, but feels free, even if not free from symptoms. In short, we see growth and emotional development that had been held up in the original situation.[145]

Although Winnicott's scheme is located within the "simplicity" of the classical system, with Winnicott, we begin to travel even further away from Freudian intra dynamics, toward a view which emphasizes the infant's relationship to the mother even more than Klein does. Winnicott's approach begins with the processes of integration out of unintegration. In this stage, the infant is completely dependent on the mother for the pleasurable

[144]Ibid., 167-8.
[145] Ibid., 168.

experiences of feeding, as well as the frustrating ones of the lack of feeding, say. In this stage, Winnicott sees the need for a good enough mother who is prepared to enable the infant to develop successfully through the process of illusion to disillusionment. What is at stake here is for the infant to be allowed, initially, to develop the illusion that it actually creates the breast that is so enjoyable to feed from. In an appropriately graded manner, the mother begins to wean the infant off her breast, thereby creating appropriate disillusionment in the infant as to its ability to create its reality at will. This is an important process if the infant is to adjust successfully to reality without disintegration, in which it could be overwhelmed by its instincts and appetites.

Two additional parts of Winnicott's theoretical scheme are personalization and reality adaptation. In personalization, the mother's actual and optimal holding and touching of the infant, help to create a sense of personal wholeness in the infant. Too much or too little handling of the infant can lead to dissociation in the infant, through which it comes to feel as though parts of its body do not belong to it.

In reality adaptation, the mother engages in skill-graded object presenting to the infant through the use of various toys and other objects. These are used by the infant as transitional objects in a transitional space between the infant and the mother, which allows the infant to develop from a phase of absolute dependence, through relative dependence, to eventual independence and a true as opposed to false self, and also to an ability to care about others. For Winnicott as for Klein, play is an essential ingredient in the quest to create an independent self, and various pathologies arise as a result of stuckness in the processes of dependence or interdependence.

For Winnicott, as for Klein, one's ability to sustain ambiguity and ambivalence consciously, is a sign of psychological health and the potential for true reparation which Klein describes as a state of concern. Winnicott acknowledges the contributions of Klein to his thinking in this area, and yet is critical of her approach in so far as he believes it focuses far too much on the infant's intra-psychic processes to the neglect of the real influences from the environment, through the infant's dependence on maternal care. For Winnicott the sort of instinctual aggression that an infant expresses, unmitigated by concern for the objects, needs to be survived by the objects in the infant's environment. These objects must not retaliate, but actually survive in the face of such aggression. Here survival by the object means that it is not angry, hostile, or attacking towards the subject, nor changing the attitude toward the subject. This is important, for if the object is unable to survive, the subject dampens its aggressive impulses in order to protect the object. This inhibits the subject from experiencing the vitality of the roots of its aggressive impulses, and therefore inhibits a certain developmental maturity such as fusion from happening.

If the object is able to survive the infant's aggression long enough, then the infant begins to develop the quality of concern for the object and self, at the same time as the bulk of its aggression is transformed into unconscious fantasies of destroying the object. It is important for a residual amount of aggression to remain in the relationships of dependency in order for the experience of the true self to occur, and in order for the creative and resultant experiences of true reparation to occur. Here, a good example is to be found in the way lovers often relate to each other. In the beginning, there is a tendency for lovers to disguise their hateful sides for fear of being rejected, and yet a small residual amount of this instinctual root is required for true self-relating in the relationship. Similarly, when things sour between lovers, there is a tendency to swing all the way over to total hate, and ignore the residual elements of love that can help to serve as the basis of true self-relating about both hate and love.

As we have already seen, Winnicott develops a focus on the role of the environment in development, which he views as an important complement to the mainly intrapsychically derived introjections and projections of infants in Klein's system. For Winnicott there is another significant difference when he is compared with Klein. First, he asserts that creativity is a primary capacity of both males and females, and the goal is to live out of it. Klein on the other hand, establishes that the reduction of instinctual anxiety through the eventual fusion of aggressive and libidinal drives is the primary goal of development.

If we return to the resurrection dream about my father, Winnicott helps me to interpret the dream in a manner that is helpful to my focus on synchronicity and the miraculous. The dream takes on meanings connected primarily with my father as a protective and supportive presence in certain aspects of my object-relations, and as a not good-enough parent in others. With the exception of his impingement on me about what to him was my lack of significant progress regarding my graduate work, and a relative lack of contribution of material resources towards my life after I turned eighteen, and a cold and distant emotional stance, he was generally loving and supportive. The dream may reflect the creative play of my imagination by which I produce an illusion of my possible reconnection with the good enough parts of him – and hence his resurrection – and yet my struggling with him around my false self, which cannot need him too much, because he leaves the scene of the resurrection in a manner similar to his cold and distant stance towards me in real life.

Again, my use of Winnicott to interpret the resurrection dream about my father helps me deepen my understanding about the tension in my psyche between the good things he provided, and how he impinged on me and did not always provide good enough parenting. As I use this approach to interpreting my resurrection dream about my father, it has beneficial implications for looking at Jesus' death and resurrection. It allows me to surface a host of ways in which Jesus feels both good enough and impinging as a source of nurture, and then to move beyond these feelings to an embrace of him as the crucified and risen Lord. As we clear up my distortions with regard to the miracle of the crucified and risen Lord, my psyche moves synchronistically towards the greater wholeness of ego-Self integration. As before with Freud and Klein, the benefits of the Winnicottian process may be viewed as aids to both the synchronistic and miraculous.

Moving on now from the benefits of Winnicott's approach (the self pole of the inter level in depth psychology) for a deeper understanding of synchronicity and the miraculous, we now look at Kohut's approach.

KOHUT

Synchronicity and the Miraculous - The Inter Level and Curative Factors

WE TURN NOW TO an overview of Kohut's[146] work to enlarge further our appreciation for how synchronicity and the miraculous can operate in our relationships on the inter level. In order to put

---

[146]Heinz Kohut (1913-1981), "founded a school of psychoanalysis that is not only a theory but a movement replete with conferences, training centers and organizations. Born in Vienna, he trained in medicine and in 1939 barely escaped the Nazis to the United States. In Chicago, Kohut trained at the Chicago Institute and became a major figure in American psychoanalysis, which included the presidency of the American Psychoanalytic Association," http://www.apsa-co.org/ctf/pubinfo/bios/kohut.html.

Kohut in perspective we must rely on Mitchell, according to whom, the many theorists of the various relational or interpersonal models are of three basic types, all of which are being considered here. First there are those who

> have contributed tools for exploring the object pole of the relational field, the manner in which various kinds of identifications and ties to other people serve as a latticework, holding together one's personal world....Klein's psychodynamic descriptions imply different ego states corresponding to different fates of internal objects....the focus, the clinical highlight, is on the object images themselves largely as internal experiences. What are the residues of the analysand's earlier experiences with others? What does he experience, consciously and unconsciously, when he does what he does with other people?[147]

Next according to Mitchell are those relational theorists who

> have contributed tools for exploring and understanding the self pole of the relational field. Thus, Winnicott focuses on the internal fragmentation and splits in self experience and the presence or absence of a sense of authenticity and reality. Kohut stresses the superordinate need of the 'self' to preserve its continuity and cohesion....Winnicott emphasizes the function of the mother in providing experiences which make possible a sense of vitalization and realization, and Kohut's 'self' is always embedded within and buoyed up by a supporting cast of 'self objects.' Nevertheless, the focus, the clinical highlight is on the nature and the subtle textures of self-reflective experience.[148]

Then finally, for Mitchell with regard to relational theorists are those who

---

[147]Mitchell, 34.
[148]Ibid.

have contributed tools for understanding the specific interactions which transpire between self and other, focusing not so much on either [object or subject] pole, but rather on the space between them. Thus, developmentalists such as Stern who have studied the 'interpersonal world' of the infant have focused on the highly subtle interactions and mutual regulation of caretakers and babies. Similarly, interpersonal psychoanalysis tends to highlight actual transactions between the analysand and others, to make detailed inquiry into what actually took place in early family relations, into what currently takes place between the analysand and others, and into the 'here and now' perceptions and interactions in the analytic relationship....The central question for the interpersonal analyst is What's going on around here?[149]

In Kohut's system, the curative factors lay down new psychological structure in the client, and yet here, this is the result primarily of the analyst's ability to understand accurately what the client's inner experience is, and successfully to communicate this understanding to the client. For Kohut,

The most general answer that self psychology gives to this question [of just how psychoanalysis cures] is a simple one: psychoanalysis cures by laying down psychological structure. And how does this accretion of psychological structure take place? The most general self psychological answer to this second question is also simple: psychological structure is laid down (a) via optimal frustration and (b) in consequence of optimal frustration, via transmuting internalization....provided that an analyst has correctly grasped the essence of [the] patient's inner state via vicarious introspection (empathy) and, in one form or another, communicated this understanding to the patient. It is my claim that even this first step of the basic therapeutic unit alone exposes the patient to a modicum of optimal frustration and thus, secondarily, to the laying down of new, that is, defect-filling or cohesion-firming psychic structures....[150]

---

[149]Ibid., 33–4.

From Kohut's perspective on the self, and still within an analytic context, attentive to the standards of insight and transference,

> The analyst's communication to the patient of [a] more or less correct understanding of the patient's inner life is optimally...frustrating because, despite the analyst's understanding of what the patient feels and [the] acknowledgement that the patient's upset is legitimate (e.g., both as a revival of an old unfulfilled need and as the manifestation of a universal need for selfobjects that persist for life), the analyst still does not act in accordance with the patient's need....It is optimal frustration rather than optimal gratification because, through the analyst's more or less accurate understanding, an empathic bond is established (reestablished) between analyst and patient that substitutes for the defacto fulfillment of the patient's need.[151]

Elsewhere, this therapeutic emphasis of Kohut's system is described as follows:

> Transmuting internalization is the filling in of structural defects of the self through the resolution of self-object transferences. Transmuting internalization occurs when there are minor empathic failures and delays of response on the part of the analyst, a significant object care-taker. The patient then has the opportunity, through selfobject transferences to the selfobject caretaker, to treat impaired self soothing, anxiety, and tension.[152]

For Kohut, several of the benefits of analysis are transmuting internalization through the minor failures of empathy on the part of the care-taker as a result of optimal frustration, and the correction of these, by which a patient learns to harness self-

[150]Heinz Kohut, *How Does Analysis Cure?*, ed. Arnold Goldberg with Paul E. Stepansky (Chicago: The University of Chicago Press, 1984), 98-9.
[151]Ibid., 102-3.
[152] Solomon, 186.

soothing, and address anxiety and tension. As we have noted before with other theorists, such positive shifts in consciousness generate positive synchronicities in terms of the ego-Self framework, as well as miracles in terms of the soul-God framework, or the lack of such shifts can generate negative synchronicities and inhibit miracles.

Synchronicity and the Miraculous - The Inter Level and Developmental Factors

In Kohut's scheme, then, he focuses on the self, which is considered as having three major aspects: "the pole of ambitions, the pole of ideals, and the intermediate area of talents and skills."[153] The self develops out of its experience of the significant others in its environment from infancy onwards who serve as selfobjects, because according to Kohut they perform certain crucial narcissistic tasks for the developing infant's sense of self, either by admiring the child's naturally emerging grandiosity, or by permitting the child to admire and idealize the selfobjects. As Kohut puts it regarding the various aspects of the self, "the pole of ambitions attempts to elicit the confirming responses of the selfobject....the pole of ideals searches for a selfobject that will accept its idealization, and the intermediate area of talents and skills seeks a self-object that will make itself available for the reassuring experience of essential alikeness."[154]

These selfobject relationships, under the right conditions of attunement and empathy on the part of the selfobjects, lead to transmuting internalizations, which are gradual step-by-step adjustments to the sense of self, through intermittent yet tolerable and easily reparable ruptures in the aforementioned empathy, a

---

[153]Kohut, 192-3.
[154]Ibid.

process which in turn leads ideally to strong and realistic self esteem in the infant and eventually adult.

In addition to this focus on the self in relational theory, Kohut makes important distinctions between his approach to development and the approach of drive theory:

Self psychology further holds, again in contrast to traditional theory, that the conception of a powerless baby, seen as existing outside a sustaining selfobject milieu, creates an artifact and that the theory derivative to this erroneous conception - that normal development proceeds from helpless dependence to autonomy and from self-love to the love of others - is therefore misleading. Self-psychology asserts that normality is properly defined by positing a meaningful sequence of changes in the nature of self-object relations throughout the course of a person's life; normality is not tantamount to the claim - the unrealistic claim - that the need for selfobjects is relinquished by the adult and replaced by autonomy and object love. We see a movement from archaic to mature narcissism, side by side and intertwined with a movement from archaic to mature object love; we do not see an abandonment of self-love and its replacement by the love for others.[155]

In the resurrection dream about my father, Kohut helps me to see the dream in a way that is helpful to my focus on synchronicity and the miraculous. The dream can be viewed as one in which my father, as the symbol of a care-taker figure and self-object, and who has in my ideal fantasy of him admired my naturally emerging grandiosity, and has allowed me to admire and idealize him, now allows me to experience optimal frustration through the empathic break that occurs after he arises from the table. I had expected him to turn to me for a joyous embrace, and yet he walks off without even a glance towards me. With regard to his walking off and leaving me behind in the dream, if I am able to discipline my initial

---

[155]Ibid., 208.

disappointment about this abandonment – this rupture in our empathic connection – this could eventually lead in me to healthy self esteem and a maturing sense of both self object love and self love. In other words, my father's leaving me behind, challenges me to become stronger and more independent without him. Although, I do not wish to deny that this abandonment is painful to me, in the end it is for my good, and I can learn to be at peace with it.

If I extrapolate my thinking about this resurrection dream involving my father onto Christ's crucifixion, resurrection, and ascension, I can see how in Kohutian terms, Christ's disciples initially are fearful at his death just as I was at the death of my father; then they are turned joyful at Christ's resurrection, again just as I was by my father's resurrection the dream; and then they are matured by Christ's ascension, by which he leaves them behind to grow into maturity through the Spirit, in a manner akin to the way in which my father walked off and left me behind in the dream.[156]

This Kohutian[157] approach to interpreting my resurrection dream about my father has beneficial implications for looking at Jesus'

---

[156]In reality, when I first heard that my father had died, and before I actually had this resurrection dream about him, I was quite concerned about where he might have gone in the afterlife; this concern eventually led me to discover the Jewish tradition of Kadish in which a son may say a set prayer every day for a year, in order to support his father's transition to heaven. See *Kaddish*, New York: Vintage Books, 1998, by Leon Wieseltier. In the dream itself, I cannot say for sure where my father goes, but in a general way it feels as if it is a good place, primarily because he is living again.

[157]This study employs critiques of synchronicity and the miraculous in order to make our eventual embrace of any particular example of synchronicity and the miraculous (i.e., such as the one involving the resurrection dream about my father) stronger. As an example of such a critique on the inter level involving Kohut's self psychology, Volney P. Gay, *Understanding the Occult: Fragmentation and Repair of the Self*, (Minneapolis: Fortress Press, 1989), 135-38, retells the same anecdotes as Aziz about the synchronistic noises from the bookcase during a meeting between Freud and Jung which we mentioned earlier in this chapter. However, Gay reduces, through

death and resurrection. It helps me to see in my relation to Jesus' death and resurrection a progression from my own narcissism and grandiosity towards a more mature self object love and self love with regard to Jesus's saving life and work as the crucified and risen Lord. Again as I clear up my narcissistic and grandiose distortions with regard to the miracle of the crucified and risen Lord, my psyche moves synchronistically towards the greater wholeness of ego-Self integration and towards soul-God integration. As before with Freud, Klein, and Winnicott, the Kohutian process may be viewed as an aid to the synchronistic and miraculous.

STERN

Synchronicity and the Miraculous - The Inter Level and Curative Factors

WE TURN NOW to a very brief overview of Stern's[158] work to add to our already rich appreciation for how synchronicity and the

his focus on self psychology (which is the "inter" level), what were putative synchronicities for Jung, to "Freud's failure to take pleasure in his brightest follower [which] evokes a rage that Jung chokes back" 137. In other words, the failure of empathy on Freud's part towards Jung, enrages Jung into an "occult defense" (the synchronistic phenomena) due to his loss of the desired and much needed selfobject (i.e., Freud). The issue here is not that Freud's "intra," or Gay's "inter" interpretations of occult phenomena are invalid under any and all circumstances. The difficulty with their approaches is that they use their "intra" or "inter" lenses, as the case may be, to attempt to discredit or interpret away, entirely, the "trans" level and its associated phenomena, such as synchronicity (and the miraculous). With regard to Freud, Jung and the bookcase noises, it should be noted that whatever anger was stirred up between Jung and Freud during this visit did not cause the synchronicity as much as trigger it. In other words, using the ego-Self framework, we know that it is the Self which causes synchronicities in order to get the ego's attention about ego states that are mis-aligned with the Self.

miraculous can operate on the inter level. With all the standard features in place regarding insight and transference, but with a focus on the intersubjective relationship between client and therapist, Stern talks about the curative efficacy of the collaborative search for, and utilization of, the central therapeutic metaphor for the client. The therapist's grasp of the metaphor which operates as a key to how the client's conflicts are organized supports the work that must be done. The therapist searches

> ...with the patient through his or her remembered history to find the potent life-experience that provides the key therapeutic metaphor for understanding and changing the patient's life. This experience can be called the narrative point of origin of the pathology, regardless of when it occurred in actual developmental time. Once the metaphor has been found, the therapy proceeds forward and backward in time from that point of origin. And for the purposes of an effective therapeutic reconstruction, the therapy rarely if ever gets back to the preverbal ages, to an assumed actual point of origin of the pathology....[159]

The work between therapist and client regarding the central metaphor, sets up a context in which the significance of the intersubjective space can be attended to. This intersubjective space between therapist and client is very much like that between a mother and her infant, but in ways distinct from Winnicott. For Winnicott, the mother must not impinge on the infant, and must provide a safe holding environment, in order for the infant's true self to emerge. For Stern, the infant's intersubjective link to its

---

[158]"Daniel N. Stern is a professor of psychology at Université de Genève and associate professor at Cornell University Medical Center in New York and author of numerous books and articles," http://www.intersubjectivity.com/stern.htm.

[159]Daniel Stern, *The Interpersonal World of the Infant: A View from Psychoanalysis and Developmental Psychology*, New York: Basic Books. 1985, 257.

mother becomes paramount, and not just the mother's ability to provide the right nurture.

> *For instance, an infant experiencing fear after wandering too far needs to know his or her state of fear has been heard. It is more than a need to be held or soothed; it is also an intersubjective need to be understood....the infant's returns to mother may be in the service of confirming that the reality and/or fantasy of intersubjectivity is being actively maintained ("Touching this castle of blocks is still scary-wonderful, isn't it, Mom?"). The creation of intersubjective sharing permits the exploration and pursuit of curiosity. Even the level of the infant's fear or distress in the situation is partially negotiated by the social referencing signals that occur in the domain of intersubjectivity, since they use the mother's feeling state as a tuner of the infant's ("is the block castle more scary than wonderful, or the other way around?").[160]*

Again with all the standard features in place regarding insight and transference, but with a focus on the intersubjective relationship between client and therapist, Stern as we saw earlier, talks about the curative efficacy of the collaborative search for, and utilization of the key therapeutic metaphor for the client:

> *The fact is that most experienced clinicians keep their developmental theories well in the background during active practice. They search with the patient through his or her remembered history to find the potent life-experience that provides the key therapeutic metaphor for understanding and changing the patient's life. This experience can be called the narrative point of origin of the pathology, regardless of when it occurred in actual developmental time. Once the metaphor has been found, the therapy proceeds forward and backward in time from that point of origin. And for the purposes of an effective therapeutic reconstruction, the therapy rarely if ever gets back to the preverbal ages, to an assumed actual point of origin of the*

---

[160]Ibid., 270–1.

179

pathology, even though one can not get at the "original edition" of the metaphor. While the developmental theory is given lip service, the practice proceeds.[161]

As we have already seen with Freud, Klein, Winnicott, and Kohut, any work that enhances the awareness of a client in treatment may lead to synchronicity and the miraculous, because such awareness as happens in treatment enhances the ego-Self connection as well as the soul-God connection implicitly. The enhancement of these connections frequently results in synchronicity regarding the ego-Self framework, and miracles regarding the soul-God framework. Therefore, employing Stern's system, we can also say that a therapist's identification and effective use of the narrative point of origin of a patient's pathology will probably also have synchronistic and miraculous effects in the treatment.[162]

---

[161]Ibid., 257.

[162]One puzzling and even paradoxical feature of our on-going discussion about how various curative systems can be aids to both synchronicity and the miraculous, is that there is an implication here that synchronistic and miraculous effects can happen whether or not the patient and therapist are aware of these effects. These synchronistic and miraculous effects might be in the body or various environmental locations, as in an example we have used before in this study, when Freud was involved in a synchronicity with Jung in which some book cases issued forth several loud noises which Jung had predicted to Freud would happen. In that particular situation, Jung was aware of the synchronicity and it had great meaning for him. However, Freud was unaware of the synchronicity. It is interesting to speculate about just who might be experiencing the meaning of a synchronicity or a miracle in a treatment, when neither therapist nor client are aware of such a synchronicity or miracle that may have happened to either the therapist, the client, or to both of them. In other words, could it be that a synchronicity or miracle will always have an observer in the Self and in God, even when the finite human beings involved are unaware of such synchronicities or miracles. This study employs critiques of synchronicity and the miraculous in order to make our eventual embrace of any particular example of synchronicity and the miraculous (i.e., such as the one involving the resurrection dream about my father) stronger. As an example of such a critique on the inter level involving Kohut's self psychology, Volney P. Gay, *Understanding the Occult: Fragmentation and Repair of the Self*, Minneapolis: Fortress Press, 1989, 135-38, retells the same anecdotes as Aziz about the synchronistic noises from the bookcase during a meeting between Freud and Jung which we

Synchronicity and the Miraculous - The Inter Level and Developmental Factors

As we have seen above regarding the three emphasizes in relational theory, Klein focuses on objects, Winnicott and Kohut on the self, and Stern on the relationship between the self and its objects. Stern assists me to see the resurrection dream about my father in a way that is helpful to my focus on synchronicity and the miraculous. In the dream, one could say that my father is playing a kind of life and death peekaboo with me to help me fortify and test my own sense of self using our inter-subjective relationship. The emphasis of this game of life and death peekaboo becomes clearer if we start off with my father as an alive person before he dies. Then when he dies that seems to be the end of the game. Then in my dream he arises from the dead, which starts the game over again. And yet in a short while he departs from the scene of his resurrection, and we are once again cut off from one another, and this again ends the game.

Using Stern to interpret my resurrection dream about my father has beneficial implications for looking at Jesus' death and resurrection. It helps me to see in my relation to Jesus' death and resurrection a kind of theological peek a boo. One day Jesus is alive,

mentioned earlier in this chapter. However, Gay reduces, through his focus on self psychology (which is the "inter" level), what were putative synchronicities for Jung, to "Freud's failure to take pleasure in his brightest follower [which] evokes a rage that Jung chokes back" 137. In other words, the failure of empathy on Freud's part towards Jung, enrages Jung into an "occult defense" (the synchronistic phenomena) due to his loss of the desired and much needed selfobject (i.e., Freud). The issue here is not that Freud's "intra," or Gay's "inter" interpretations of occult phenomena are invalid under any and all circumstances. The difficulty with their approaches is that they use their "intra" or "inter" lenses, as the case may be, to attempt to discredit or interpret away, entirely, the "trans" level and its associated phenomena, such as synchronicity (and the miraculous). With regard to Freud, Jung and the bookcase noises, it should be noted that whatever anger was stirred up between Jung and Freud during this visit did not cause the synchronicity as much as trigger it. In other words, using the ego-Self framework, we know that it is the Self which causes synchronicities in order to get the ego's attention about ego states that are misaligned with the Self.

the next he is dead, then he is alive again, then he departs into heaven and is promised to be returning. What helps me to stay connected to Jesus in spite of his appearing and disappearing is my growing faith in the constancy of his saving life and work as the crucified and risen Lord. As this faith in his constancy is enhanced, I also come to anticipate that miracles can and will happen to us as affirmations of this constancy. Also, in terms of the ego–Self framework, as I experience a deepening of the constancy of the Self, I come to expect this sense of constancy to be reaffirmed for us through an anticipation of synchronicities. In this manner, as before with Freud, Klein, Winnicott, and Kohut, Stern's approach may be viewed as an aid to our simultaneous embrace of synchronicity and the miraculous.

Moving on now from the benefits of Stern's approach (also the intersubjective pole of the inter level in depth psychology) for a deeper understanding of synchronicity and the miraculous, we now look at Jung and Ulanov on the trans level.

Synchronicity and the Miraculous – The Trans Level
(Jung and Ulanov)

In the method used in this study to integrate the various levels of theory addressed here – Freud's theory (on the intra level), and Klein, Winnicott, Kohut, and Stern (on the inter level) – all shed light on our simultaneous appreciation of synchronicity and the miraculous as illustrated above. With the theoretical systems of Ulanov and Jung, we begin to travel further away from exclusively intra and inter territory, and harness these theorists toward a view which emphasizes the trans approach to a simultaneous embrace of synchronicity and the miraculous.

Let us turn first to an overview of Jung's work as a foundation on which to build our appreciation for how synchronicity and the miraculous can operate on the trans levels of the psyche. C.G.

Jung's *Synchronicity: An Acausal Connecting Principle* is the foundational work on synchronicity in depth psychology. In this work, Jung draws connections between synchronicity, mantic activities in divination, extra sensory perception (ESP), other psychic and parapsychological phenomena, the relationship in monadism between microcosm and macrocosm, and astrology. One of his stated aims here is to develop a quantitative and statistical method based on an astrological experiment to distinguish between chance groupings of events and those with underlying acausal connections which are truly synchronistic. This is how he describes the difference between chance runs and synchronicities:

> *Runs or series which are composed of quite ordinary occurrences must for the present be regarded as fortuitous. However wide their range may be, they must be ruled out as acausal connections. It is, therefore, generally assumed that all coincidences are lucky hits and do not require an acausal interpretation. This assumption can, and indeed must, be regarded as true so long as proof is lacking that their incidence exceeds the limits of probability. Should this proof be forthcoming, however, it would prove that there are genuinely non-causal combinations of events for whose explanation we should have to postulate a factor incommensurable with causality. We should then have to assume that events in general are related to one another on the one hand as causal chains, and on the other hand by a kind of meaningful cross-connection.*[163]

Also, it is noteworthy that in this work, Jung refers to Albertus Magnus on the subject of magic by quoting him, in part, as follows:

> *I discovered an instructive account [of magic] in Avicenna's Liber sextus naturalium, which says a certain power to alter things indwells in the human soul*

---

[163]Jung, 11.

and subordinates the other things to her, particularly when she is swept into a great excess of love or hate or the like....Whoever would learn the secret of doing or undoing...things must know that everyone can influence everything magically if he falls into great excess.[164]

After citing Albertus Magnus in this manner, Jung goes on to say

This text shows clearly that synchronistic ("magical") happenings are regarded as being dependent on affects. Naturally Albertus Magnus, in accordance with the spirit of his age, explains this by postulating a magical faculty in the soul, without considering that the psychic process itself is just as much "arranged" as the coinciding image which anticipates the external process. This image originates in the unconscious and therefore [does] not spring from our own thinking.[165]

What is significant to note here in this study about synchronicity and the miraculous, is that although Jung associates synchronicity with magic, as in the textual example above, as well as with divinatory, prophetic, precognitive, intuitive, psychic, and paranormal activity, he does not here specifically connect synchronicity with the miraculous as such.

Roderick Main in his very helpful selections of Jung's texts entitled *Jung on Synchronicity and the Paranormal*, illuminates how elsewhere in Jung's *Synchronicity: An Acausal Connecting Principle*, Jung does indeed draw a few fleeting connections between synchronicity and the miraculous when reflecting on the results of his quantitative and statistical astrological experiment to explore synchronicity:

---

[164]Ibid., 32.
[165]Ibid., 33.

> *That anything so improbable as the turning up of three classical moon conjunctions, should occur at all, however, can only be explained either as the result of an intentional or unintentional fraud, or else as precisely such a meaningful coincidence, that is, as synchronicity....What happened in this case was admittedly a curiosity, apparently a unique instance of meaningful coincidence. If one is impressed by such things, one could call it a minor miracle. Today, however, we are obliged to view the miraculous in a somewhat different light. The Rhine experiments have demonstrated that space and time, and hence causality, are factors that can be eliminated, with the result that acausal phenomena, otherwise called miracles, appear possible.[166]*

In a text of his entitled "The Miraculous Fast of Brother Klaus," Jung says the following:

> *The fact that Brother Klaus, on his own admission and according to the reports of reliable witnesses, lived without material sustenance for twenty years is something that cannot be brushed aside however uncomfortable it may be. ...Such things naturally cannot be understood with our present knowledge of physiology. One would be well advised, however, not to dismiss them as utterly impossible on that account. There are very many things that earlier were held to be impossible which nevertheless we know and can prove to be possible today.*
>
> *Naturally I have no explanation to offer concerning such phenomena as the fast of Brother Klaus, but I am inclined to think it should be sought in the realm of parapsychology. I myself was present at the investigation of a medium who manifested physical phenomena.[167]*

Although in these references to Brother Klaus's fast, Jung does refer to either synchronicity or the miraculous explicitly, nor to any connection between them, nevertheless, he is referring to

---

[166]Ibid., 100-1. See Roderick Main, *Jung on Synchronicity and the Paranormal*, (Princeton: Princeton University Press, 1997).

[167]Main, 162.

marvelous phenomena with both psychology and theological significance.

In a writing of Jung's referred to as the "Letter to Dr. H.," we find a much more explicit effort on Jung's to connect synchronicity and the miraculous when he says:

My modus procedendi is naturally empirical: how to give a satisfactory description of the phenomenon "Christ" from the standpoint of psychological experience?

The existing statements about Christ are, in part, about an empirical man, but for the other and greater part about a mythological God-man. Out of these different statements you can reconstruct a personality who, as an empirical man, was identical with the traditional Son of Man type, as presented in the then widely read Book of Enoch. Wherever such identities occur, characteristic archetypal effects appear, that is, numinosity and synchronistic phenomena, hence tales of miracles are inseparable from the Christ figure. The former explains the irresistible suggestive power of his personality, for only one who is "gripped" has a "gripping" effect on others; the latter occur chiefly in the field of force of an archetype and, because of their aspatial and atemporal character, are acausal, i.e., miracles. (I have just lectured at Eranos on synchronicity. The paper will soon appear in the acts of the Institute.) This remarkable effect points to the "psychoid" and essentially transcendental nature of the archetype as an "arranger" of psychic forms inside and outside the psyche. (In theoretical physics the archetype corresponds to the model of the radioactive atom, with the difference that the atom consists of quantitative, the archetype of qualitative, i.e., meaningful, relationships, the quantum appearing only in the degree of numinosity. In physics the quale appears in the irreducible quality of the so-called discontinuities, as for instance in the quantum or in the half-life of radioactive substances).[168]

Although Jung does connect synchronicity and the miraculous in the above text, it is clear that developing a sustained focus on the

---

[168]Ibid., 164.

connection between synchronicity and the miraculous is not one of the stated intentions of Jung in his overall work. This absence in Jung's work itself is rather curious, and yet it is also evident in other significant discourses on Jung's pioneering work. For instance, Robert Aziz in his helpful book, *C.G. Jung's Psychology of Religion and Synchronicity*, outlines the basic features of synchronistic events in a systematic manner as follows, completely based on the ego-Self framework, without any references to the miraculous in terms of the soul-God framework. These then are the essential features Aziz outlines: 1. Unconscious contents related to a synchronistic event emerge into consciousness in a compensatory manner with regard to the ego. 2 At the conscious level, the subject possesses a set of awarenesses related to the compensatory synchronicity. 3. There is an objective compensatory event which corresponds in some manner to the unconscious compensatory contents emerging within the subject. 4. The objective compensatory event is the only compensator of the ego. This assertion is intended to highlight that when Jung "speaks of the 'psychic state of the questioner,' he is clearly not referring to the presence of a specific compensatory content which will in turn be mirrored in the casting of the *I Ching*, that is to say, he is not speaking of a situation in which the compensatory content is experienced both inwardly and outwardly. Rather, he is referring to a situation in which the compensatory content is synchronistically represented outwardly only...."[169] This seems intended to highlight a keener distinction about acausality, as well as distinctions between figurative and literal representations of the synchronicity. 5. The inner state and the objective synchronistic event may be synchronous in terms of clock time as well as spatially near each other. The objective event may be distant in time and/or space in

---

[169]Aziz, 63.

relation to the inner state. 6. The inner state and objective event are not causally related to each other. 7. The synchronistic event is meaningful to the one who experiences it because a) the inner and outer events have meaningful parallels; b) the synchronistic event has a numinous charge associated with it; c) there is significance to the subjective interpretations made of this type of event; and d) there is an archetypal level of meaning to the experience. Again, what is noteworthy for this study on the relationship between synchronicity and the miraculous, is that no mention is made by Aziz in these clear formulations about the possibility of a link between synchronicity and the miraculous.

JUNG

Synchronicity and the Miraculous – The Trans Level and Curative Factors

AT THE TRANS LEVEL, Jung's psychoanalytic work on the compensatory relationship between the ego and the Self is foundational for an appreciation of the amazing and wondrous nature of synchronicities, as well as for our focus in this study on the simultaneous appreciation of both synchronicity and the miraculous. Of special significance is Jung's synchronistic story about a female patient which he describes as follows:

> *The problem of synchronicity has puzzled me for a long time, ever since the middle twenties, when I was investigating the phenomena of the collective unconscious and kept on coming across connections which I simply could not explain as chance groupings or "runs." What I found were "coincidences" which were connected so meaningfully that their "chance" concurrence would represent a degree of improbability that would have to be expressed by an astronomical figure.*

By way of example, I shall mention an incident from my own observation. A young woman I was treating had, at a critical moment, a dream in which she was given a golden scarab. While she was telling me this dream I sat with my back to the closed window. Suddenly I heard a noise behind me, like a gentle tapping. I turned round and saw a flying insect knocking against the window-pane from outside. I opened the window and caught the creature in the air as it flew in. It was the nearest analogy to a golden scarab that one finds in our latitudes, a scarabaeid beetle, the common rose-chafer (Cetonia aurata), which contrary to its usual habits had evidently felt an urge to get into the dark room at this particular moment.[170]

In this text of Jung's, we see a convergence and integration of elements from his patient's inner life (what I call the intra level of her dream), the inter level of their relationship through which he listens to her dream and hands her the scarab from out of their objective physical environment. Further on, Jung provides this interpretation of the entire event which introduces more fully the transcendent or trans element present in the collective unconscious:

It was an extraordinarily difficult case to treat, and up to the time of the dream little or no progress had been made. I should explain that the main reason for this was my patient's animus, which was steeped in Cartesian philosophy and clung so rigidly to its own idea of reality that the efforts of three doctors - I was the third - had not been able to weaken it. Evidently something quite irrational was needed which was beyond my powers to produce. The dream alone was enough to disturb ever so slightly the rationalistic attitude of my patient. But when the "scarab" came flying in through the window in actual fact, her natural being could burst through the armour of her animus possession and the process of transformation could at last begin to move. Any essential change of attitude signifies a psychic renewal which is usually accompanied by symbols of rebirth in the patient's dreams and fantasies. The scarab is a classic example of a rebirth symbol. The ancient Egyptian Book of

[170]Jung, *Synchronicity: An Acausal Connecting Principle*, 21-2.

> What Is in the Netherworld describes how the dead sun-god changes himself at the tenth station into Khepri, the scarab, and then, at the twelfth station, mounts the barge which carries the rejuvenated sun-god into the morning sky. The only difficulty here is that with educated people cryptomnesia often cannot be ruled out with certainty (although my patient did not happen to know this symbol). But this does not alter the fact that the psychologist is continually coming up against cases where the emergence of symbolic parallels cannot be explained without the hypothesis of the collective unconscious.[171]

The synchronicity principle in Jung's story about the scarab above, which is organized within the ego-Self framework, tells us that not only can we experience an inner change in the depths of the unconscious (the woman's dream - the intra level), but that the objective psyche will begin responding to us in some significant way based on the acausal level of reality (the scarab at the window - the trans level), and that such changes may be mediated for us by other people (Jung handing the woman the scarab - inter level). In Chapter Four we will explore more fully the soul-God framework on the intra, inter, and trans levels regarding the miracle of rebirth that we can experience in Christ, and which is a parallel to Jung's approach to the ego-Self framework here involving synchronicity and what we are calling the intra, inter, and trans levels about psychological rebirth. For now, we will turn to a brief exploration of how Jung treats the sacrifice of the mass as symbolic of the reciprocal sacrifice that goes on between the ego and the Self in the ego-Self framework.

---

[171] Ibid., 23-4.

Synchronicity and the Miraculous - The Trans Level and Developmental Factors

In order to set the stage for Jung's treatment of the sacrifice of the mass as symbolic of the reciprocal sacrifice that goes on between the ego and the Self in the ego-Self framework, let us take a broader look at Jung's foundational theoretical framework of the compensatory relationship between the ego and the Self, as well as his approach to archetypes, all of which can aid us in our efforts to support the simultaneous embrace of synchronicity and the miraculous. As noted in Chapter One, in Jung's theory, the psyche has two major centers, the ego being that in the conscious personality, and the Self that in the total psyche. In addition to the ego complex and the Self archetype there are many other complexes, some of which are the persona, the anima, the animus, and the shadow.[172] Archetypes are considered to operate at several levels: the instinctual, the psychophysical, the psychological, and the spiritual. Furthermore archetypes are innate aspects of the psyche that determine the pathways along which the psyche will unfold in conjunction with environmental factors. Thus in this scheme, the Self is the central

---

[172]"Archetypes" refer to universal patterns which, although they cannot themselves be represented, are discerned in the psyche through archetypal images such as father, mother, King, Queen, God and the like. "Complex" refers to a collection of ideas or images in the psyche which possess a strong emotional charge and are governed by archetypes. "Anima" refers to the unconscious and feminine aspects of a man's psyche. "Animus" refers to the unconscious and masculine aspects of a woman's psyche. "Persona" refers to the social role by which the ego relates to the external world. "Psychoid" refers to the unconscious dimension of the psyche in which there is a unity underlying the space-time-energy-matter-psyche continuum. "Shadow" is an unconscious aspect of the psyche, made up of both positive and negative characteristics which the ego rejects or avoids. See James A. Hall's, *Jungian Dream Interpretation: A Handbook of Theory and Practice*, (Toronto, Canada: Inner City Books, 1983), 120-1, and Andrew Samuel's, *Jung and the Post-Jungians*, (New York: Routledge, 1985), 29-30.

191

organizing archetype of the total psyche, and exerts a compensatory effect on the ego as it emerges from an undifferentiated state within the psyche. The Self can relate to the ego with positive approval, or with negative challenges and threats as in dreams for instance.

The process outlined above is basically about the on-going reconciliation of opposites, anima-animus; self-ego; shadow-persona; God-humans; evil-good, and so on. These reconciliations follow a dialectical process in which a thesis leads to an anti-thesis, which in turn leads to a synthesis, or the transcendence of the two opposites involved, which then starts the process over anew.

Within this overarching system of his, Jung also examines the psychological implications of the mass, by detailing the functions of the sacrificer, who in the actual rite is the priest who offers a sacrifice of thanksgiving and praise to God for the life, passion, death, and resurrection of Christ. He explains how neither the priest nor the congregation gathered for the rite are really worthy to offer sacrifices to God, but have nevertheless been chosen for their roles by God, who also established the rite to begin with.

Jung also notes that the bread and wine used in the rite represent several important symbolic features which are basically the products of agriculture, the fruits of human toil and skill, and the daimon of nature or the essence of what gives life to growing things. These features are compressed and compacted into the rite as a way of bringing it closer to the nature of a true sacrifice.

Jung takes pains to explain what he considers to be a true sacrifice, in that he says it must be the giving up of something which one values. It must be something which one deliberately chooses to offer to another, and the loss of which causes one suffering. These are the requirements of a genuine sacrifice.

He also describes Abraham's near sacrifice of Isaac, as something that would have been relatively painless for Isaac, when compared with the deep agonies Jesus must have suffered on the cross, by having his heart and pleural cavity punctured, and having been left to die a slow and tortuous death on the cross for six hours between two thieves. Jung makes the point that, the crucifixion between the two thieves represents the deepest form of humiliation for Jesus and God in several ways. First it represents the execution of a criminal, which is aimed as much at injuring and humiliating the father as it is at the son. This is because the killing of the son represents the symbolic killing of the father/King who is perceived by the people to have failed in his task of protecting them. Therefore he and any of his family are killed and gotten rid of in order that the people may take matters into their own hands and set things straight.

In this manner Jung attempts to draw out the depth and magnitude of God's sacrifice of his son Jesus as compared to other human sacrifices, and Jung also makes the point that the sacrifice in the Mass has been designed to present it in the most inspiring and beautiful manner possible without causing it to lose any of its power as a sacrifice. He compares this approach to sacrifice, with other more primitive and gruesome sacrifices, which while bearing the essential features of the Christian rite of sacrifice, lose their power to make a favorable imprint on the psyche because of the obnoxious and grotesque violence they contain.

In Jung's view, the sacrifice in the Mass then, represents the deepest giving, loss, and suffering that God could engage in to work out the atonement of human sin. It symbolizes God giving up God's self without ultimately losing this self as center of divinity, and yet still making a genuine sacrifice.

Jung's great emphasis in all of this was on translating the treasures of the Christian tradition into realities that can be appropriated for actual living through people's awareness of the many important phenomenological realities that are embedded in the rites, rites which have been so ordained by the archetype of the Self albeit with human collaboration.

What we have discovered through this study, is that we are not merely translating Christian concepts about the miraculous into psychological terms involving synchronicity, nor are we translating psychological concepts about synchronicity into Christian concepts about the miraculous. However, it appears that Jung's use of the symbolism of the mass is a vehicle for him to translate theological concepts about death and rebirth into phenomenological and psychological understandings. For us in this study though, we seek to make distinctions between the psychological and the theological such that our simultaneous embrace of them leaves us richer than our translations of either one of them into the other would.

If we return to our earlier review about Jung's treatment of synchronicity and the miraculous (as shown above regarding brother Klaus), we see that while he did not make a thorough-going analysis of synchronicity and the miraculous simultaneously, in the few places he addressed them together, he basically equated them. By implication, then, Jung's treatment of the symbolism in the mass, is primarily about ego-Self dynamics which, by implication, point to the dynamics of synchronicity.[173] Using Jung's approach by

---

[173]Thus far in the research for this study, we are yet to find an actual example of an account of synchronicity in relation to the symbolism of mass as treated by Jung. It would be interesting to explore if and how other Jungians have explored synchronicity in relation to the symbolism of the mass. Also, we might consider issues of transubstantiation as possible leads in a similar direction, although regarding both synchronicity and the miraculous simultaneously in relation to the mass, but beyond the scope of the present study. In other words, on the trans level we have the actual body and blood of the crucified and risen Christ; on the inter level, the actual bread and the wine are the life-bringing manifestations (accidents, in Aristotelian terms) of the actual substance of the crucified and risen Christ who is made real and present in the elements when they are consecrated by the priest. On the intra level, he recipient of the communion elements then partakes synchronistically and miraculously in the body and blood of Christ.

itself, we might be tempted to simply equate the miraculous with the dynamics of the ego–Self relationship in our understanding of the mass – this would not be about the simultaneous embrace we are aiming for in this study. What Jung does is apply the ego–Self framework to an understanding of the symbolism of the mass. What we are aiming for is to combine his treatment based on the ego–Self framework and synchronicity, with an assessment of the death and resurrection of Jesus based on the soul–God framework and the miraculous. Again, this specific nuance of our simultaneous embrace of synchronicity and the miraculous will be taken up more fully in Chapter Four from the side of the intra, inter, and trans levels regarding the miraculous from the soul–God framework.

For Jung, human growth and development are essentially about differentiation and integration, a process that takes place along the ego–Self axis under the orchestration of the Self. The Self sacrifices itself to become known to the ego, and the ego sacrifices itself to accommodate the promptings of the Self. This pattern of mutual sacrifice and genuine giving within the psyche itself is what the sacrifice in the mass represents.

The facilitation of individuation is at the core of the process of analysis. According to Edward Edinger

> *Psychological development in all its phases is a redemptive process. The goal is to redeem by conscious realization, the hidden Self, hidden in unconscious identification with the ego. The repetitive cycle of inflation and alienation is superseded by the conscious process of individuation when awareness of the reality of the ego-Self axis occurs.*[174]

---

[174]Edward F. Edinger, *Ego and Archetype: Individuation and the Religious Function of the Psyche*, (Boston: Shambhala, 1972), 103.

Therefore on the one hand, in analysis, the analyst supports the analysand to open his or her ego to the Self. On the other hand, analysis can also be viewed as a living ritual which reflects the manner in which the sacrifice of the mass works; a ritual in which an analysand (as the congregation celebrating the rite under the priest's leadership) opens up to the process within his or her psyche by which the Self within sacrifices to the ego, while the ego in turn sacrifices to the Self. The analyst (like the priest in the rite), is not worthy as such to be doing the task, but nonetheless serves as custodian of a process that has been established and orchestrated by the Self, and which continues through the cooperation of the analysand and the analyst in the various offerings of dream interpretation, active imagination, and the like.

ULANOV

The Trans Level – Developmental and Curative Factors

AS INDICATED IN Chapter One, Ann Ulanov is of help in explicating the connection between inner psychological events and outer physical ones in synchronicities.

Ulanov says the following:

> *The full significance of synchronicity on the objective level – of what such a postulated acausal connecting principle which is accessible only as yet to a non-rational, subjective experience of meaning would mean about the nature of reality itself – is yet to be discovered. Jung is on the border-line of knowledge here, though on the basis of existing evidence, we can say that "subjective" experience is a doorway to objective reality; and, that non-rational coincidences grasped by intuitive, emotional, sensitive faculties convey aspects of objective reality which are inaccessible to our ratiocinations.*[175]

For Ulanov, the understanding of the Self, the Center of the psyche, is a supremely important aspect the healing process of analysis. Ulanov also clarifies, in a manner reminiscent of Hegel's drive towards systems of higher synthesis and integration, how Jung employs the term "transcendent" in his work.

> Transcendent, then means two things in the workings of Jung's idea of the transcendent function. It means specifically the spontaneous psychic process where our ego confronts and converses with a counter position in the unconscious, represented by a symbol, or better, a personification....This conversation leads to a third thing arising from the conflict of the two, something that both expresses and transcends the two opposing viewpoints. The arrival of this "third" always impresses us as marvelous, a gift, even though the strenuous work that went before readies us to receive it.[176]

Conversation, dialogue, unifying integration, wholeness, healing, and sometimes synchronistic events and signs occur as

> We hover over the gap between ego process and Self process. When the new begins to show itself in image form, we pause, look, contemplate, in order to integrate into a new level of unity parts of ourselves and of life outside us that were hitherto unknown to us....The conversation between ego and Self becomes our daily meditation.
>
> ....
>
> When this happens, reality seems to reform itself. Odd coincidences of events that are not causally related occur, impressing us with their large and immediate meaning: what Jung called synchronicity. Outer and inner events collide in significant ways that open us to perceive what Jung calls the unus mundus, a

[175]Ann Belford Ulanov, *The Feminine in Jungian Psychology and Christian Theology* (Evanston, IL: Northwestern University Press, 1971), 76.

[176]Ann Belford Ulanov, *The Functioning Transcendent* (Wilmette, IL: Chiron Publications, 1996), 8.

wholeness where matter and psyche are revealed to be but two aspects of the same reality. Clinically, I have seen striking examples of this. A man struggled in a conversation with a childhood terror of being locked in a dark attic as punishment for crying out too often to his parents when he was put to bed at night. Eventually, he reached the key to unlock a compulsive fetish that he now saw had functioned as the symbol to bridge the gap between his adult personality and his abject childhood terror in the locked attic. When this new attitude emerged out of his struggling back and forth with the fascination of the fetish on the one hand and his conscious humiliation and wish to rid himself of this compulsion on the other, an outer event synchronistically occurred. The attic room in the house of his childhood was struck by lightening and destroyed – but only the attic part of the house![177]

And yet such wonderful synchronistic signs and the inner archetypal symbols related to them, that come to us from the transcendent function, are of no benefit in and of themselves. Depth psychology and theology must intertwine if such experiences are to be of any lasting good:

It is not enough just to appreciate the transcendent function and marvel at the new symbols that arise with it. We must live them, use them, bind them back into personal and communal life if we are to submit to the religious attitude. The transcendent function is the process through which the new comes about in us.[178]

From the above, it is quite clear that Ann Ulanov embraces synchronicity in the context of the ego–Self framework. At the same time, Ann Ulanov also guides us to go beyond merely marveling at the new symbols that arise before us synchronistically through the Self and the trans level. In fact, she encourages us to connect the

---

[177]Ann Belford Ulanov, "Jung and Religion: The Opposing Self," in *The Cambridge Companion to Jung*, ed. Polly Young-Eisendrath and Terence Dawson (Cambridge, UK: Cambridge University Press, 1997), 310–11.

[178]Ibid., 310.

new symbols that arise for us back to the religious attitudes of our personal and communal lives through the imaginative function. One could say that she also encourages us, through the use of our imaginative function, to embrace the soul-God framework and the miraculous. One place in which she (together with Barry Ulanov), provides us with a clear example of this, in a very direct manner, is in the description of the resurrection our bodies must one day experience in real and concrete terms. If we combine Ulanov's work on synchronicity, with her treatment of the resurrection through the work of our imagination, this enables us to engage more fully in a simultaneous embrace of synchronicity and the miraculous.

There is a handsome paradox in the fact that a religion can survive only by facing and dealing with death. The Judeo-Christian way is precise and rooted as it must be in the body, in time, in history: it is the way of resurrection in the flesh.

In the flesh? Yes, that is the whole point. We are created in the flesh; we are re-created in the flesh. That is the Christian faith, that is the figure of Jesus, God in the flesh. That is the scandalous fact at the center of everything for those who believe, the fact that the body in which we live our lives, the body in which we see others living their lives, is also the body of whatever it is that comes after this life. We call what comes eternal life, not eternal death. There can be no such thing as eternal death – even the weakest imagination can see that. If death is an end, a finality without reprieve, an absolute nothing, then nothing is the only word for it. Can one say eternal nothing? Perhaps, but all it can mean is nothing.

Ulanov is inviting us to engage our imaginations in the realities of the resurrection. Engaging the resurrection through imagination is not normal in analysis nor even in very many religious environments either. However, it is crucial to the lives we live in the flesh.

Everything we know we know in the flesh. Even the abstractions with which we must deal when we talk to each other have their meaning for us because they are connected to experiences we have had or can accept that others have had in the flesh. Do we speak of fulfillment, of emptiness, of drabness, of beauty, of truth, of goodness? Yes, of course we do, but we mean something precise when we say those fine round abstract words. We mean, whether we are prepared to admit it at the time or not, whether we can bring what we mean to fill consciousness in ourselves or not, something we have known in the flesh. We have in mind – or nerve, or gland, or spirit - a particular completion we have known, with an idea, with a belief, with a religious experience, a fulfillment we have felt in the flesh somewhere, somehow. And if we have any conviction at all when we speak of emptiness, it is because we have known its corroding vacancies in some form or another directly; we have known it in the flesh

Ulanov takes us deeper into our understanding of why the resurrection of the body is so necessary; it is necessary because everything we do, we do basically in the flesh – what possible meaning could eternal life have for us if it does not continue in the flesh, albeit the flesh in resurrected form?

It is because of the astonishing fact that each of us is himself or herself and nobody else, and that we know that to be a fact as we meet each other and come to know each other, in the flesh, that resurrection must be in the flesh. That doesn't mean we can be reduced to the flesh. We are very much more than the flesh. But what we are we know, and others know, because we reveal ourselves in the flesh. That is what must survive if anything survives, the miraculous amalgam of flesh and the spirit which is the human person. If we survive, we must do so in our fleshly specificity, with our particular thickness or thinness, our wisdom, our strength, our stupidity, our weakness, our love, our hope for love, our graces, our movings toward grace, our movings away. What we must find when we find ourselves forever is everything we have been, including what we tried to be, for even that incompleteness is ours; its failure to achieve being was part of our being.

When we look at our lives this way, comtemplating death, which is to say our death, that least abstract of things, we really find ourselves, yes even here below, find ourselves with some of the tinctures of what we will find when we find ourselves forever. What do we find? A name. A body. A life. A person who lived a life with others, few or many, achieved much or not so much or little, but one who clearly has lived a life to which a name and a body and a term of days can be attached. A person thought worthy to be, or else there would be no such person.[179]

As we look at death and the resurrection, Ulanov reminds us of what we all ponder sometimes: Jesus was great enough to achieve the impossible, i.e., resurrection. How in the world do we get to that as mere mortals?

Looking at life in the shadow of death – and all of us must at some time, in time, come to do that – is inevitably to face the possibility of life after death, of rebirth. This is for many, even unbelievers, a stumbling block. Jesus, it may be, accomplished that, but he was God made man. Perhaps Lazarus and a few others whom Jesus touched can be allowed rebirth, but the rest of us? Come on! That strains the imagination.

What "right," Pascal asks, do those who are unbelievers, atheists perhaps, "have to say that one cannot rise again?" Good scientist that he is, he asks the hard-nosed questions: 'Which is more difficult, birth or resurrection; that what has never been should be, or that what has once been should recur? Is it more difficult to come into existence than to return to it? Habit makes the one seem easy for us, want of habit makes the other seem impossible; popular reasoning!....For Pascal, for all of us who live after the events of the gospels, and especially the resurrection, it is possible to be disdainful of those who will not believe, and worse still, those who will not ask themselves such questions as he does about birth and death. How cruel it is, with the example of Jesus and all who have believed in him and followed him, to have to go

---

[179]Ann and Barry Ulanov, *The Healing Imagination: The Meeting of Psyche and Soul*, (Daimon Verlag, 1999), 140-2, passim.

201

back into the same witlessness, the same fear and doubt, the same gaps in which so many of his immediate company were thrown after the crucifixion. Death can do that to us. Death will do that to us. It will bring everything we believe into question and reinforce all the ugly edges of our unbelief.

Death seems to annihilate any hope we might have in our resurrection, for at first, the crucified Jesus in his death, although he is the one who promises us that we have eternal life through his death and resurrection, seems to have disappeared forever when he first dies.

In the face of death all our imaginings about God seem to fall into the gap. In our time in history, how many have said that God is dead, God has disappeared, God is nowhere to be found. The stories of Jesus's death and resurrection tell us the same: his body was nowhere to be found. The visible outward manifestation of his presence, and the great high values he embodied, all gone with the missing corpse. But the story goes on to tell us that he rose again and disappeared again, transformed, to the women who came to care for his body, and then appeared once more for his disciples. The great high values come again, embodied again, but in such changed form no one recognizes them at first, not even those who loved Jesus in the flesh....[180]

Regardless of whether or not our imaginations are up to the task of comprehending that the resurrection is intended for us as well as for Jesus, we must press on to grab a hold of this promise by faith. The disciples were able to touch and to see the Risen Lord for themselves, although we do not have that privilege yet:

[180]Ibid., 142–3, passim.

Jesus risen appears to two of the disciples in Mark, and again to a pair on the way to Emmaus. None of them recognizes him which can be taken to mean that a darkness of understanding, a thickness of feeling stand in the way of finding and recognizing the transformed, the resurrected. We need to be given special power and courage and determination to find it and see it and take it in. At Emmaus Jesus opens the disciples' eyes when he takes bread, breaks it and gives it to them. To Thomas who cannot even believe when Jesus stands there before him, Jesus goes even further, saying, Put your hand in my wound. Know me, he is saying, in the flesh. To all the disciples Jesus says, Touch me. I am a man, he is saying; a spirit does not have hands and feet.[181]

Ulanov, then, provides us with an approach to synchronicity through the ego-Self framework and depth psychology on the intra, inter, and trans levels. Her work also calls us, through the soul-God framework in theology, to embrace the ultimate miracle of resurrection from the dead, both of Jesus, and also of ourselves on the intra, inter, and trans levels. Borrowing from Ulanov's work, the link used to connect synchronicity and the miraculous and the two frameworks which support them can be said to be that of the imagination. Ulanov's embrace of both synchronicity and the miraculous in her work, and especially also, her embrace of the ego-Self framework and the soul-God framework, is the foundation which has made this entire study of the simultaneous embrace of synchronicity and the miraculous in depth psychology and theology possible.

In this chapter, we have been exploring the simultaneous embrace of synchronicity and the miraculous from the perspective of several seminal and representative depth psychologists. In Chapter Four we turn to an exploration of the simultaneous

---

[181]Ibid., 144–5.

embrace of synchronicity and the miraculous from the perspective of several important theologians.

4. THEOLOGY

THIS CHAPTER INVESTIGATES the relationship between synchronicity and the miraculous from the side of theology. The main goal of this chapter is to demonstrate significant aspects of the different approaches to the miraculous on the intra, inter, and trans levels of the soul-God framework, and to begin to show how an integrated approach to these levels can aid us in our quest to enhance our simultaneous embrace of synchronicity and the miraculous.

As we established in the introduction to this study, there are at least 6 significant parallels between synchronicity and the miraculous based on the ego-Self framework and the soul-God framework. Furthermore, these parallels can be reformulated into a recognition of three levels of discourse in the psyche about synchronicity and the miraculous, which also have parallels in discourses about the soul with regard to synchronicity and the miraculous. We have named these three levels of discourse in the psyche or in the soul, the intra, the inter, and the trans levels. Although originally derived from depth psychology, we are not approaching these levels in theology from a depth psychological perspective. In other words, we are not privileging depth psychology as the lens through which we explore these three levels in theology. Furthermore, we are not equating or collapsing the 3 levels as they are manifest in depth psychology with the manner in which they are manifest in theology. Rather, we are using these terms to designate that the levels, regardless of discipline or discourse, possess certain general similarities. In actually addressing each of the levels specifically within a given discipline or discourse, the unique features of the level are then brought forward.

The intra level whether in depth psychology or theology refers to a rigorously exclusive and closed (often scientific) way of defining how things work such that synchronicity and the miraculous are rejected as in some way phony. The inter level refers to a somewhat more open (often humanistic) way of defining how things work, based mostly on human relatedness, and tends to either reject or be somewhat ambivalent about synchronicity and the miraculous. The trans level refers to a very open (and often supernaturalistic) way of defining how things can work which is much more apt to embrace synchronicity and the miraculous. The basic usefulness of having identified these three levels in depth psychology with regard to synchronicity and the miraculous, is that they have allowed us to posit that we should be able to discern them analogs in theology with regard to synchronicity and the miraculous.

On the intra level, Feuerbach's work is used briefly to illustrate the delusional ways of the heart and mind which serve as his basis for rejecting the miraculous. Furthermore, on the intra level, this chapter also looks at additional ways in which theology has often opposed miracles in order to avoid credulity. Specifically, Kelsey's summary of those who stand against Christian healing is presented here to highlight some of the most significant views within theology against the miraculous in Christianity.

On the inter level, we focus briefly on Kee and then more extensively on Hume in order to understand the ways in which people interact with one another through their use of evidence about the miraculous. On the trans level, this chapter focuses on the work again of Kelsey, Easton, and Ulanov[182], to look at how we might embrace the miraculous through a deeper understanding of the soul–God dynamic.

One of the basic premises of the method of integration presented here regarding the intra, inter, and trans approaches to the miraculous, is that there are benefits to understanding the primary concerns of each of these theory levels, and that their essence can be integrated into a more holistic approach. Therefore, the method of integration presented here provides a way to organize and evaluate hermeneutical systems displaying the intra, the inter, and the trans levels of theological orientation to the miraculous. This holistic approach then is a basis for our exploration of the simultaneous embrace of synchronicity and miraculous in these levels.

As has been indicated throughout this study thus far, synchronicity and the miraculous can benefit tremendously from each other. Ideas and even lived experiences of synchronicity may be able to make the miraculous, for those Christians who desire to enrich and magnify their faith in the resurrection of Jesus, more accessible in their day to day lives. On the other hand, ideas about the miraculous may be able to support our understandings of synchronicity to include a fuller embrace of the utmost miracle which, for certain Christians, is the resurrection.[183]

---

[182]As has been indicated in Chapter Three, Ann Ulanov's work embraces both the ego–Self framework and the soul–God framework, and is the basis upon which this study has been able to evolve to its current focus on the simultaneous embrace of synchronicity and the miraculous in depth psychology and theology. Ulanov's distinctive double embrace of the ego–Self framework and the soul–God framework as well as her embrace of synchronicity and the miraculous is why her work appears as an important model in both the depth psychology approach of Chapter Three and the theology approach of Chapter Four.

[183]With the right adjustments to account for each different religious and cultural context this simultaneous embrace of synchronicity and the miraculous could also be

It should be noted here, however, that although God and the miraculous are embraced in a positive manner by Kelsey, Easton, and Ulanov, and while this serves as a much needed support for the wonder-working ways of the divine in the human soul – something which is not reducible to deception alone as certain other theorists maintain – most theological schools of thought about the miraculous, typically, have not correlated the miraculous and synchronicity with each other in an extensive manner.

A sustained investigation of how to integrate the best insights of the intra aspects (briefly represented by Feuerbach here) of theology on the miraculous, with the inter aspects (represented by Kee and Hume), as well as the trans aspects (represented by Kelsey, Easton, and Ulanov), can lead to more comprehensive and effective strategies for guiding the soul in the process of salvation. For the Christian, such guiding strategies are in need of being integrated more completely with psychotherapeutic strategies which hold on to the core uncovering of the numerous psychological defenses that we all possess with regard to the ego-Self as well as the soul-God framework on the intra, inter, and trans levels regarding synchronicity and the miraculous. This study seeks to support such integration. As in our approach to synchronicity and the miraculous from the side of depth psychology in Chapter Three, our aim here is to approach the miraculous and synchronicity from the side of theology without collapsing them into each other.

To be careful to integrate and demonstrate parallels between synchronicity and the miraculous, rather than collapsing them into each other, challenges us to a discipline of constantly asking ourselves how the idea and experience of miracle supports and enlivens the idea and experience of synchronicity, and how the idea and experience of synchronicity supports and enlivens that of

applied to Hinduism, Buddhism, Islam, and Judaism in addition Christianity.

miracle. As we have seen, synchronicity and the miraculous support each other when synchronicity prompts us to view the miraculous as plausible and palpable on a regular if not daily basis, while the miraculous stimulates and even prods us to confront the resurrection of Jesus, also more regularly. If we fall to the temptation as so many of us frequently do, simply to equate synchronicity and the miraculous, we then tend to forego the reciprocal advantages they can give to each other.

The relative lack on the intra and inter levels in theology of positive conceptions of the relationship between synchronicity and the miraculous has reasons analogous to those addressed in Chapter Three on depth psychology. In an irony similar to that demonstrated in depth psychology when it comes to synchronicity and the miraculous, the positive contributions of the those schools of theology cause a zealous avoidance of the evils of credulity when considering the miraculous on the intra and inter levels. In other words, the avoidance of positive conceptions of the miraculous in theology has been due largely to the desire to hold fast only to what can be depended on as psychologically and philosophically (or scientifically) valid.

In theological and philosophical discourse, miracles are usually not considered as special expressions or signs from God, but are described largely as forms of superstition, magic, myth, deception, or as primitive and unscientific misunderstandings of naturally (as opposed to supernaturally) occurring phenomena. These approaches to the miraculous are tremendously helpful when it comes to dealing with the many types of misjudgment that the over-eager can apply to their experiences of so-called miraculous phenomena. However, the disadvantage of such skeptical approaches by themselves is that human experience is replete with well-documented miracles[184] which are not reducible merely to errors in human perception. Miracles need not be only and always errors in psychological, philosophical, and scientific acuity certain theologians, psychologists, scientists, and philosophers make them out to be.[185]

As noted in Chapter Three, Jung, von Franz, and Ulanov detail for us our relationship to the objective psyche and its way of signaling and speaking to us through synchronicities. This objective psyche, or our experience of it, is distorted by our neuroses, but

[184]Certain theologians reject the miraculous; by implication they would probably also reject what we are describing here as the depth psychological parallel to the miraculous, i.e., synchronicity, if they were even aware of it. Given that human experience is replete with well-documented synchronicities, these abundantly documented depth psychological parallels to the miraculous should give us pause about dismissing either synchronicities, so readily, or their theological parallels i.e., the miraculous. In other words, synchronicities can serve as an independently confirming experience category for the miraculous – we are not saying here that they are identical to the miraculous, we are saying that because they parallel the miraculous from a different perspective (i.e., the depth psychological), they make it a bit harder to simply dismiss their parallel, the miraculous, without asking why there is this parallel system. In other words there is something here about synchronicity and the miraculous that has to be reckoned with.

[185]See also Eugen Drewermann, *Discovering the GodChild Within: A Spiritual Psychology of the Infancy of Jesus,* translated by Peter Heinegg, (New York: The Crossroad Publishing Company, 1994), 75-6 who says the following regarding the despairing in this life: "Only when the figure of Christ meets (has met) them so that they experience themselves as 'newborn' can they believe in the man from Nazareth as '(re)born from the virgin.' And only when people discover the figure of Christ as an opportunity to start all over, ending a life that in truth looks more like a slow death, will they be able to call the person of Christ divine. For what would God be if not the wellspring of life, the source of light, the condition of truth (Jn. 8:12; 14:6)? To that extent the *miracle stories* of the New Testament, say, can serve as examples of the sort of experience that a person can and must have to come to know and to confess Jesus as the Son of God. For those who thanks to Christ recover the courage to stand on their own two feet (Jn. 5:1-9) and to regain the use of their 'withered' hands (Mk. 3:1-6)....for all such Christ *is* the Son of God, the place where heaven comes close to earth, the high priest (Heb. 414-16), the king of kings (Rev. 17:14; 19:16)."

nonetheless it is as if it requires that we learn to deal with it on its own terms. The objective psyche, and therefore synchronicity as well, are basically ignored in the Freudian and object-relations schools. Nor do most Jungian schools correlate synchronicity and the miraculous with each other in a sustained and simultaneous manner, although these Jungian schools do embrace the objective psyche and synchronicity as more than just manifestations of neurosis. While those depth psychologists who embrace the objective psyche and its attendant synchronicities may be uncomfortable making truth claims about God and miracles based on these phenomena, perhaps we can say that it is one of the tasks of this study to help theologians to be more familiar with how understanding the objective psyche can enrich our appreciation of the God of salvation for the Christian, and how understanding synchronicity can enrich our appreciation of the miraculous, all without collapsing these various categories. [186] Also, depth

---

[186]It is beyond the scope of this study to apply our integration of the ego-Self and soul-God frameworks, as well as the simultaneous embrace of synchronicity and the miraculous, to the many miracles of Jesus, beyond our preliminary initial treatment of the resurrection of Jesus. However, the following miracles of Jesus promise to be fruitful avenues for future study in this regard: 1) The Healing of Ten Lepers (Luke 17:11-19); Jesus Walks on Water (Matthew 14:22-23; Mark 6:45-52; John 6:16-21); The Miraculous Catch (Luke 5:11; John 21:3-14); The Miracle at Cana (John 2:1-12); The Multiplication of the Loaves (Mark 6:35-44; 8:1-10; Matthew 14:15-21; 15:32-39; Luke 9:12-17; John 6:3-15); The Healing of Man Born Blind (John 9:1-41); The Possessed Man among the Gerasenes (Matthew 8:28-34; Mark 5:1-20; Luke 8:26-39); The Raising of Lazarus (John 11:1-45). Why these miracles in particular?: 1)These miracles have been written about more frequently and at more length and so there is more commentary about them to be explored; 2) The number and variety of miracles reflect a range of physical, emotional, social, and spiritual issues and problems. This range of miracles is also intended to help amplify the definition of the miraculous; 3) These particular miracles reflect the intense difficulties of the various problems they address, and so it is perhaps less likely that these miracles and the difficulties they address might be explained away as other than what they are.

psychologists could be made more familiar with how God can enrich our appreciation of the objective psyche and how miracles can enrich our appreciation of synchronicity, again without collapsing these categories.

The Intra, Inter, and Trans Levels in Theology in Relation to Synchronicity and the Miraculous

The next sections of this chapter highlight intra, inter, and trans levels of theology that shed light on the miraculous. Also, these sections of the study highlight how the intra, the inter, and the trans levels, each in their own distinct ways, help us to deepen and enrich our approach to a simultaneous embrace of both the miraculous and synchronicity. By combining the work done in Chapter Three in depth psychology and synchronicity with that done in Chapter Four in theology and the miraculous, we set the stage to explore synchronicity and the miraculous in an integrated way on the intra, the inter, and the trans levels in Chapter Five from the perspective of African American social cultural formation with regard to the Bible and psychotherapy.

Also, it must be noted here, that unlike in Chapter Three on depth psychology where we looked at the development and cure of the psyche, it is not feasible here in theology to delve into the curative and developmental factors regarding the soul. This is because I am better prepared in depth psychology than I am in theology to do this. Also, this is a preliminary opening up of the topic on the side of theology, and no doubt there is a rich literature to borrow from in mysticism with regard to the development and cure of the soul when the time is right. What is actually presented then in these sections on the intra, inter, and trans levels in theology, are general themes about the rejection or acceptance of the miraculous and synchronicity in ways that parallel what was presented about the rejection or acceptance of synchronicity and the miraculous on these levels in depth psychology.

Synchronicity and the Miraculous – The Intra Level: Feuerbach and Kelsey

In the vast literature on the miraculous, we have many thinkers who reject the miraculous either close to the manner in which Freud did as some sort of wish-fulfillment fantasy, or more generally based on their scientific assumptions. Feuerbach is representative of the former, and Kelsey provides us with cogent summaries of the latter.

FEUERBACH

Synchronicity and the Miraculous – The Intra Level

FROM THE SIDE of theology, while Ludwig Feuerbach[187], as with Freud, rejects the miraculous as real per se, nevertheless he is of use to us in this study about synchronicity and the miraculous, in that he assists us to be appropriately suspicious of any delusional attractions we might have to synchronicity and the miraculous. Feuerbach's *The Essence of Christianity*, rejects the miraculous, in a chapter entitled, "The Mystery of Faith – The Mystery of Miracle," where he develops the idea that the miraculous is absurd with the following remarks:

---

[187]Ludwig Feuerbach (1804 - 72), was a "German philosopher....He originally studied Protestant theology at Heidelberg but soon moved to Berlin where for two years he studied philosophy with Hegel....in his most celebrated work, *The Essence of Christianity* (1841), translated by George Eliot in 1853, Feuerbach directed anthropology against religion," http://www.xrefer.com/entry/552050.

> And the glory of the Son consists in this: that he is acknowledged and reverenced as the being who is able to do what man is unable but wishes to do. Activity towards an end is well known to describe a circle: in the end it returns upon its beginning. But miraculous agency is distinguished from the ordinary realization of an object in that it realizes the end without the means, that it effects an immediate identity of the wish and its fulfillment; that consequently it describes a circle, not in a curved, but in a straight line, that is, the shortest line. A circle in a straight line is the mathematical symbol of a miracle. The attempt to construct a circle with a straight line would not be more ridiculous than the attempt to deduce miracle philosophically. To reason, miracle is absurd, inconceivable; as inconceivable as wooden iron or a circle without a periphery.[188]

At the conclusion of this chapter, Feuerbach provides the following paragraph to drive home the absurdity of the miraculous in terms which present the miraculous as mere "wishes of the heart":

> If the explanation of miracles by feeling and imagination is superficial, the charge of superficiality falls not on the explainer, but on that which he explains, namely on miracle; for seen in clear daylight, miracle presents absolutely nothing else than the sorcery of the imagination, which satisfies without contradiction all wishes of the heart.[189]

Feuerbach's view about the miraculous here appears to be similar to Freud's approach in that they both reject the miraculous, an approach we are referring to as the intra level, where we are cautioned not to allow our desire for miraculous experiences to fool us into accepting them as real.

---

[188]Ludwig Feuerbach, *The Essence of Christianity*, Translated by George Eliot. (Buffalo, NY: Prometheus Books, 1989), 130.

[189]Ibid., 134.

From a theological direction, Feuerbach, as Freud did for us from a psychological direction, can serve as a voice of caution to us to screen our experiences of the miraculous for the work of "the sorcery of the imagination." If I look at the resurrection dream involving my father and first presented in Chapter Three, Feuerbach says to me that my heart wishes for my father to be alive and thus makes it so through my belief as expressed in the dream that he is alive somehow. By first questioning this dream and the wish for my father to be alive even though he is dead, I strengthen my ultimate acceptance and embrace of the miraculous and of synchronicity because I have allowed myself to test my assumptions in the most critical psychological and theological furnaces, and in allowing myself to explore my own doubts and those of others, what I am left with is in the end, much more solid than if never exposed to these voices of suspicion.

Furthermore, by using a broad foundation in this study based on both the ego-Self framework and the soul-God framework, and recalling what we established in Chapter Three as the basis by which synchronicity can help us to accept the miraculous, we see that in the end, perhaps Feuerbach has too narrow a view which excludes how people may approach and benefit from embracing the miraculous without falling victim to "the sorcery of the imagination." Our simultaneous approach in this study provides us with both the benefits of the hermeneutic of suspicion in psychology and theology, and at the same protects us from the blind spots that appear to exist in these hermeneutics of suspicion with regard to the miraculous and synchronicity.

KELSEY

Synchronicity and the Miraculous - The Intra Level

MORTON KELSEY[190] PROVIDES excellent accounts of why the miraculous has been rejected even within Christianity itself, as well as for why the similarities between the miraculous and synchronicity have not been attended to more fully.

Ignored or rationalized are other elements of the Christian message – the healings done by Jesus and his followers (which alone account for one fifth of the narrative portions of the gospels), the out-pouring of the Holy Spirit along with other strange phenomena at Pentecost and in apostolic times, the dreams and visions, the references to angelic and evil spirits in the New Testament, indeed the whole emphasis on the interrelation of body, soul, and spirit. One begins to wonder how it is possible to take the ethical and moral teachings of Jesus seriously when nearly half the verses of the New Testament must be avoided because these other things – chiefly healing – intrude into them. In my book Encounter With God I provide a detailed analysis of these aspects of the New Testament. In lecturing I demonstrate this analysis with a copy of the New Testament in which these passages have been cut out with a razor. This demonstration is nearly always greeted with an explosion of laughter. It comes as a shock to most people to see that most of the powerful passages of scripture are cut out.

Modern Christians, however, have found several quite acceptable ways of avoiding the unmodern elements in these stories.[191]

---

[190]See http://www.newcitypress.com/Todayissues/material.htm: "Morton Kelsey has achieved much success as an author, teacher, poet and psychologist. He is Professor Emeritus at the University of Notre Dame, and was an active priest in the Episcopalian Church for many years." Kelsey himself is quite open to, and accepting of, the miraculous.

[191]Kelsey, 9-10.

The various reasons Kelsey gives for the contemporary rejection of the miraculous healings in the Bible as follows: a) The New Testament writers were in error regarding the facts they were attempting to describe; b) the miracle stories were added later by the more credulous early church; c) in our age, mostly, we doubt supernatural healing as it is not part of our scientific world view and so we dismiss miracle stories; d) the healings were not really of actual physical conditions – the blind were hysterically blind, the lepers were suffering from allergies, the lame were psychologically bound, and the dead were in a coma or catatonic state; e) these stories are accepted only for their allegorical meanings.

Kelsey also summarizes several theological rationalizations about the role of God and the church in healing that are often given by those attempting to establish that there are valid reasons to reject miracles: a)"God is responsible for sickness. There is no indication that evil or what might be expressed as the devil or demons may be the cause of any of it. Since there is apparently no other place for it to come from, sickness, along with other adversity and calamity, even though produced by material cause and effect must have been sent or allowed by God for a reason. A natural calamity is known in British law as an act of God;" b) "God as Father shows his love to us as human by needful correction and chastisement which is what sickness is;" c) sicknesses are punishments due to breaking God's law and commandments; d) when sickness occurs the focus should be on the spiritual salvation of the person not on the actual physical or emotional problems involved – therefore there is no need to care for miracles; e) the Christian minister has no healing function; f) dispensationalism – God used to heal miraculously but no longer does.

As we saw above with Feuerbach, our approach in this study to the simultaneous embrace of synchronicity and the miraculous is based on both the ego-Self framework and the soul-God framework, which allows us to perceive more easily the gaps in the understanding of those who attempt to dismiss the miraculous for all the reasons Kelsey enumerates.

Synchronicity and the Miraculous – The Inter Level: Kee and Hume

As described earlier, the inter level tends to be based on issues of human relatedness and can appear to either reject or be somewhat ambivalent about the miraculous. Kee and Hume helps us to explore several different dimensions of the inter level with regard to our simultaneous embrace of synchronicity and the miraculous in this study.

KEE

Synchronicity and the Miraculous – The Inter Level

HOWARD CLARK KEE[192] in his *Medicine, Miracle and Magic in New Testament Time* sheds light on the influence of existentialism with

---

[192]"Howard Clark Kee is Emeritus Professor of New Testament at Boston University. Among his many publications are *Evolution of the Synagogus* (1999), *The Cambridge Companion to the Bible* (editor, 1998), and *Removing Anti-Judaism from the Pulpit* (editor, 1996)," http://www.centuryone.com/0927-X.html. While the Bible generally eschews magic, there is debate about whether or not the miracles in the Bible involve magical practices: "Although commentators have sought to find traces of magic in the healing stories of Jesus (such as his use of spittle) or of the Apostles (such as their invocation of the name of Jesus), the worldview of the writers of the Gospels and Acts is fundamentally religious rather than magical. None of the characteristic features of magic that we have observed in the sources is to be found in New Testament writings, though there are traces of magic-type thinking in some of the healing stories and a kindred outlook behind the punitive miracles. All instances are in Acts; in six out of the eight stories, punitive and magical features are mingled," Howard Clark Kee, *Miracle in the Early Christian World: A Study in*

regard to the way in which the miraculous is regarded. However, Kee also makes it quite clear that not only do existentialist Bible scholars such as Bultmann, subtly reject the miraculous in the end, but that their brand of existentialism also focuses primarily on the *relational* (and thus inter) dimension of the metaphorical implications of Jesus' miraculous works:

> The strategy of Bultmann was formally similar to that of Harnack, even though his philosophical predilections lay elsewhere than in the Kantian or Hegelian spheres. His own equivalent of Harnack's essence was Jesus, which was perhaps more appropriately titled in its English translation, Jesus and the Word. There we read that the essence of Jesus was his call to decision, with the result that those who heed his call die to this world and enter in the moment of decision into the life of the age to come. Terms like "die" and "world" and "age to come" are all understood metaphorically to point to the surrender of values which contemporary society and culture cherish, replacing them instead by the attitudes of love, compassion, service which Jesus taught [emphasis mine] and which were embodied in his life and his obedience "unto death," in Paul's phrase from Phil 2:9-10. So long as that reading of the gospel tradition is set forth as a modern derivative interpretation, its beauty and potential power can only be admired. But when this abstract construct is presented as being not only the essence of the actual message and career of Jesus but also the norm by which historical judgments are to be reached as to what is central in the gospel tradition and what is peripheral, the method must be recognized for what it is: a reductionist circular argument. The essence for Bultmann and his followers derives from the skilful use of an appealing philosophical option – existentialism, especially that of Martin Heidegger – and this provides the criteria for, or at least the stated justification for, historical judgments about the development of the gospel tradition. Naturally, such phenomena as miracles, exorcisms, acts of divine intervention in the historical sphere have no place in such an approach to historical reconstruction.[193]

Sociohistorical Method, (New Haven: Yale University Press, 1983), 214-5. Also, see *The Greek Magical Papyri in Translation: Including the Demotic Spells*, (Chicago: The University of Chicago Press, 1992), ed. Hans Dieter Betz.

In this passage we see not so much a focus on the intra level of the rejection of the miraculous in which our innermost fantasies and wishes are projected outward onto our own theological constructions. Instead we see a focus on the relational aspects of the gospel where are about the attitudes of love, compassion, and service which Jesus taught, which although not bad in itself, is used to replace, minimize, and ultimately reject a trans focus on divine and miraculous intervention in human affairs. This sort of approach to the miraculous is a partial and therefore inadequate one.

When we turn this relational approach to the miraculous to the dream in which my father miraculously arises from death, the benefits are that I am urged to focus more intently on forgiving my father; having compassion towards him; and loving more deeply and richly than I might otherwise work at doing without this relational aspect of Jesus's ministry. At the same time, my entering more fully into a loving and forgiving relationship towards my deceased father based on the gospel, then has benefits for my ego-Self experience which may lead to synchronicities, as well as benefits for my soul-God experience which may lead to the miraculous.

HUME

Synchronicity and the Miraculous – The Inter Level
Part I: Hume on the Miraculous

THE PURPOSE OF THIS section of the chapter is to look at ways in which arguments for and against miracles highlight the ways in

---

[193]Howard Clark Kee, *Medicine, Miracle, and Magic in New Testament Times,* (New York: Cambridge University Press, 1986), 77-78.

which humans interact with one another when they are reporting this evidence. Hume's[194] emphasis on human interaction and relatedness in the sharing of evidence about the miraculous is what makes this section on Hume about the inter level. This section of the chapter also serves as an innovative way to investigate Hume's argument about miracles in relation the ego-Self framework and the soul-God framework regarding synchronicity and the miraculous.

This next section of the chapter is based on Hume's treatise, "Of Miracles." The first part of this section is a systematic description of the text "Of Miracles," which is required here to establish Hume's approach to miracles as I see it. The second part of this section is a brief and selective summary and analysis of possible objections to Hume's approach to miracles. The third, and final, part of this section is a brief survey of what several other voices have to say about Hume's approach to miracles.

In "Of Miracles," Hume works within the Enlightenment project represented, in part, by the work of Locke, to try to argue that the testimony one might receive about miracles is always dubious on rational grounds. Nonetheless, he seems to conclude his argument with the assertion that miracles are needed for the Christian faith, and that they are a positive and acceptable basis for the Christian faith. How does Hume come to maintain these two seemingly opposite views? I will now attempt a systematic description of the

---

[194]David Hume (1711 - 76), was a "Scottish philosopher, essayist, and historian. Perhaps the greatest of eighteenth-century philosophers, Hume aimed to place 'Logic, Morals, Criticism, and Politics' on a new foundation: the 'science of man' and the theory of human nature. Famous for his scepticism in metaphysics, he also insisted that human nature places limits on our capacity for skepticism. In morals, Hume insists on the reality of moral distinctions, though our judgements are ultimately founded only in human sentiment. In all areas, Hume's concern is to expose the limitations of reason, and to explain how we make the judgements we do, in the absence of the illusory support of reason," http://www.xrefer.com/entry.jsp?xrefid=552346&secid=.1.-&hh=1#s.1.-

text "Of Miracles," in order to determine what Hume actually says about miracles, as a way to start answering this question.

In his treatise, "Of Miracles," Hume first establishes that although experience is our only guide in attempting to reason about "matters of fact," it is not an infallible guide. This infallibility is caused by the variableness with which expected effects arise from their alleged causes. In other words, experience generally confirms that certain causes give rise to certain predictable effects, but that there are exceptions. Therefore, the exceptions cause broad ranges of doubt or confidence about our reasoning based on our experience of "moral evidence". Thus even when we are reasoning about what experience teaches us to expect, our confidence will vary.

It is prudent therefore, when experience has consistently borne out that a certain cause gives rise to a certain effect, to continue to reason that the correlation between cause and effect will continue to be so for future events. Past experience serves as the rational proof for continued correlation. When past experience is not so consistent, then a weighing of pertinent past events is needed to establish which effect is most probable to arise from a particular cause.

Hume applies this argument about reasoning from experience to the treatment of testimony from eye–witnesses and spectators. He claims that reasoning about such testimony is the most "common...useful and even necessary..." form of reasoning in human life.[195] He is aware that, for some, such testimony may not be adequately rooted in the relations between causes and effects. Nonetheless, he believes that experience allows us to conclude that humans generally produce good testimony because they have good

---

[195]William L. Rowe and William J. Wainwright, eds., *Philosophy of Religion: Selected Readings*, (New York: Harcourt, Brace Jovanovich, Inc., 1973), 385. Also, see Rowe's *Philosophy of Religion: An Introduction*, (Encino, CA: Dickenson Publishing Company, Inc., 1978).

memories, are truthful, and do not want the shame of being found to be untruthful.

Thus, some testimonies will serve as proof if their cause-effect correlations are well attested by past experience. Other testimonies will be subject to a calculus of probability based on other evidence to the contrary. Evidence may be contrary due to the following reasons: it comes from several different witnesses; it is presented in different ways; and the variability in the characters of witnesses. Testimony is suspicious if witnesses are too confident or too hesitant about their testimony; few in number; not trustworthy; have a vested interest in what they present; or contradict one another.

Based on these preliminary considerations, Hume discusses testimony about "extraordinary or marvelous" occurrences. Such testimony will be received skeptically, with the degree of skepticism inversely proportional to the degree of the usualness of the reported event. In other words, the more usual the event, the less skepticism it will be received with, and vice versa. We cannot simply accept the testimony as true in such a case because, testimony is not accepted a priori as a valid account of a certain reality. Rather, experience shows us that testimony can be trusted with a high degree of probability if it concerns events that are usual. Thus when testimony concerns something unusual, it is actually opposed to the normal experience correlating cause and effect, and this opposition to usual experience is enough to diminish the authority of the testimony.

Next, Hume turns to testimony concerning purportedly miraculous events. Miracles violate the laws of nature. If they were normal occurrences or even marvelous ones they would not be called miracles. Since the laws of nature are firmly and unalterably established by experience, testimonies regarding miracles are completely lacking in any authority or validity. On the basis of this reasoning, Hume advances the following maxim:

That no testimony is sufficient to establish a miracle, unless the testimony be of such a kind, that its falsehood would be more miraculous, than the fact, which it endeavors to establish: And even in that case there is a mutual destruction of arguments, and the superior only gives us an assurance suitable to that degree of force, which remains, after deducting the inferior.[196]

He gives the following example as an application of the maxim. Someone tells him he saw a dead person raised to life. The testimony is weighed to consider which is more probably the case: has the witness lied or been deceived; or has the witness actually seen someone raised from the dead? Which is the more miraculous: that someone was actually raised from the dead, or that the testimony about such an occurrence is false? Because resurrections do not normally occur in everyday experience, while human deceptions do, the greater miracle is for someone to have been raised from the dead. The lesser miracle is that the testimony is false. According to Hume's maxim, the greater miracle is always to be rejected in favor of the lesser. Therefore, in this example the testimony is somehow false and is rejected.

Hume indicates that he has made an extreme and unwarranted concession (simply for the sake of a clearer argument) by assuming that in his example, there might even have been a possibility that rejecting the testimony would have been more miraculous than the event it reported. According to Hume, experience shows that there are no testimonies about miracles (that come from sufficiently public events or prudent, educated, honest, reputable people) that

---

[196]Ibid., 387.

satisfy the general requirements needed to give us confidence in testimony.

For Hume, an additional reason to reject such testimony is found in the common human tendency to enjoy the element of "surprize and wonder"[197] associated with recounting testimonies about miraculous events. Thus, people testify (sometimes with second-hand information) about miraculous events, even though they do not believe they occurred, simply from the vanity and enjoyment of being admired by others for delighting their hunger for "surprize."

According to Hume, religionists may passionately (and with good intentions or not) present testimonies about miracles they do not believe, simply to capitalize on their effects for advancing their overall religious mission. The hearers of such testimonies do not generally examine them critically, because they do not feel they have the ability to penetrate such religious matters. Religionists often take advantage of such conditions for obscurantism.

Another reason to reject testimony about the miraculous is that miracles arise in primitive societies predisposed to accepting and transmitting such testimonies in authoritative ways. Miracles are thereby seen in all manner of natural events (such as battles and famines). Later, enlightened peoples are correctly able to see that such testimonies are not supernatural at all, but are again the result of the ineradicable attraction in humans for "surprize."

Yet another reason for rejecting testimony about miracles is based on the fact that different religions give testimonies from within their traditions as a way of rejecting the validity of other competing religions. If they all testify to miracles, in this manner, then they reject the miracles of one another, "...which likewise destroys the credit of those miracles, on which that system was established...."[198]

---

[197]Ibid., 388.

With these basic reasons for not accepting testimony about any miracle, Hume presents this maxim: "...no human testimony can have such force as to prove a miracle, and make it a just foundation for any such system of religion."[199] He emphasizes that his concern is to establish that miracles cannot serve as a valid rational basis for one's belief in a religious system. Furthermore, he explains that it is still conceivable that there may be miracles that are provable through human testimony; testimony which meets all the requirements for placing confidence in such testimony, because enough veracious people, in sufficiently public settings attest to the testimony. Nevertheless, Hume insists that he would still refuse to accept such overwhelming testimony, because it would, from his experience, be a greater miracle to believe such testimony, than to believe that there was some knavery or delusion afoot with regard to it.[200]

[198]Ibid., 389.

[199]Ibid., 390.

[200]In an interesting contrast to Hume's views on testimony, let us note what Easton says about testimony regarding miracles. His comments here hearken back to the discussion in Chapter One on the comparisons between Easton's view of the miraculous and Peat's view of synchronicity as both these pertain to disruptions of our accustomed ways of experiencing nature: "The credibility of miracles is established by the evidence of the senses on the part of those who are witnesses of them, and to all others by the testimony of such witnesses. The witnesses were competent, and their testimony is trustworthy. Unbelievers, following Hume, deny that any testimony can prove a miracle, because they say miracles are impossible. We have shown that miracles are possible, and surely they can be borne witness to. Surely they are credible when we have abundant and trustworthy evidence of their occurrence. They are credible just as any facts of history well authenticated are credible. Miracles, it is said, are contrary to experience. Of course they are contrary to our experience, but that does not prove that they were contrary to the experience of those who witnessed them. We believe a thousand facts, both of history and of science, that are contrary to our experience, but we believe them on the ground of competent testimony. An atheist or a pantheist must, as a matter of course, deny the possibility of miracles; but to one who believes in a personal God, who in his wisdom

In his conclusion, he seems to explain that his objective has been to show that it is invalid for adherents of the "Christian Religion," to defend the religion on the basis of attempted rational proofs and testimonies about miracles.[201] He does this, not as one might suppose, because he is opposed to Christianity, but precisely because he wants to defend it as a religion based on faith, not on reason. He explains that Christianity is not designed to be defended by reason, and any attempts to do so might actually be harmful to it.

He summarizes the various sorts of miracles that appear in the Pentateuch. In order to be rigorous in his reasoning here, he assumes that the accounts of miracles in the Pentateuch are the result of human testimony. He then applies his first maxim about miracles (presented above) to the accounts. He asserts that in order to accept the Bible as valid testimony, one has to conclude that accepting its bizarre accounts is a smaller miracle than rejecting the events it purports to recount. Instead, it is far more reasonable, according to Hume, to reject the events the Bible reports as being untrue. His main goal up to this point has been to underscore his view that Christianity cannot be established on rational proofs of these types of miracles that exist in the tradition.

Hume is much more trusting with regard to prophecies as miracles. These are miracles because they exceed ordinary human ability to forecast future events. They are to be tested using all the criteria outlined above. Apparently, they are found by Hume to be "...real miracles, and as such only can be admitted as proofs of any revelation. If they did not exceed the capacity of human nature to foretell future events, it would be absurd to employ any prophecy as an argument for a divine mission or authority from heaven."[202]

may see fit to interfere with the ordinary processes of nature, miracles are not impossible, nor are they incredible" *Easton's Bible Dictionary.*
    [201]Ibid., 391.

Therefore, it seems that prophecies are less problematic for Hume as a basis for faith than the other types of miracles described, although Hume does not say this. Nor does he indicate exactly how they pass the test of his first maxim. It cannot be that he accepts them because he naively thinks that biblical prophecies are necessarily true; for he implies that he understands the mechanisms of anachronistic revisions when he says of the Bible that it is "...a book written in an age when they were still more barbarous, and in all probability long after the facts which it relates...."[203] Thus, he could indict prophecies as deceptive rewrites of history after the fact, but he chooses not to.

Thus at the end of Hume's "Of Miracles," we see that he has not been trying to disavow all miracles as the basis for Christianity. Instead, he appears to have disavowed as the basis of Christianity rational proofs of those testimonies about miracles that are not prophecy. Indeed, there is yet another type of miracle that he implies he accepts and sees as the real basis of Christianity: this type is the miracle of conversion to the Christian faith. Hume indicates that without this miracle one cannot come to faith. However, it is not a rational proof, but a supra-rational experience that, while actually militating against one's better rational judgments, is nonetheless inexorable. Thus he can say of this type of miracle that it "...subverts all the principles of his understanding, and gives him a determination to believe what is most contrary to custom and experience."[204]

---

[202]Ibid., 392. Hume's argument here might seem to be weak at this point because he really does not explain why prophecies are valid miracles. However, he does not necessarily contradict his earlier assertion that no testimony regarding a miracle can serve as a rational proof of religious claims. This is because he is so vague here, that he could be conceivably defended as consistent, if by prophecy we take him to mean a miracle per se, and not a testimony about a miracle.

[203]Ibid., 391.

[204]Ibid., 392.

To some, Hume may not appear impressive in his general argument about miracles for the following reasons. First, it seems unreasonable for Hume to assert that one's experience is representative regardless of testimony to the contrary. This is one of the weakest points of Hume's argument. As pointed out earlier, Hume insists that regardless of how many respectable witnesses might present him with testimony for a particular miracle, he would still hold their testimony to be false.

In addition, Hume might be overstating his case that what one takes to be the laws of nature will rarely be altered on the basis of other people's testimony. In other words, Hume's position about our confidence in the immutability of the laws of nature might be too rigid. There are those who believe we change our minds all the time with regard to what we assume are the laws of nature. For such people then, Hume's argument is inadequate because he fails to distinguish between the different levels of regularity that we experience, and fails to recognize that there are varying degrees of regularity from level to level. In other words, at the level of ordinary everyday human affairs, there is a high degree of change in the regularity of our perception of the laws of nature. On the other hand, at the level of the physical processes that govern the universe, there seems to be less change in the regularity of the laws of nature.

My basic disagreement with those arguing against Hume along such lines arises from the fact that Hume, in "Of Miracles," is not primarily concerned with developing a general theory of the regularity of experience as such. Rather, he uses his arguments about regularity and testimony to try to assert that religion cannot be proved rationally, or be successfully established, on the basis of testimonies about miracles. Hume's concern is with miracles, which according to him are highly unusual occurrences that violate well established patterns of regularity. By implication then, his theories about testimony are not concerned with the everyday events about which we often change our minds, as some of his detractors suggest. The context of Hume's argument seems to make it clear that he is concerned about the miracles reported by religious traditions, and not primarily about testimony from everyday life.

Another major concern in his treatise might be in Hume's contradictory early rejection and then later acceptance of miracles. I believe that the contradiction is only apparent rather than real. Hume's views about miracles are best represented as a variety of opinions on a continuum, rather than as just two polar and opposite views.

Hume's spectrum of views on miracles starts out at one end, with a probabilistic calculus regarding the validity of testimony about miracles. Next, based on this calculus, he asserts that testimonies about miracles fail as successful rational proofs of the validity of the claims of various religions. Next, Hume asserts that although *testimonies* about miracles are not successful at a *rational* level, certain *miracles* themselves (such as prophecy and conversion) are proper and acceptable through *faith*. And thus, at the other end of the spectrum, faith itself is described by Hume as an ineffable, yet proper, miracle that humans can experience, even though it is not rationally provable or demonstrable. Hume's attack is on testimonies as rational proofs of religion; his attack is not on all miracles themselves, nor does he attack faith, or one's faith in certain miracles.[205]

---

[205]It is startling to realize how little support there is in the literature for these conclusions about Hume's continuum of views on miracles. Almost every available commentator on Hume, seems to suggest or conclude that Hume did not personally accept miracles, at the rational level, on faith, or any other way. One perspective somewhat similar to mine regarding Hume is expressed by Ernest Mossner when he says, "The purpose of the essay "Of Miracles," despite a few linguistic lapses on the part of the author, is to determine, not the philosophical issue of the possibility of miracles, but the evidential issue "that no human testimony can have such a force as

Part II: An Interpretation of Hume Based on the Ego-

to prove a miracle, and make it a just foundation for any...system of religion" Mossner, 1980, 286-7.

Antony Flew also lends some support to my position that Hume's main goal was to denounce the use of testimony about miracles as proof of a religion, but not to attack miracles themselves. But for reasons that I do not understand, he completely ignores what Hume says about his belief in prophecy, conversion, and faith. This is what Flew says: "...Hume was engaged with a question of evidence rather than a question of fact. What he was trying to establish was not that miracles do not occur, although he does make it very plain that this was his own view as well as that of all other men [sic] of sense; but that, whether or not they did or had, this is not something we can any of us ever be in a position positively to know" Flew, 1986, 80.

John Gaskin seems to contradict Flew's assertion that "other men of sense," and perhaps Hume, do not believe that miracles occur. Also, Gaskin refers to Hume's statements regarding his belief in miracles, but is ambivalent about their true intention. Gaskin indicates that Hume, "...does not say that no reasonable man can believe in any religion. A reasonable man can have a belief which goes beyond the evidence, but his belief will subvert 'all the principles of his understanding' and be brought home to him 'by the immediate operation of the Holy Spirit.' This operation Hume graciously - or sarcastically - leaves undiscussed as, simply, 'a miracle' " Gaskin, 1978, 125.

Contrary to what I have tried to establish here, about Hume's smooth transition of ideas, Nicholas Capaldi views Hume's treatise as confusing, and simply assumes that it is a direct attack on miracles. He says, "Suffice it to say that Hume's position is quite exasperating to many readers....One might even speculate that Hume presented the argument against miracles...because this made the attack on the arguments for God's properties all the more uncomfortable to the reader" Capaldi, 1975, 177.

Michael Levine also assumes that Hume's treatise is an attack on miracles. Also, contrary to what Hume himself attempts to say about the ineffable role of faith in one's belief in miracles, Levine insists that Hume's treatise is primarily useful in the broader context of reasoning about the causation of miracles. Levine says: "...the concept of a miracle is not independent of the concept of causation. God, or his agents, cause miracles. However, Hume's analysis of causation is particularly important in his arguments against miracles....This is because for Hume, all reasoning about empirical matters of fact - present, past, future, and counterfactual situations as well - should be regarded as a kind of causal reasoning. Such reasoning must therefore take account of his analysis of the causal relation and must not violate or ignore the principles of reasoning extrapolated from it" Levine, 1989, 4.

It is difficult to understand why Levine puts all these ideas together here about how to use Hume's approach to miracles. Hume seems to believe in miracles (such as prophecy and conversion), rather than to attack them. Also, Hume asserts that miracles

Self and Soul-God Frameworks

We have seen from the above treatment of Hume's "Of Miracles," that he is not opposed to all miracles as such, as the basis for Christianity. Rather he seems to be against rational proofs of those testimonies about miracles that are not prophecy which are used as the basis for Christianity. There is a type of miracle that Hume suggests he accepts as the real basis of Christianity. This is the miracle of conversion to the Christian faith. Without this miracle one cannot come to faith. And yet this miracle of conversion is not a rational proof, but a supra-rational experience which inexorably pulls one against one's better rational judgments. And this is why Hume can say of this type of miracle that it "...subverts all the principles of his understanding, and gives him a determination to believe what is most contrary to custom and experience."[206] Hume uses concepts such as supra-rational experience; "being pulled inexorably against one's better judgments;" and "having the principles of one's understanding subverted...," all of which appear to be phrases related to the fourth parallel we presented between synchronicity and the miraculous in Chapter One.

We saw in Chapter One that the fourth parallel between synchronicity and the miraculous is about how miracles and synchronicities can disrupt our understanding of how nature works. We saw from the two perspectives of Peat and Easton, that in both synchronicity and the miraculous, it is not the way in which things work that is violated, but rather, it is our *limited understandings* (and even our understandings based on our best assumptions) about the

---

have a cause. However, the cause of miracles (such as conversion), according to Hume in "Of Miracles," is itself the miracle of faith, which he says it is futile to reason about because "...it subverts all the principles of his understanding...." Rowe, 392.

[206]Rowe, 392.

way things work that get disrupted by synchronicities or the miraculous.

When we interpret Hume through the soul-God framework, we can see him, in a manner similar to Easton, describing the miracle of faith, and we see that Hume's suprarational experience is very much akin to Easton's infinite personal will where the miraculous is concerned. Alternatively, when we interpret Hume through the ego-Self framework, we can see allusions in his thinking about prophecy to synchronicity which for Peat gives "us a glimpse of that beyond our conventional notions of time and causality."

It appears that for Hume prophecy is a plausible and acceptable type of miracle. What allows us then to say that references to prophecy in Hume's thinking about the miraculous are also implicit references to our more contemporary understandings of synchronicity? For the answer to this we must turn once again to von Franz's story of the empress and her servitor in Chapter One.

As we indicated in Chapter One, the empress in the story there is parallel to a king of Israel; the servitor is parallel to an Israelite prophet; the servitor speaks with clarity and authority about the causal link between the empress's distortions and the dire synchronistic fate of her empire as reflected in the unseemly volcano, and also calls her to repent and turn from her distortions. The prophets of Israel, likewise, call the kings and their people to repent and the prophets also announce God's miraculously bestowed favor or disfavor (manifested through natural phenomena) based on whether or not the people respond to God appropriately.

Thus theology helps us to understand the miraculous as a manifestation of the dynamics between the soul and God, while depth psychology amplifies for us that these theological dynamics are parallel to synchronicities which are based on the subjective richness of the relationship between the ego and the Self. Thus, in a way that Hume was probably not completely conscious of, he appears to have been open to those miracles of foretelling known as prophecy, perhaps, we can speculate, because as is the case with most people, he had probably experienced for himself what we refer to today as synchronicities. It is not completely outrageous for us to suggest that Hume himself may have had experiences on the trans level which would have made him a believer in the supra-rational possibilities by which future events can be miraculously and synchronistically foretold. Why do I make this speculation here? It seems to me that Hume, in his acceptance of faith and prophecy as the two most legitimate forms of the miraculous for him, is expressing what most humans experience at one time or another, i.e., that there is something bigger than themselves to which they are accountable (the rudiments of faith and the miraculous), and also that uncanny foretellings (the rudiments of synchronicity) can happen to anyone.

Prophecy in the way Hume means it, clearly refers to a type of foretelling of events. This type of prophetic foretelling is analogous to an aspect of Ulanov's definition of synchronicity when she says (as noted in Chapter One) that:

> Examples of synchronistic events occur frequently in analysis of unconscious contents where meaningful parallelism between psychic and physical events takes place. A dream may refer to life events which happen after the dream rather than before it. Similar or identical thoughts or dreams may occur in different places at the same time. [207]

One of the biggest concerns of Hume's detractors, has to do with the way he seems to contradict himself, first by appearing to reject all miracles, and then later by appearing to accept certain miracles.

[207]Belford, 108.

Earlier, I demonstrated, in a transitive analysis of the relevant aspects of his text that Hume is best represented as treating miracles on a continuum, rather than merely as having two polar opposite and contradictory views. The thesis and method of this book allow us to speculate that Hume's spectrum of views represents his attempt to grapple with the different levels of the psyche and the soul, (i.e., the intra, inter, and trans levels) as he shifts from examining the validity of testimony about miracles (which reflects the intra levels regarding a person's honesty), to assertions that testimonies about miracles fail as successful rational proofs of the validity of the claims of the various religions (reflecting the inter level based on how people convey and receive information with one another), to assertions that although *testimonies* about miracles are not successful at a *rational* level, certain *miracles* themselves (such as prophecy and conversion) are proper and acceptable through *faith* (reflecting trans levels).

Thus it appears we can discern analogs in Hume's work on the miraculous to the intra, inter, and trans levels of the psyche, as well as to synchronicity, and thus by implication to the relationship between synchronicity and the miraculous. None of this is at all obvious if the arguments Hume presents are analyzed in the usual philosophical manner. However, by passing his argument through the ego–Self and soul–God frameworks, and under the guidance of the thesis being elucidated here, Hume's argument is quite coherent, and even true to the manner in which the psyche and soul when taken as a whole (by integrating the intra, inter, and trans levels) function with regard to the miraculous and synchronicity or their analogs.

Synchronicity and the Miraculous - The Trans Level: Easton and Ulanov

What does it look like for us to consider the miraculous more fully from the perspective of those whose minds are made up about it in a favorable way; who embrace and affirm the existence and reality of miracles from a positive direction in theology. What do they say about the miraculous, and how does what they say correlate with synchronicity?

EASTON

Resurrection of Christ

AS WE SAW EARLIER in Chapter One, the resurrection is of the utmost importance to the Christian. According to Easton the resurrection is

> One of the cardinal facts and doctrines of the gospel. If Christ be not risen, our faith is vain (1 Cor. 15:14). The whole of the New Testament revelation rests on this as an historical fact. On the day of Pentecost Peter argued the necessity of Christ's resurrection from the prediction in Ps. 16 (Acts 2:24-28). In his own discourses, also, our Lord clearly intimates his resurrection (Matt. 20:19; Mark 9:9; 14:28; Luke 18:33; John 2:19-22).

---

[208]According to Easton, "Ten different appearances of our risen Lord are recorded in the New Testament. They may be arranged as follows: (1.) To Mary Magdalene at the sepulchre alone. This is recorded at length only by John (John 20:11-18), and alluded to by Mark (Mark 16:9-11). (2.) To certain women, "the other Mary," Salome, Joanna, and others, as they returned from the sepulchre. Matthew (Matt. 28:1-10) alone gives an account of this. (3.) To Simon Peter alone on the day of the

The evangelists give circumstantial accounts of the facts connected with that event, and the apostles, also, in their public teaching largely insist upon it.[208]

The resurrection is a public testimony of Christ's release from his undertaking as surety, and an evidence of the Father's acceptance of his work of redemption. It is a victory over death and the grave for all his followers.

The importance of Christ's resurrection will be seen when we consider that if he rose the gospel is true, and if he rose not it is false. His resurrection from the dead makes it manifest that his sacrifice was accepted. Our justification was secured by his obedience to the death, and therefore he was raised from the dead (Rom. 4:25). His resurrection is a proof that he made a full atonement for our sins, that his sacrifice was accepted as a satisfaction to divine justice, and his blood a ransom for sinners. It is also a pledge and an earnest of the resurrection of all believers (Rom. 8:11; 1 Cor. 6:14; 15:47-49; Phil. 3:21; 1 John 3:2). As he lives, they shall live also.

It proved him to be the Son of God, inasmuch as it authenticated all his claims (John 2:19; 10:17). "If Christ did not rise, the whole scheme of redemption is a failure, and all the predictions and anticipations of its glorious results for time and for

---

resurrection. (See Luke 24:34; 1 Cor. 15:5.) (4.) To the two disciples on the way to Emmaus on the day of the resurrection, recorded fully only by Luke (Luke 24:13-35). (5.) To the ten disciples (Thomas being absent) and others "with them," at Jerusalem on the evening of the resurrection day. (John 20:19-24). (6.) To the disciples again (Thomas being present) at Jerusalem (Mark 16:14-18; Luke 24:33-40; John 20:26-28. See also 1 Cor. 15:5). (7.) To the disciples when fishing at the Sea of Galilee. Of this appearance (John 21:1-23). (8.) To the eleven, and above 500 brethren at once, at an appointed place in Galilee (1 Cor. 15:6; compare Matt. 28:16-20). (9.) To James, but under what circumstances we are not informed (1 Cor. 15:7). (10.) To the apostles immediately before the ascension. They accompanied him from Jerusalem to Mount Olivet, and there they saw him ascend "till a cloud received him out of their sight" (Mark 16:19; Luke 24:50-52; Acts1:4-10). It is worthy of note that it is distinctly related that on most of these occasions our Lord afforded his disciples the amplest opportunity of testing the fact of his resurrection. He conversed with them face to face. They touched him (Matt. 28:9; Luke 24:39; John 20:27), and he ate bread with them (Luke 24:42, 43; John 21:12, 13). (11.) In addition to the above, mention might be made of Christ's manifestation of himself to Paul at Damascus, who speaks of it as an appearance of the risen Saviour (Acts 9:3-9, 17; 1 Cor. 15:8; 9:1)" *Easton's Bible Dictionary.*

eternity, for men and for angels of every rank and order, are proved to be chimeras. 'But now is Christ risen from the dead, and become the first-fruits of them that slept.' Therefore the Bible is true from Genesis to Revelation. The kingdom of darkness has been overthrown, Satan has fallen as lightning from heaven, and the triumph of truth over error, of good over evil, of happiness over misery is for ever secured." Hodge.

With reference to the report which the Roman soldiers were bribed (Matt. 28:12-14) to circulate concerning Christ's resurrection, "his disciples came by night and stole him away while we slept," Matthew Henry in his "Commentary," under John 20:1-10, fittingly remarks, "The grave-clothes in which Christ had been buried were found in very good order, which serves for an evidence that his body was not 'stolen away while men slept.' Robbers of tombs have been known to take away 'the clothes' and leave the body; but none ever took away 'the body' and left the clothes, especially when they were 'fine linen' and new (Mark 15:46). Any one would rather choose to carry a dead body in its clothes than naked. Or if they that were supposed to have stolen it would have left the grave-clothes behind, yet it cannot be supposed they would find leisure to 'fold up the linen.'"[209]

General Resurrection of the Dead

Apart from the resurrection of Jesus in particular, what of the general resurrection of the dead? *Easton's Bible Dictionary* says the following:

Christ's resurrection secures and illustrates that of his people.[210] (1.) Because his resurrection seals and consummates his redemptive power; and the redemption of

---

[209]*Easton's Bible Dictionary.*

[210]According to *Easton's Bible Dictionary*, the resurrection "Will be simultaneous both of the just and the unjust (Dan. 12:2; John 5:28, 29; Rom. 2:6-16; 2 Thess. 1:6-10). The qualities of the resurrection body will be different from those of the body laid in the grave (1 Cor. 15:53, 54; Phil. 3:21); but its identity will nevertheless be preserved. It will still be the same body (1 Cor. 15:42-44) which rises again. As to the

our persons involves the redemption of our bodies (Rom. 8:23). (2.) Because of our federal and vital union with Christ (1 Cor. 15:21, 22; 1 Thess. 4:14). (3.) Because of his Spirit which dwells in us making our bodies his members (1 Cor. 6:15; Rom. 8:11). (4.) Because Christ by covenant is Lord both of the living and the dead (Rom. 14:9). This same federal and vital union of the Christian with Christ likewise causes the resurrection of the believer to be similar to as well as consequent upon that of Christ (1 Cor. 15:49; Phil. 3:21; 1 John 3:2). Hodge's Outlines of Theology.[211]

We have seen that synchronicity and the miraculous are parallel in that, among other things, they are both disruptions in our understanding of how reality can work. From the soul-God perspective we can say that for some Christians, based on the Bible, the resurrection is the greatest miracle, and therefore, given the parallels between synchronicity and the miraculous, logically at least, we can say that from the ego-Self perspective the resurrection can be described as the greatest synchronicity for this group of Christians.

Furthermore, we are promised, that as Christians we participate in the resurrection of Jesus, and that we will actually be resurrected ourselves one day. Therefore if the resurrection of Jesus is the greatest synchronicity from the ego-Self perspective as suggested above, then by our living authentically in the heart of our faith which says that "if you confess with your lips that Jesus is Lord and believe in your heart that God raised him from the dead, you will be saved," we then also participate in this the greatest synchronicity.

The reason it is useful here to integrate synchronicity and the miraculous with regard to the resurrection, is that synchronicity

---

nature of the resurrection body, (1.) it will be spiritual (1 Cor. 15:44), i.e., a body adapted to the use of the soul in its glorified state, and to all the conditions of the heavenly state; (2.) glorious, incorruptible, and powerful (1 Cor. 15:54); (3.) like unto the glorified body of Christ (Phil. 3:21); and (4.) immortal (Rev. 21:4)."

[211]*Easton's Bible Dictionary.*

involves the space-time-matter-energy continuum more palpably for us than mere words about the resurrection can. This aspect of synchronicity – that it helps us experience and understand how the transcendent participates in the physicality of our our existences - enables us to understand the resurrection of Jesus (and of ourselves one day) in more concrete physical terms, in a manner akin to Ulanov's description of the resurrection as presented in Chapter Three.

Furthermore, our integrated model based on the intra, inter, and trans levels in depth psychology and theology can be put to use here with regard to the resurrection as the ultimate miracle for the Christian from the soul-God perspective, which we are saying has a parallel ultimate synchronicity for the Christian from the ego-Self perspective. To see how this might parallel of ultimacy might operate on the intra, inter, and trans levels, let us return to Jung's example of the synchronicity involving the woman with the scarab beetle that we first saw in Chapter Three.

We established in Chapter Three that this synchronicity involved the intra level on which the woman had a dream about a scarab beetle. We also saw that her describing the dream to Jung, as well as his interpretation of it, involved the inter level. And then we saw that the actual scarab showing up at the window involved the trans level. So our confession of faith from Romans 10:9 which says "if you confess with your lips that Jesus is Lord and believe in your heart that God raised him from the dead, you will be saved," can be seen in the light of this scarab beetle synchronicity in relation to the parallel between the resurrection as the ultimate miracle from the soul-God perspective, and as the ultimate synchronicity from the ego-Self perspective. Believing in one's heart that God raised Jesus from the dead represents the intra level, and can be seen as a parallel to the woman's dream about the scarab. Confessing with one's lips that Jesus is Lord can be seen as a parallel to the woman's sharing of her dream with Jung which is on the inter level. The promised salvation as a result of believing in one's heart and confessing with one's lips is a parallel on the trans level to the scarab showing up at the window. We are promised through this confession of faith that in theological terms based on the soul-God perspective, we will be saved and participate in the resurrection of Jesus through our own bodily resurrection. At the same time, from the ego-Self perspective, we know that this confession will culminate in the ultimate space-time-energy-matter synchronicity which we frequently experience foretastes of in the smaller seemingly less significant everyday synchronicities, of which this scarab synchronicity is an example.

Synchronicities happen in a growth-inducing albeit surprising ways. By embracing our creeds, doctrines, sacraments and other instruments of Christian growth, we put into play triggers that yield the miraculous results (from the soul-God perspective) we are promised by God, and which we experience from the ego-Self perspective as synchronicities due to the acausal connecting principle. and which all ultimately point to and symbolize Christ's resurrection from the dead.

Our redemption by God through the death and resurrection of Jesus can be seen from the soul-God perspective as a parallel to the acausal redemptive process from the ego-Self perspective. *Easton's Bible Dictionary* describes the theological side of the parallel as

---

The purchase back of something that had been lost, by the payment of a ransom. The Greek word so rendered is apolutrosis, a word occurring nine times in Scripture, and always with the idea of a ransom or price paid, i.e., redemption by a lutron (see Matt. 20:28; Mark 10:45). There are instances in the LXX. Version of the Old Testament of the use of lutron in man's relation to man (Lev. 19:20; 25:51; Ex.

21:30; Num. 35:31, 32; Isa. 45:13; Prov. 6:35), and in the same sense of man's relation to God (Num. 3:49; 18:15).

There are many passages in the New Testament which represent Christ's sufferings under the idea of a ransom or price, and the result thereby secured is a purchase or redemption (Compare Acts 20:28; 1 Cor. 6:19, 20; Gal. 3:13; 4:4, 5; Eph. 1:7; Col. 1:14; 1 Tim. 2:5, 6; Titus 2:14; Heb. 9:12; 1 Pet. 1:18, 19; Rev. 5:9). The idea running through all these texts, however various their reference, is that of payment made for our redemption. The debt against us is not viewed as simply canceled, but is fully paid. Christ's blood or life, which he surrendered for them, is the "ransom" by which the deliverance of his people from the servitude of sin and from its penal consequences is secured. It is the plain doctrine of Scripture that "Christ saves us neither by the mere exercise of power, nor by his doctrine, nor by his example, nor by the moral influence which he exerted, nor by any subjective influence on his people, whether natural or mystical, but as a satisfaction to divine justice, as an expiation for sin, and as a ransom from the curse and authority of the law, thus reconciling us to God by making it consistent with his perfection to exercise mercy toward sinners" (Hodge's Systematic Theology).[212]

We see a parallel to the acausal element in this forensic and ransom approach to Jesus' death in Easton's quoting of Hodge above to say "Christ saves us neither by the mere exercise of power, nor by his doctrine, nor by his example, nor by the moral influence which he exerted, nor by any subjective influence on his people, whether natural or mystical, but as a satisfaction to divine justice, as an expiation for sin, and as a ransom from the curse and authority of the law, thus reconciling us to God by making it consistent with his perfection to exercise mercy toward sinners." Again, the soul-God parallel to the ego-Self acausal element in this article of Christian faith is found in the idea that Christ's redemptive and reconciling work[213] is legal matter arranged

---

[212]*Easton's Bible Dictionary.*

[213]According to *Easton's Bible Dictionary*, **"Justice of God** [is] That perfection of his nature whereby he is infinitely righteous in himself and in all he does, the

between God and Christ with no contribution from, or participation on the part of, sinful humanity, except in so far as we are the beneficiaries of this redemptive process if we choose it.

ULANOV

IF WE RETURN FOR a moment to the notion that some things improve[214] our experience of the synchronistic dimension of the miraculous, and other things are hazardous[215] to it we see the

righteousness of the divine nature exercised in his moral government.... **Atonement**....does not occur in the Authorized Version of the New Testament except in Rom. 5:11, where in the Revised Version the word 'reconciliation' is used. In the Old Testament it is of frequent occurrence. The meaning of the word is simply at-one-ment, i.e., the state of being at one or being reconciled, so that atonement is reconciliation. Thus it is used to denote the effect which flows from the death of Christ. (Ex. 32:30; Lev. 4:26; 5:16; Num. 6:11), and, as regards the person, to reconcile, to propitiate God in his behalf....Christ's satisfaction is all he did in the room and in behalf of sinners to satisfy the demands of the law and justice of God....**Justification** [is] A forensic term, opposed to condemnation. As regards its nature, it is the judicial act of God, by which he pardons all the sins of those who believe in Christ, and accounts, accepts, and treats them as righteous in the eye of the law, i.e., as conformed to all its demands....The sole condition on which this righteousness is imputed or credited to the believer is faith in or on the Lord Jesus Christ. Faith is called a 'condition,' not because it possesses any merit, but only because it is the instrument, the only instrument by which the soul appropriates or apprehends Christ and his righteousness (Rom. 1:17; 3:25, 26; 4:20, 22; Phil. 3:8-11; Gal. 2:16)."

[214]According to *Easton's Bible Dictionary*, **Holiness** "In the highest sense belongs to God (Isa. 6:3; Rev. 15:4), and to Christians as consecrated to God's service, and in so far as they are conformed in all things to the will of God (Rom. 6:19, 22; Eph. 1:4; Titus 1:8; 1 Pet. 1:15). Personal holiness is a work of gradual development. It is carried on under many hindrances, hence the frequent admonitions to watchfulness, prayer, and perseverance (1 Cor. 1:30; 2 Cor. 7:1; Eph. 4:23, 24)...." See also, **Sanctification, Prayer, and Heaven.**

[215]According to *Easton's Bible Dictionary*, "**Damnation** In Rom. 13:2, means 'condemnation,' which comes on those who withstand God's ordinance of magistracy. This sentence of condemnation comes not from the magistrate, but from

following, according to Ann and Barry Ulanov, about openness to prayer and the imagination:

At moments of impasse, whether in psyche or soul, in prayer or social action, we do not believe that if we surrender to the darkness that engulfs us new visions, solutions, or energies will suddenly burst upon us. We feel helpless to fix things, resourceless. And yet in this dying, in this death, there is a suddenness, the suddenness of absolute beginnings: the resurrected one comes across the gap to meet us. He brings a whole new picture that we could not reach ourselves. It breaks in upon us, this new picture, like him who brought it. It creates new life.

Such breaking-in can happen in our prayer and imaginative life. Or it can happen socially, where a new possibility, completely different from what we have expected, shows itself in political and social worlds. The early work of Martin Luther King, Jr., meeting violence with nonviolence, meeting racist division with a vision of love, reaching both oppressors and oppressed, showed us such a breaking-in. It happens psychologically too, when a new image of sexuality, spirituality, or aggression leaps up in us, suddenly throws us to the ground, causing total reversion from what we were before, a new conversion. Jungian psychology offers vivid illustration of this experience both in theory and in practice. It comes in the exercises of Jung's active imagination, where we open our attention to whatever the psyche shows us and engage in imaginative dialogue with an autonomous other. To see this other as other, our ego must remain firmly settled in its own ground and commitments, and know that there is no preordained outcome to the imaginative encounter. That is what makes the method so scary, so dangerous.

The autonomy of the unconscious shocks us, may even pull us under, so that we lose our foothold in reality. Then no dialogue is possible. And even if we escape that danger, we must recognize that the way the other side "speaks" will be very different from speech as we usually meet it, within ourselves or with others [reflecting the intra, inter, trans levels]. It may communicate through frightening

---

God, whose authority is thus resisted. In 1 Cor. 11:29 (R.V., 'judgment') this word means condemnation, in the sense of exposure to severe temporal judgments from God, as the following verse explains....See also, **Death, Sin, Satan,** and **The Final Judgment.**

images or seductive ones. It may communicate through our body, making us feel exhilarated or full of aches and pains. It may shout back at us through noisy symptoms or may entirely elude us, looking to fold its skirts and disappear into the desert. The unconscious has its own logic which is not always the same as our conscious one. That is what we learn when we dare a full prayer life. Sooner or later come struggle and fear. We know that the Spirit really exists and God really has come into our world. Something must happen. But what? And will we be up to it? These are fearful questions we ask when we seek God's presence, with no holds barred.[216]

Ulanov and Ulanov provide us with a way of opening up to the unconscious, through prayer, the imagination, and social action, in such ways that the unconscious meets us with healing and redemption, and yet does so in ways that are beyond our control - i.e., through the disruptions of the synchronistic and miraculous addressed above.

These scary synchronistic or miraculous disruptions to our habitual ways of experiencing the world – these signs of new and resurrected life – may be communicated to us by the unconscious "through frightening images or seductive ones. It may communicate through our body, making us feel exhilarated or full of aches and pains. It may shout back at us through noisy symptoms or may entirely elude us, looking to fold its skirts and disappear into the desert. The unconscious has its own logic which is not always the same as our conscious one."

What brings the religious object close – and closer than close, right within us – is when it breaks all the boundaries of time and space to share our subjectivity with us. That is the astonishing truth of the faith and its psychological and spiritual strength. We live as one in the human and the divine, each of us, because the divine became

---

[216]Ann and Barry Ulanov, *The Healing Imagination*, 157-8.

human....The psychological reach of this central fact of the faith is stunning. It is what resolves impasse and dissolves ambiguity. It is resurrection in the flesh, here and now, as well as in the eternal distance. We possess the life that was laid down for us. We have been crucified with Christ, as Paul says of himself in the grand statement explaining himself to the Galatians, and yet we live in the flesh, now. "I live now, not I, but Christ in me," are the famous words that say so much, that insist that we have been resurrected, that the violence of the crucifixion has been matched, and overmatched, by the violence done to our habitual ways of thinking and feeling and understanding. We who live now, not we, but Christ in us, have been reborn.[217]

By deepening our understanding of the parallels between synchronicity and the miraculous on the intra, inter, and trans levels of the ego-Self and soul-God frameworks, we have come closer to understanding how the resurrection can be seen both as the ultimate miracle and as the ultimate synchronicity for a certain type of Christian. In this manner, we are much closer to understanding how Jesus, the resurrected One, "breaks all the boundaries of time and space to share our subjectivity with us." This disruption of all the boundaries of time and space evidenced in both miracle and synchronicity happens in ultimate ways for us through "the violence of the crucifixion [which] has been matched, and overmatched, by the violence done to our habitual ways of thinking and feeling and understanding. We who live now, not we, but Christ in us, have been reborn."

We now turn in Chapter Five to a consideration of the ways in which the soul-God and ego-Self frameworks with regard to synchronicity and the miraculous on the intra, inter, and trans levels can be discerned in contemporary African American social cultural formation.

---

[217]Ibid., 160-1.

5. AFRICAN AMERICAN SOCIAL CULTURAL FORMATION

Na Yesu firi hó baa Galilea po ho. Na ókóó bepó so kótenaa ase hó. Na nkurófoó akuakuo pii de mpakye, mmbuafoó, anifirafoó, emum ne afoforó pii baa ne nkyen, na wóde wón beguu ne nan ase, na ósaa wón yadeɛ no yɛɛ nkurófokuo no nwanwa, berɛ a wóhunuu sɛ emum rekasa, na mpakye ho sane, na mmubuafoó nanteɛ, na anifirafoó hunu adeɛ; na wóhyeɛ Israel Nyankopón animuonyam (Mateo 15: 29-31)

Na óbarima bi a óde Simon wó kuro no mu a akane no na ódi asumansɛm, na óyɛ ne ho sɛ obi a óyɛ kɛseɛ maa Samaria man no ho dwirii wón. 'Ono na wón nyinaa, ɛfiri nketewa soó kósi akɛseɛ soó tie no ka sɛ : Oyi ne Nyankopón ahoóden kɛseɛ no. Na wótiee no ɛfiri sɛ óde akómfosɛm no maa wón ho dwirii wón akyɛ.Na wógyee Filipo a óka Nyankopón ahennie ne Yesu Kristo din ho asɛmpa no diiɛ no, mmarima ne mmaa maa wóbóó wón asu. Na Simon no ara nso gye dii, na wóbóó no asu no, óde ne bataa Filipo ho; na óhunuu nsɛnkyerɛnneɛ ne ahoódennɛɛ akɛseɛ a óyóeɛ no, ne ho dwirii no. (Asomafoó No Nnuma 8: 9-13).

Twɛrɛ Kronkron – Asante (Holy Scriptures in the Akan – Asante - language of Ghana, West Africa)

AND JESUS WENT ON from there and passed along the Sea of Galilee. And he went up on the mountain, and sat down there. And great crowds came to him, bringing with them the lame, the maimed, the blind, the dumb, and many others, and they put them at his feet, and he healed them, so that the throng wondered, when they saw the dumb speaking, the maimed whole, the lame walking, and the blind seeing; and they glorified the God of Israel (Matthew 15: 29-31)

But there was a man named Simon who had previously practiced magic in the city and amazed the nation of Samaria, saying that he himself was somebody great. They all gave heed to him, from the least to the greatest, saying, "This man is that power of God which is called Great." And they gave heed to him, because for a long time he had amazed them with his magic. But when they believed Philip as he preached good news about the kingdom of God and the name of Jesus Christ, they were baptized, both men and women. Even Simon himself believed, and after being baptized he continued with Philip. And seeing signs and great miracles performed, he was amazed (Acts 8: 9-13).

The New Oxford Annotated Bible (RSV).

This chapter explores the relationship between synchronicity and the miraculous in African American social cultural formation with regard to the Bible and biblical psychotherapy.[218] As in previous chapters, the exploration of the relationship between synchronicity and the miraculous in this chapter is approached on the intra, inter, and trans levels. For the intra level we look at Albert Cleage's rejection of Christ's resurrection. For the inter level we engage Edward P. Wimberly's *Counseling African American Marriages and Families.* For the trans level we examine Clarence Walker's *Biblical Counseling with African Americans: Taking a Ride in the Ethiopian's Chariot.* For the trans level we also examine two personal anecdotes about synchronicity and the miraculous, relevant to

---

[218]See the introduction for explanations of why African American social cultural formation is included in this study, as well as for a description of the term "biblical psychotherapy" in this context. Cleage, Walker, Wimberly, and Lee are used in this study because they each exemplify the "theory level" in which I have placed them. As with other sources for this study, I have discovered these sources as relevant to the various theory levels in a serendipitous manner. Future work might employ more powerful analytics to distinguish between religious experience and religious belief, as well as to go beyond using the Bible in terms of confessional issues, and to explore with greater texture and a sense of history, the psycho-social social-cultural dimensions of African American group dynamics and patterns. The more limited purpose of this study has been to get the exploration started about African American social cultural formation in relation to synchronicity and the miraculous in depth psychology and religion with regard to the intra, inter, and trans levels.

African American social cultural formation and psychotherapy from my own practice.

In summary then, this chapter seeks to deepen the exploration of how certain significant African American theological and psychotherapeutic commentators regard (or fail to regard) a simultaneous consideration of synchronicity and the miraculous on the intra, inter, and trans levels of discourse this study maintains one can observe. One purpose of this exploration is to advance learning about the relationship between depth psychology, the Bible, and African American religious experiences[219] of

---

[219]See Theophus H. Smith, *Conjuring Culture: Biblical Formations of Black America* (New York: Oxford University Press, 1994). He describes conjure as the linkage of "magical and supernatural elements on the one hand, with medicinal practices and natural processes on the other....reflection on conjure in its full ethnographic and phenomenal reality requires that we hold in concert both its therapeutic or benign referents and its occult and malign attributes," 5-6. Furthermore, Smith integrates conjure, shamanism, biblical cosmology, black social prophetism, ethics, and therapy: "The traditional black preacher has also felt commissioned to address the congregation's collective moral integrity, alongside its external strength in the form of socio-political empowerment and freedom. Not infrequently, these compound tasks have united in one person the role of theological ethicist, a social activist, and a therapeutic practitioner in the community. We may speculate that, conversely, other social character types in black communities have shared the preacher's shamanic role – not only ethicists and activists but also other charismatic figures, including orators and musical performers. These social characters can also claim to induce psychosocial transformations in their audiences and constituencies....In these diverse contexts one can observe not only distinguished individuals but also groups that function as agencies of psychosocial cure. Here we may refer particularly to the cure of disorders generated by the oppression of racism," 162-3. This reference to "distinguished individuals and groups that function as agencies of psychosocial cure," with regard to the African American experience of racism can be applied to Spike Lee, his documentary, "4 Little Girls," and the community of individuals and family members involved in the project which is addressed in Chapter Five of this study. See also, George Brandon, *Santeria from Africa to the New World: The Dead Sell Memories*, ed. John McCluskey Darlene Clark Hine, Jr., and David Barry Gasper, Blacks in the Diaspora (Bloomington, IN: Indiana University Press, 1997). Philip M.

synchronicity and the miraculous as signs of God's healing power and liberating action in the face of racial oppression and injustice in contemporary society. It is hoped that the insights garnered from these investigations can be applied more broadly to the even further and fuller refinement of strategies for improved functioning in African American and other communities.

CLEAGE

Synchronicity and the Miraculous in an African American Approach to the Resurrection: The Intra Level

IN THIS STUDY, Cleage[220] represents the intra level of the African American approach to the Bible because he sees the Christian faith in the resurrection as a misguided projection of hope into an afterlife that does not exist, (in a manner akin to Feuerbach and Freud). Cleage views the bodily resurrection of Jesus as a distortion intended to distract oppressed Blacks from fighting for their liberation from injustices in this life. The resurrection myth accomplishes this by promising release from all afflictions in a

Peek, ed. *African Divination Systems: Ways of Knowing*, ed. Charles S. Bird and Ivan Karp, African Systems of Thought (Bloomington, IN: Indiana University Press, 1991). Karen McCarthy Brown, *Mama Lola: A Vodou Priestess in Brooklyn*, ed. Mark Juergensmeyer, Comparative Studies in Religion and Society (Los Angeles: University of California Press, 1991). E. E. Evans-Pritchard, *Witchcraft, Oracle and Magic among the Azande* (Oxford: Clarendon Press, 1937). John Middleton, *Magic, Witchcraft, and Curing* (Garden City, NY: Natural History Press, 1967).

[220] Albert G. Cleage, *The Black Messiah*, (Africa World Press, 1989). "Albert Cleage Jr., died in 2002, at 88, and was an "influential black Detroit clergyman who helped elect the city's first black mayor, Coleman Young....founded the Shrine of the Black Madonna and preached that Jesus was a black revolutionary descended from a dark-skinned tribe of Israelites,"

http://www.cnn.com/SPECIALS/2000/year.in.review/story/obits/.

future heaven. The myth asserts that because Jesus met his death in the knowledge that he would be resurrected to ultimate glory in the future, ordinary Black people, oppressed by whites, need only focus on personal piety, while enduring suffering and injustice, in the hope that, like Jesus, their glory will eventually come with bodily resurrection after death.

However, according to Cleage, the empty tomb was not that meaningful for the disciples because Jesus had educated them to understand the resurrection not as a matter of individual survival but in terms of the survival of the blacks as a collective otherwise known as the Nation. In other words, Jesus' resurrection was not a personal bodily one, but was a mythical story actually referring to the resurrection of the Black Nation.

Thus for Cleage, Jesus was black, and his mission was to serve as a this-worldly revolutionary zealot. He fought just as much against the individualism, materialism, and complacency of his own Black brothers and sisters, as against the racism of the white (Roman) political oppressors of his people. His ultimate goal was to energize his black compatriots into a liberative nation-building effort.

According to Cleage, the revolutionary nature of the person and work of Jesus needs to be understood, reclaimed, and applied to the conditions of white oppression of blacks in America and the world at large. White hegemonic control of the world for the last five hundred years has caused this revolutionary black Jesus to be concealed. As a result, the early Black Church, afflicted by slavery, passivity, and other-worldliness (rooted in a misguided belief in the bodily resurrection in the after-life), did not possess the true knowledge of its black liberator.

For Cleage, various forms of oppression and passivity still exist. The white enemy continues to undermine the strongmen of Jesus' Black Nation by sending them to war and the penitentiaries. Those who strive to build the Nation are often undermined in their efforts by those of the Nation who are self-satisfied and materially secure. The secure are often co-opted by the white oppressor to hinder progress in the Black Nation.

If we look at Cleage from the soul-God perspective already developed in this study thus far, he like his parallels, Freud, in depth psychology, and Feuerbach, in theology, rejects the miraculous. If we look at him from the ego-Self perspective, we see that he does not acknowledge synchronicity. Here then is a black man, Cleage, with a decidely black view, who is parallel to Freud, in that he rejects the miraculous. In other words, Freud and Cleage appear to agree on the defensive function of such beliefs as the resurrection. This is significant to understand here because there are large segments of African Americans who think like Cleage does, and normally would be turned off, automatically, by white approaches to depth psychology and theology, because for them, the Bible, psychotherapy, synchronicity and the miraculous, as advanced by whites, are not categories that connect to the core of their black experience. In other words, without being sensitive and alert to the issues raised by Cleage on the intra level here, it might be difficult to get the commitment from blacks who could benefit from the theological and psychological approaches to synchronicity and the miraculous being presented in this study.

WIMBERLY

Synchronicity and the Miraculous in African American Biblical Psychotherapy: The Inter Level

IN APPLYING THE METHOD of integration underlying this book to contemporary African American social cultural formation with regard to biblical on the inter level we now turn to Edward P. Wimberly's *Counseling African American Marriages and Families.*

For Edward P. Wimberly, an African American professor of pastoral care and counseling at the Interdenominational Theological Center in Atlanta, there are three approaches to scripture when doing counseling with African American marriages and families. These three approaches are as follows:

1) **The Propositional Model** – this approach "emphasizes cognitive uses of scripture that formulate truth into objective realities and call for rational and behavioral allegiance by its adherents."[221]

2) **The Experiential-Expressive Model** – this approach focuses "on the inner feelings, attitudes, and experiences of people. It draws on the experiences of people and makes scripture secondary when understanding family relationships."[222]

3) **The Cultural Linguistic or Narrative Model** – this approach focuses on "the narrative orientation to life and demonstrates how narrative organizes life and informs experience. Rather than seeking sanctions for marital and family relationships in theological propositions or in the experience of marital partners or family members, this approach looks to scripture as narrative to inform marital and family life."[223]

Wimberly understands that these three models are not necessarily mutually exclusive, although he tends to favor the narrative approach to scripture:

---

[221]Edward P. Wimberly, *Counseling African American Marriages and Families* (Louisville, KY: Westminster John Knox Press, 1997), 2.

[222] Ibid.

[223]Ibid

> *The relationship among these three forms of organizing material and family experience is not necessarily exclusive. They represent divergent aspects of organizing experience and can inform how people in marriage and families utilize religious values. The concern here is that propositional statements are made about male and female relationships and relationships between family members that exclude the experiences of other family members and produce dysfunctional families. Moreover, focusing on individual experiences of family members could lead to making one family member's experience normative for all family members. This too could end up in marital and family dysfunction. However, the narrative approach to utilizing scripture holds out the potential for developing marital and family interactive patterns that allow for each family member to grow and develop.*[224]

Wimberly goes on to suggest that propositional and experiential-expressive approaches to scripture are much less dynamic than the narrative approach where the concern is with how scripture actually engages in their real and lived experiences. The benefit of the narrative approach to scripture, is that it corrects the potentially stultifying effects of the propositional model, and also corrects the overly subjective approaches people can have about experience. According to Wimberly,

> *...a narrative approach that understands the function of scripture in interaction with human beings offers an important way to approach marriages and families. It is especially useful with families that have a tendency to make rigid propositions about male and female role relationships. Consequently, narrative theology and narrative approaches to scripture will be utilized to give direction for assessing and intervening with African American marriages and families that have the tendency to develop inflexible role boundaries rooted in propositional understandings.*[225]

---

[224]Ibid.
[225] Ibid., 2-3.

Wimberly continues as follows:

> *Narrative approaches to marital and family life are more consistent with how African American families have brought meaning to their lives in the past. Scripture has been very important in the African American church and in African American families, and the method of bringing meaning to the lives of people has been relating their lives to the dominant stories of the Bible. For example, it is not unusual to hear storytellers of family history tell the family history in relationship to the Christian story, especially the exodus story. Consequently, narrative approaches, where people bring meaning to their lives by relating them to biblical stories and plots, have been very important in African American family traditions.*[226]

Wimberly is not opposed to propositional approaches to scripture. Rather, he is concerned about employing a holistic approach to using the Bible. As he puts it,

> *This does not mean, however, that propositional approaches are not necessary. Rather, it emphasizes a more holistic approach that involves both sides of the brain. Propositional or rational uses of scripture alone are not sufficient to inform the family and marital life of many African Americans. Consequently, the narrative perspective permits African American marriages and families to be more flexible with regard to roles and family patterns as they respond to the problems that they confront.*[227]

From Wimberly's approach to the use of the Bible in psychotherapy certain significant observations emerge. Wimberly is

---

[226]Ibid., 3.

[227]Ibid. Wimberly also focuses in some detail, throughout his work, on the following therapeutic issues: African American male hierarchical leadership; gender issues; the impact of slavery and racism on African American families; biculturalism; transgenerational dynamics; and parentification.

aware of the unconscious processes of the ego in the therapeutic process when he applies his scripturally-derived ethic of holistic love to counsel a husband who has been involved in an extra-marital affair. Wimberly says the following:

> The major theological issue that needs to be addressed is the analysis of extramarital affairs in light of the norm of liberated holistic growth and the ethic of love. This calls for the assessment to go beyond propositional theology that prohibits adultery and move to an examination of the impact of adultery on the growth and development of both partners in the marriage. Propositional laws against adultery may seem arbitrary and put a damper on human freedom and expression. Yet when the impact of it on actual lives is understood, values prohibiting adultery make sense.[228]

Wimberly goes on to add that

> [the client] explored the impact of the extramarital affair on his personal growth. Up until the affair, he did not realize that he was not dealing realistically with his midlife crisis. Having the affair helped him to suddenly realize that his life needed to be assessed and that he needed to make some major adjustments in it. He admitted his shortcomings, and he discussed with his wife what he needed to do about getting his personal life together. Therefore the norm and ethic that permeated the pastoral counseling relationship helped [the client] transform the negative affair into something positive for growth.[229]

---

[228]Wimberly, *Counseling African American Marriages and Families*, 107.

[229]Ibid., 110-111. Wimberly appears to be emphasizing here not so much an absolute position that adultery is always wrong, but more the position that in this particular case where it caused harm through mistrust and lack of awareness, its effects were damaging and thus had to be remedied.

Here Wimberly is aware of the unconscious dynamics that can work against a client when he illustrates that his client "did not realize that he was not dealing realistically with his midlife crisis." Again Wimberly shows his awareness of unconscious dynamics when he says his client was helped "to suddenly realize that his life needed to be assessed and that he needed to make some major adjustments in it." And finally, Wimberly emphasizes unconscious dynamics when he says his client "admitted his shortcomings, and he discussed with his wife what he needed to do about getting his personal life together."

Wimberly's approach to psychotherapy demonstrates an implicit understanding of all three theory levels (the intra, the inter, and the trans levels) and their implications for the practice of psychotherapy with African Americans. He implicitly acknowledges inter levels of theory and practice when he says that therapeutic interventions regarding adultery need to "move to an examination of the impact of adultery on the growth and development of both partners in the marriage." His understanding, albeit somewhat muted, of the trans level comes across when he says that "the norm and ethic that permeated the pastoral counseling relationship helped [the client] transform the negative affair into something positive for growth." The norm and ethic of love he is referring to here has eschatological roots in the coming Kingdom of God which is the trans level. Although there is an implicit focus on the trans dimensions of healing and scripture in Wimberly's work, there is no direct reference to synchronicity or the miraculous in his approach to psychotherapy with African Americans.

Wimberly's approach to psychotherapy can be described as largely on the inter level with slight aspects of the intra as well as tinges of the trans levels. The purpose of this study is to provide both therapists and clients with more options for wholeness in depth psychology and theology through the robust integration of the soul–God and ego–Self frameworks, with the attending intra, inter, and trans understandings of synchronicity and the miraculous being addressed in this study.

WALKER

Synchronicity and the Miraculous in African American Biblical Psychotherapy: The Trans Level

IN APPLYING THE METHOD of integration underlying this book to contemporary African American social cultural formation with regard to biblical psychotherapy on the trans level we turn to Clarence Walker's *Biblical Counseling with African Americans: Taking a Ride in the Ethiopian's Chariot*.

Clarence Walker, a licensed marriage and family therapist, with a Ph.D. in counseling from Trinity Theological Seminary, and an M.S.W. from Temple University, organizes his approach to counseling around Acts 8:23-39[230], and states that his purpose in

---

[230]It seems to be more coherent to cite the text as Acts 8: 26-40 – "Then an angel of the Lord said to Philip, 'Get up and go toward the south to the road that goes down from Jerusalem to Gaza.' (This is a wilderness road.) So he got up and went. Now there was an Ethiopian eunuch, a court official of the Candace, queen of the Ethiopians, in charge of her entire treasury. He had come to Jerusalem to worship and was returning home; seated in his chariot, he was reading the prophet Isaiah. Then the Spirit said to Philip, 'Go over to this chariot and join it.' So Philip ran up to it and heard him reading the prophet Isaiah. He asked, 'Do you understand what you are reading?' He replied, 'How can I, unless someone guides me?' And he invited Philip to get in and sit beside him. Now the passage of the scripture that he was reading was this:
'Like a sheep he was led to the slaughter,
and like a lamb silent before its shearer,
so he does not open his mouth.
In his humiliation justice was denied him.
Who can describe his generation?

Biblical Counseling with African Americans: Taking a Ride in the Ethiopian's Chariot, "is to set forth the issues, principles, and interventions of counseling as revealed by the Holy Spirit through God's Word, and apply them in the counseling of African-Americans, especially in terms of marriage counseling and family therapy."[231]

For Walker, Philip's meeting with the Ethiopian eunuch as recounted in Acts 8:23-39 is more than a message rallying devout Christians to evangelism and "soul-winning." For Walker, this passage "is a wonderful illustration of Bible-based counseling as it relates to black counselees."[232] In 17 of the 18 chapters in his book, Walker uses short fragments of the Acts 8:23-39 passage to introduce each of the chapters. In the general heading that introduces the first part of his book, Walker provides the following title: "COUNSELING ISSUES WITH BLACK COUNSELEES." Thus in Chapter One, Walker's chapter title is "ETHNICITY ISSUES," with the subtitle "A Man of Ethiopia" (Acts 8:27). Walker then applies this Bible fragment to the theme of ethnicity in counseling as follows:

For his life is taken away from the earth.'
The eunuch asked Philip, 'About whom, may I ask you, does the prophet say this, about himself or about someone else?' Then Philip began to speak, and starting with this scripture, he proclaimed to him the good news about Jesus. As they were going along the road, they came to some water; and the eunuch said, 'Look, here is water! What is to prevent me from being baptized?' He commanded the chariot to stop, and both of them, Philip and the eunuch, went down into the water, and Philip baptized him. When they came up out of the water, the Spirit of the Lord snatched Philip away; the eunuch saw him no more, and went on his way rejoicing. But Philip found himself at Azotus, and as he was passing through the region, he proclaimed the good news to all the towns until he came to Caesarea."

[231]Clarence Walker, *Biblical Counseling with African Americans: Taking a Ride in the Ethiopian's Chariot,* (Grand Rapids: Zondervan Publishing House, 1992), 9.
[232]Ibid.

> One of the first challenges faced by Philip in Acts 8: 27 was the fact that the Eunuch was an Ethiopian, a man of a different ethnicity and nationality. This same issue confronts the non-black counselor seeking a therapeutic relationship with black counselees. If counselors are to experience a successful chariot ride through the course of counseling, it is important that they recognize the possible impact of ethnicity. When this factor is not taken into consideration, it may lead to mistaken presumptions concerning behavior observed in counseling. Often blacks are viewed through ethnocentric glasses and evaluated by white middle-class norms.
>
> On the other hand, counselors can be influenced by ethnicity in stereotyping African-Americans as a people. This notion is just as counterproductive as the view that depreciates the importance of racial factors.[233]

In Chapter Two, Walker's chapter title is "GENDER ISSUES," again with the subtitle "A Man of Ethiopia" (Acts 8:27). This time, Walker ties this Bible fragment into the counseling process in the following manner:

> We discover in Acts 8:27 that Philip arose and went to join this "man of Ethiopia." He not only had to deal with the issue of ethnicity regarding the eunuch, but also with the fact that he was a man from Ethiopia. Gender is a significant issue in therapy, affecting the efficacy of the counseling process and outcome.
>
> For black men, the issue of masculinity has been a sensitive factor for them in America....Gender may surface as an issue in the counseling process as therapy progresses, in some cases preempting other issues. This is especially possible when exploring black men's sense of masculinity or black/female dynamics in general.[234]

---

[233]Ibid., 13. In subsequent chapters, Walker applies the same basic headlining approach outlined above to introduce issues pertinent to the therapeutic issues as follows: Chapter Three, SEXUAL ISSUES: "An Eunuch" (Acts 8:27); Chapter Four, POWER ISSUES: "Of great authority" (Acts 8:27); Chapter Five SOCIO-ECONOMIC ISSUES: "Who had the charge of all her treasure" (Acts 8:27); Chapter Six, ENVIRONMENTAL ISSUES: "And had come to Jerusalem" (Acts 8:27); Chapter Seven, RELIGIOUS ISSUES: "Had come to Jerusalem for to worship" (Acts 8:27).

[234] Ibid., 25.

In the general heading that introduces the second part of his book, Walker provides the following title: "THE COUNSELING PROCESS AND BLACK COUNSELEES: TEN BIBLICAL PRINCIPLES." In Chapter Eight, DIRECTIVE ENGAGING: "He arose and went" (Acts 8: 27), the first chapter of this new section of his book, Walker's headlining method takes on a different focus as he moves away from issues that come up in therapy with African Americans, to a focus on the actual processes that apply in therapy. In the opening paragraphs of Chapter Eight, Walker says the following in tying the Scripture fragment to the particular counseling process of directive engaging he is focusing on here:

The first of Philip's activities is found in verse 26: "And the angel of the Lord spake unto Philip, saying Arise, and go toward the south unto the way that goeth down from Jerusalem unto Gaza, which is desert." This particular activity has been labeled "directive engaging." Engaging means initiating a counselee to the counseling process. Directive means the leading of God as the act of engaging. Philip was directed by the angel of the Lord to pursue his mission with the eunuch.

In like manner, all Christian counselors must be sensitive to God's leading as they enter into a relationship with black counselees. This discussion will center on the role of God's leading in the engaging process, difficulties engaging blacks, methods of engaging, and some suggestions for white counselors. If the counseling process does not begin correctly, there is a strong possibility that it may not proceed or terminate well. Directive engaging helps assure a good start.[235]

In Chapter Nine, AFFECTIVE JOINING: "Then the Spirit said unto Philip, Go near, and join thyself to this chariot" (Acts 8:29), Walker describes the second principle in his biblical counseling process as follows:

---

[235]Ibid., 71.

> The second principle in the counseling process I want to discuss is affective joining. This principle is reflected in Acts 8: 29 when the Spirit instructed Philip to join himself to the Ethiopian's chariot. This joining is now more than physical – it is affective, an emotional juncture. Joining is the connectedness, the rapport between counselor and counselee. It is the formation of the therapeutic alliance. Here again we see the necessity of God's leading through his Holy Spirit. It was the Spirit who motivated Philip to join with the Ethiopian. As in directive engaging, it is the Spirit who prompts and enables us as counselors to join with counselees. The onus was on Phillip, not the eunuch, to initiate the joining. We cannot rely on counselees, who are understandably apprehensive, anxious, and emotionally spent, to make the effort, although they certainly have an important part in the process. To succeed in making the transition to joining, counselors must respect the Ethiopian's chariot and explore the appropriate method for entering it.[236]

Walker's approach to the use of the Bible in psychotherapy with African Americans can be organized according to the following themes underlying this study. Walker is indeed aware of the universal unconscious dynamics the ego, and this is clear in the way he describes how clients get stuck. Walker cleverly adapts the text fragment, "Philip opened his mouth, and began at the same scripture," (Acts 8:35), to suggest that it implies that Philip "recognized where the eunuch was stuck in his reading of Isaiah.

[236]Ibid., 77. In the chapters that follow, Walker once again applies the same basic headlining approach outlined above to introduce issues pertinent to the therapeutic process as follows: Chapter 10, ACTIVE LISTENING: "Philip ran thither to him, and heard him read the prophet Esaias" (Acts 8:30); Chapter 11, EXPLORATIVE QUESTIONING: "Understandest thou what thou readest?" (Acts 8:30); Chapter 12: CORRELATIVE BEGINNING: "Philip opened his mouth, and began at the same scripture" (Acts 8:35); Chapter 13: INTEGRATIVE WITNESSING: "Preached unto him Jesus" (Acts 8:35); Chapter 14: OBJECTIVE PROCEEDING: "As they went on their way" (Acts 8:36); Chapter 15: EFFECTIVE COUNSELING: "Philip said, If thou believest with all thine heart" (Acts 8:37); Chapter 16: COOPERATIVE INVOLVING: "And he commanded the chariot to stand still: and they went down both into the water, both Philip and the eunuch; and he baptized him" (Acts 8:38); Chapter 17: POSITIVE TERMINATING: "The Spirit of the Lord caught away Philip, that the eunuch saw him no more" (Acts 8:39).

Philip assessed the eunuch's level of understanding and began there."[237] In other words Philip correlated his entry into the process of transformation with the eunuch on a level accessible to the eunuch, given the eunuch's level of being stuck. Walker goes on to highlight the manner in which unconscious blockage retards healing as follows:

> The process of discerning how black counselees get stuck is not different from discerning how non-black counselees get stuck during the counseling process. Counselees who avoid a certain issue or subject, or who cannot alter their perception of a problem to consider an alternative solution are stuck in their journey toward healing. Other signs of counselees getting stuck are lack of empathy with their partners; inability to see their own contributions to problems; unwillingness to change; chronic failure to do therapeutic assignments; and continual sabotage of the counseling process. Therefore, counselors must be alert to redundant behavioral, intrapsychic, and systemic patterns that indicate counselees are stuck.[238]

Walker's psychotherapeutic work demonstrates an implicit understanding of all three theory levels (the intra, the inter, and the trans levels from depth psychology), and their implications for the practice of psychotherapy with African Americans. His understanding of the intra and inter levels comes across, for instance, when he says "counselors must be alert to redundant behavioral, intrapsychic [or intrapersonal], and systemic [or interpersonal] patterns that indicate counselees are stuck."[239] His understanding of the trans level (from a soul-God perspective) comes across when, as noted earlier, he declares that "It was the Spirit who motivated Philip to join with the Ethiopian. As in

---

[237] Walker, *Biblical Counseling*, 91.
[238] Ibid., 91-92.
[239] Ibid.,92.

directive engaging, it is the Spirit who prompts and enables us as counselors to join with counselees."[240] [241]

Walker implicitly refers to what we can consider as parallels to the miraculous when he refers to God's direction to Philip (and thus to the counselor) as being mediated by an angel:

The first of Philip's activities is found in verse 26: 'And the angel of the Lord spake unto Philip, saying Arise, and go toward the south unto the way that goeth down from Jerusalem unto Gaza, which is desert.' This particular activity has been labeled 'directive engaging.' Engaging means initiating a counselee to the counseling process. Directive means the leading of God as the act of engaging. Philip was directed by the angel of the Lord to pursue his mission with the eunuch [emphasis mine].[242]

Walker's approach to psychotherapy and the Bible is predominantly on the trans level, although it also has significant aspects of the intra and inter levels. His work is implicitly holistic and integrated rather than explicitly so, and neither does he refer to synchronicity or the miraculous explicitly. What such analysis points out then, is the need for counselors to be more explicitly attuned to synchronicity and the miraculous on the intra, inter, trans levels regarding the soul-God and ego-Self frameworks. The danger in not listening or screening for such phenomena more consciously and explicitly is that this can communicate a lack of deeper openness about such phenomena to clients, who in turn, may mute their attention to such forms of healing experience and guidance in counseling. This makes the efficacy of the healing process less holistic, and thereby weaker for all involved.

---

[240] Ibid., 77.

[241] Ibid., 55.

[242] Walker, *Biblical Counseling*, 71.

Two Personal Anecdotes about Synchronicity and the Miraculous Revisited: The Trans Level

In light of the above discussion regarding the work of Cleage, Wimberly, and Walker, (as well as the treatments of synchronicity and the miraculous in Chapters Three and Four), it seems appropriate to revisit the two examples from my own practice of psychotherapy first used in Chapter Two to demonstrate my own deepening awareness of synchronicity and the miraculous, and now to illustrate both synchronicity and the miraculous in the context of psychotherapy with African Americans.

In the case of the couple who became pregnant after many years of difficulty in doing so, of course this story cannot be taken merely at face value to be a convincing and actual miracle in the biblical sense of something dramatic and supernatural on the trans level of the soul-God framework; which is not to say that the conception was not synchronistic or miraculous either. However, some might choose to see the wife's infertility as a psychosomatically triggered resistance to becoming pregnant (on the intra level) which was eased when she started addressing the backlog of problems in the marriage (on the inter level). Others might suggest that my survey and my own interest in the topic of synchronicity and the miraculous induced in this couple an interest in the topic, as well as a desire to please me by offering me something useful for my survey project. One of the purposes of this study has been to create a useable and accessible system that allows us to integrate all three levels – the intra, inter, and trans levels - when teaching and learning about synchronicity and the miraculous in the context of psychotherapy.

In the dream about Professor Wimbush, it is quite clear to me that my dream images later on appeared to have been a foretelling of a deepening of my role with regard to healing work in an African and African American context. One lasting effect of the dream is that it has helped me to understand how prophetic visions (the trans level) in biblical literature might have arisen. The foretelling of events that I experienced through this synchronistic and miraculous (given the supernatural powers of the wisdom figure described in Chapter Two) sequence of situations, happened to me without much deliberate preparation other than through my doctoral and clinical focus on synchronicity and the miraculous, and the mediation of a wisdom figure (the trans level) appearing to me in a dream. In other words, I was not particularly aware of or confident about the supernatural and the miraculous as it is purported to occur in the Bible. However, my own determined and long-term focus on the study of synchronicity and the miraculous was finally yielding some small measure of fruit regarding actual experiences of the miraculous.

How much more if one were to have been called by God to be a prophet, and was graced with an ability to be God's spokesperson across the ages as were the biblical prophets? What supernatural and miraculous healing and redemptive power might such a calling from God confer, especially if one were to meet this calling with on-going spiritual discipline and purification? And what if one were to have been sent as God's Son, Jesus, pure and holy, and with all power to save, redeem, and heal from the beginning, and with a mission to disrupt humanity's narrow, dull, blind, and limited view of God's ways? What synchronistic and miraculous possibilities might emanate from a person with such power? What synchronistic and miraculous power might eventually ensue from the life of a person following Jesus as a loyal disciple where ever life took him or her, be it in politics, in academia, in business, in the work of a laborer, in the pain of prison, or in the psychotherapist's office? Might this power be great enough to raise people from the dead?

None of these discussion levels (intra, inter, or trans in the soul-God and ego-Self frameworks) can or should be dismissed or ignored lightly. The main reason for including these stories here is because they represent examples of African Americans engaging in discourse about synchronicity and the miraculous in the context of psychotherapy and the Bible.

This is significant because these examples bring into play many of the ingredients underlying the overall study in this chapter: teaching and learning about synchronicity and the miraculous with regard to the intra, inter, and trans levels, as well as with regard to psychotherapy, the Bible, and African American social cultural formation. In other words, these two anecdotes are representative of the ways in which this study seeks to deepen the exploration of the manner in which African Americans and others experience synchronicity and the miraculous with regard to healing and redemptive experiences.

LEE

Synchronicity and the Miraculous in Spike Lee's "4 Little Girls"

FROM ANOTHER PERSPECTIVE regarding contemporary African American social cultural formation, we have very potent, albeit brief, references to what can be considered as a synchronicity and the miraculous[243] in Spike Lee's[244] award-winning documentary,

---

[243]It should be stressed here that what we are doing is exploring the ways in which people refer to the miraculous and what we may discern as synchronicity in the context of African American social cultural formation.

[244]Spike Lee (born Shelton Jackson Lee) made a name for himself in 1986 with the hit independent film *She's Gotta Have It*, a frank comedy about the many lovers of an independent Brooklyn woman. The film established Lee as a rising young black

267

"Four Little Girls."[245] This Academy Award-nominated documentary tells the story of the notorious Birmingham, Alabama, church bombing on Sept. 15, 1963, in which one 11-year-old and three 14-year-olds, members of the 16th Street Church choir, were killed by a white man who planted a powerful bomb in their church basement. Using a combination of news clips, personal photographs of relatives of the girls, and various witnesses to many of the events described in the film, Lee takes us through the events of the day the bomb killed the four girls. He provides a context for his film within the civil rights movement in the South, and vividly depicts various marches, songs sit-ins and arrests, as well as the killings. Many have said that these killings, more than any other events, forced all of America to take a hard look at its racism, and that these killings also spurred on the civil rights movement like never before.

What follows now is a presentation of sections of the transcript which can be seen as serving in the manner a clinical verbatim might in a clinical pastoral education module. In other words, we can use it to slow down the pace of communication in order to analyze various parts of the theological and psychological processes at work.

There are three basic sections of transcript that we will explore briefly. The first one involves a synchronistic dream that happened about two weeks before the church was bombed. The second portion

---

filmmaker, a rarity at the time, and his skills and independence, along with his outspoken African-American perspective and feisty public persona, kept him in the public eye...." http://www.who2.com/spikelee.html.

[245]Roger Ebert, the film critic, says of the film, "The little girls had gone to church early for choir practice, and we can imagine them, dressed in their Sunday best, meeting their friends in the room destroyed by the bomb. We can fashion the picture in our minds because Lee has, in a way, brought them back to life, through photographs, through old home movies and especially through the memories of their families and friends."Copyright©ChicagoSun-TimesInc. http://www.suntimes.com/ebert/ebert_reviews/1997/10/102404.html

of the transcript involves commentary about the bombing from various civil rights leaders leading up to Jesse Jackson's references to the crucifixion and resurrection as a motif underlying the bombing and the subsequent rallying of the African American community. The third section of the transcript involves Lee's asking questions of the various family members most closely affected by the bombing, questions of an almost pastoral and psychotherapeutic nature.

What is noteworthy about these sections of the film, is that they contain a synchronistic dream, Jackson's reference to the resurrection, and Lee's somewhat pastoral and psychotherapeutic line of questioning directed at affected family members, all in the context of a significant African American social crisis of major defining proportions.[246] These elements represent the type of integration we have been seeking to address throughout the study, and it is remarkable that Lee, as the director of the film, and as a lay person both theologically and psychologically, nonetheless includes them in the final cut of the film.

------

[246]Again, see Theophus H. Smith, who in his *Conjuring Culture: Biblical Formations of Black America*, describes the shamanic healing functions of black "charismatic figures, including orators and musical performers. These social characters can also claim to induce psychosocial transformations in their audiences and constituencies....In these diverse contexts one can observe not only distinguished individuals but also groups that function as agencies of psychosocial cure. Here we may refer particularly to the cure of disorders generated by the oppression of racism,"162-3. As mentioned earlier, this reference to "distinguished individuals and groups that function as agencies of psychosocial cure," with regard to the African American experience of racism can be applied to Spike Lee and this documentary.

Abridged Transcript of the Documentary Film, "4 Little Girls"
Part I – A Reference to a Synchronistic Dream

In the following sections of the transcript of the film, we see an account of a synchronistic dream that a mother is described as having had about a bloody tragedy in the church roughly two weeks before the bomb exploded there (lines 2, 3, 4, and 5 below). It is a synchronicity because the mother, after she had had the dream, used it to warn her children to stay away from the church because she felt quite strongly that something terrible was going to happen there soon. When in fact, the church was actually bombed about two weeks later, the synchronicity was then in the fact that she had had this deeply meaningful inner experience on the intra level, that she had communicated it to her children on the inter level, and then that the church had been bombed in a way that had tremendous significance on the trans level, given that the mother had foreknowledge of it without in any way having caused it.

> 1. Chris McNair[247] (father of Denise, one of the four
>   girls killed – reminiscing about their last meal

---

[247]Marc Savlov, in a review for "The Austin Chronicle," dated April 6, 1998, says the following about the film: "There is a defining moment in Spike Lee and Sam Pollard's Academy Award-nominated *4 Little Girls*, a documentary about the 1963 Ku Klux Klan bombing of the 16th Street Baptist Church in Birmingham, Alabama which ended the lives of four girls. This moment provides a bridge between the legendary and near-mythical status of the civil rights movement of the 1950s and 1960s and the intimate and very human reality of the individual men and women who were involved in its textbooks, this micro-analysis of the nuts and bolts of the battle-like process is a refreshing revelation, indeed. His expertise in both fields is evidenced by one particularly powerful interview with George Wallace. Using such narrative devices as jump cuts, different film stocks, and varying focal lengths, the scene cuts to the heart of the horror of George Wallace and everything he stood for in a little more than a minute of screen time. It represents a penultimate example of the fusion of high drama and documentary. Despite the fact that they were conducted 23

together, the night before the bomb blast which killed her and three others)

"It was like the last supper with Christ and his disciples."

2. Barbara Nunn (Denise's Childhood friend)

"Two weeks before the church was bombed my mother was in the kitchen and we were getting ready for church and all those of things and she was standing there at the sink and she turned around and said to Ray my oldest brother, Ray I know you've been going out there leading those demonstrations, leaving school and going to down to Birmingham....mama just wants to ask you this – don't go back into 16th street Baptist church cause God has shown me something terrible is going to happen there."

3. Mother Queen Nunn (Barbara's mother)

"I dreamed seemingly out of a clear blue sky that there was going to be something terrible happening at 16th street. And I saw a lot of blood and I mentioned it at breakfast table – it was on a Saturday morning and I said please I don't want any of you....I said Ray, I Don't

---

years after the fact, the interviews with the four girls' family members contain a startling immediacy. And each individual reflects back on the events with a remarkable bearing of both internal fortitude and grace that, despite all of the hate and chaotic insanity directed toward them, comes with the self-awareness of their moral certainty and rightness in the face of evil. Unlike the racist forces aligned against them, 'They didn't have a pathology' explains Pollard. 'They didn't walk around thinking 'We need to figure out a way to hate white people as much as they hate us.'" http://www.filmvault.com/cgi-bin/pop.pl?p=austin.

want you nowhere near 16th Street Baptist Church."

4. Barbara Nunn

"And Ray went Ma!!!...."don't tell the children any superstitious stuff like that." She said, "No. God has shown me I dreamed it last night it was just blood coming all out of that church, and it was blood just pouring out of that church....And I don't want any of my blood spilled." We were all looking like...I guess Ray didn't respond...Next thing she fell on her knees."

5. Mother Queen Nunn

"And I started crying because it seemed so real to me in the dream
Well when this happened I think we all thought about it."

Commentary:

In line 2 we can see a clear reference to the soul-God framework in action when Barbara Nunn reports that her mother had said to Barbara's brother "don't go back into 16th street Baptist church cause God has shown me something terrible is going to happen there." Mother Queen Nunn clearly felt strongly connected enough to God in this way, that she took her dream as a realistic warning about something bad that would soon happen at the church. It seems pretty clear that in spite of Mother Nunn's impassioned pleas to her chirldren in the light of her dramatic dream, they were skeptical about her concerns, and labeled her dream "superstitious stuff." Viewed from the ego-Self framework, it is clear that Mother Nunn was somehow open to the Self in such a way that she received a synchronistic dream, which others in the family who having more ego-resistance, were skeptical of. Mother Nunn stayed aware of the dream and tried to communicate the essence of its importance to the others in her life. From a soul-God perspective, she took the dream as a direct warning from God that something bad was about to happen, and that protective measures were called for.[248] Mother Nunn makes it clear in line 5 that when the bombing actually occurred, they all remembered that she had seen this in her dream.

Part II – A Reference to the Crucifixion and Resurrection

Further down in the transcript (line 19), The Rev. Jesse Jackson is quoted as saying that, "The bad news is four innocent babies were killed; the good news is we were able to transform a crucifixion into a resurrection – new life, new hope, new energy, and more determination." Before we get to this part of Jesse Jackson's script, it is instructive to provide more from the other civil rights interviewees involved at the time as a way of creating a bigger context.

> 6. Nicholas Katzenbach (Former US Attorney General)
> "The bombing of the churches in Birmingham with the death of the little girls was just an act of terrorism in my judgment and those are in many as we know today the hardest ones to resolve and the cruelest because they don't

---

[248]See four examples of similar messages in Matthew 1:18 to 2:23, in which angels mediate various forms of guidance and warnings from God to Joseph and the Magi as the incarnation of the Christ-child is in danger of bebeing thwarted several different times. The correlation between Mother Nunn's dream and these miraculous biblical warnings is part of the reason this study focuses on an integrated approach to synchronicity and the miraculous as a way of supporting a robust and healthy faith in biblical miracles.

care who it is that gets killed as long as there's some symbolism in what they're doing."

7. Rev. Andrew Young (SCLC)

"It just seemed pointless; it wasn't going to stop the movement; it just took the lives of four beautiful innocent little girls."

8. Diane Nash (SCLC and ex-wife of civil rights activist, the Rev. James Bevel)

"My former husband and I, Jim Bevel, were in Eddington, NC. The SCLC was carrying out a voter registration project."

9. Rev. James Bevel

"And in fact I was scheduled to preach that Sunday morning and so when the church blew up we heard about it before I got to church."

10. Diane Nash

"And we felt that in order to respect ourselves as an adult man and woman we could not let little girls be killed."

11. Rev. James Bevel

"It was like somebody had hit me with hot steel... and I felt personally insulted because it was like they knew those children was using that church and they really felt insulted because the children have defeated them, right? so it's like they're coming back on the children to say we will teach you a lesson and my point is no we will teach you a lesson."

12. Diane Nash

"We felt that there were two things we could do. The first option is that we felt confidant that we could find out who was responsible for having killed those girls and we could make certain that they got killed that was option one."

13. Rev. James Bevel

"I said look I'm going to have to get out of the movement and kill these guys we are not going to let guys come in to the community blow up our churches and kill our children – we're not going to do it."

14. Diane Nash

"The second option was that if blacks in Alabama got the right to vote they could protect their children."

15. Rev. James Bevel

"Now that's where – this bombing of the church – is where the Selma right to vote movement was born."

16. Coretta Scott King (reading a letter from Martin Luther King, Jr. to the McNairs):

"Dear Mr. and Mrs. McNair:

Here in the midst of the Christmas season my thoughts have turned to you. This has been a difficult year for you. The coming of Christmas, when the family bonds are normally more closely knit, makes the loss you have sustained even more painful. Yet, with the sad memories there are the memories of the good days when Denise was with you and your family.

As you know many of us are giving up our Christmas or are severely limiting them as a memorial for the great sacrifices made this year in the freedom struggle. I know there is nothing that can compensate for the vacant place in your family circle, but we did want to share a part of our sacrifice this year with you. Perhaps there is some small thing dear to your heart in which this can play a part.

Sincerely Yours,

Martin Luther King, Jr."

17. Janie Gaines

"When I was going to school after she had died when I was goin' to school you know how you just remember such a good time you used to have and you know you going to have a good time when you go home because you going to get with your sister – that was the type of relationship we had. I knew that when I got home me and Addie was going to have us a good time playing and I rushed home that evening from school thinking that I was rushing home to get with Addie and I had remembered that Addie was dead, and that thing hurted me, it hurted me so deep 'til.........(long pause) it's not easy because we had put so much of this behind us we don't remember.......(long pause) we just don't remember anymore you know what I'm saying? But you know how you felt. You may not remember the details on what step by step what I had to go through but I do know that it affected me so bad."

18. Walter Cronkite (Special Correspondent CBS News)

"I don't think the white community really understood the depths of the problem or the depths of the hate of the Klan and its friends in the south and in the north too for that matter until that incredibly mean terrible crime of blowing up kids in a Sunday school basement. Up to that time, I think, it was looked at primarily as an interesting kind of a social development that would come along somehow or other in the generations to come. At that moment that that bomb went off and those four little girls were blasted and buried in the debris of that church America understood the real nature of the hate that was preventing integration, particularly in the south but also throughout America – this was the awakening."

19. Rev. Jesse L. Jackson, Sr. (Founder of the Rainbow Push Coalition)

"The bad news is four innocent babies were killed; the good news is we were able to transform a crucifixion into a resurrection – new life, new hope, new energy, and more determination."

20. Three Different Overlapping Television Announcers

"First Announcer: one hundred twenty years of history suddenly destroyed; five churches with black congregations have burned in Alabama this year – look at some of the damage in Green county; Second Announcer: just last week somebody torched this church in the nearby town of Tyler; this is one of dozens of southern predominantly black churches that burned within the last year and a half – President Clinton now wants to know if the fires are racially motivated."

21. Rev. Jesse L. Jackson, Sr.

"What's painful to me if you look at the story today is that they're burning churches again."

22. Rev. Reggie White (Green Bay Packers)

"I guess more than anything that really bothered me was when I found out how many other churches they burned since 1994 – there were over 22 churches in the south that had burned down. People kept saying it was not a conspiracy and things like that. But the thing that I believe is that it's a conspiracy of the mind – once you burn one down, other people gonna burn others down."

Commentary

In line 6, we see Nicholas Katzenbach, a former US Attorney General, emphasize how cruel an act the bombing was. He also offers something of a psychological perspective on why people commit such acts of terrorism – they do it for the symbolic message it communicates more broadly. In line 7, the Rev. Andrew Young (SCLC), is defiant about the fact that the there was no way that the bombing would have stopped the movement – from this perspective the bombing then seemed pointless.

In lines 8 to 15 we hear from Diane Nash and the Rev. James Bevel how compelling it was for them to consider various ways in which to strike back at the terrorists – it was a point of pride, dignity, and the desire to put a clear message that the most vulnerable in the African American community had fierce protectors. In line 16 we see the efforts of Martin Luther King, Jr. to serve the families of the victims as a true pastor with moving and noble words of comfort and solace.

In line 17, Jaine Gaines gives us a look at the psyche's desire to repress the fierce pain of such a trauma when expresses her heartbreak about often forgetting when she would get after school that her sister had been killed – she would go looking for her so they could play. She also provides us with a window into the trauma this buried into her psyche when she says "it's not easy because we had put so much of this behind us; we don't remember.......(long pause) we just don't remember anymore, you know what I'm saying? But you know how you felt. You may not remember the details on what step by step what I had to go through but I do know that it affected me so bad."

In line 18 Walter Cronkite expresses something of the white perspective when he says, "I don't think the white community really understood the depths of the problem or the depths of the hate of the Klan and its friends." This point by Cronkite is especially important because so often, blacks feel the dimension of hatred and opposition they experience from whites is ignored or minimized by whites, precisely because whites do not experience the same levels of racism that blacks do. Then in line 19, Jesse Jackson uses the archetypal motif of the death and resurrection of Christ to describe how the black community used this adversity to create opportunity. This is particularly noteworthy because no else interviewed uses this motif. I am not saying that Jackson's reference is to an actual miracle of bodily resurrection as such in the circumstances the film depicts.

What I am saying is that it is remarkable to me that this film includes references to both a synchronicity as seen earlier regarding lines 1-5, and the miraculous (i.e., Jackson's reference to the crucifixion and resurrection of Jesus), and my interest is in whether or not Lee sees these as connected, and therefore deliberately includes both references in order to imply a connection between the synchronistic dream and Jackson's reference to the crucifixion and resurrection of Jesus, or whether it was a more of an unconscious process for Lee. Lines 20-22 show us that the same spirit of violence is alive and well decades later and this is often quite shocking to realize for many people both black and white.

Part III – References to the Soul-God Framework and Psychological Healing

In this next section of the transcript, we see Lee engaged as a counselor of sorts, investigating the nature of the healing from anger that the mother of one of the victims underwent.

> 23. Junie Collins (Addie Mae's sister)
>
> "It wasn't God that brought the bombing on. A lot of people would think well God did this and God did that it's just like there's a God of good we have a god of evil too. And it's no part of God... when we realize that God has our best interest and he has a plan for each one of us, a plan that's good and not for evil, then we can begin to come and receive healing."
>
> 24. Maxine McNair
>
> "A friend of mine who's a pastor said God has a will for everything Maxine you just have to go with it and you can't ask him why, because he has a divine plan, and you know that so don't ask just go on and do what you know is right to do."

25. Alpha Robertson (mother of Carole, one of the victims of the bombing)

"I've worked hard not to feel anger and hatred, but I did and I just had to work on it, and I had to kind of keep my spirits up so that I could help my husband to keep his up, and, you know, the other folk around me, and we had good friends and family who gave us a lot of support and I just had to work with it and pray."

26. Spike Lee

"Did it take a number of years for that to happen for you to arrive at that."

27. Alpha Robertson

"Yes gradually it came about because the hating of people wasn't going do me any good. It would hurt me worse than it would them, so I think I conquered it; every now and then it still comes out though – not hatred but anger."

28. Spike Lee

"How does it come out?"

29. Alpha Robertson:

"I don't know....in different ways....that's a tricky question" (laughter).

30. Spike Lee

"I'm not trying to be Mike Wallace now."

31. Alpha Robertson

"Or Ed Bradley huh?"

32. Spike Lee

"Or Ed Bradley....I just wanna...."

33. Alpha Robertson

"Well I guess it's a question that deserves an answer,
    I guess – you asking me how does it come out.
    Sometimes it comes out in ways that I'm not
    even conscious of. You know if you're
    thinking about something and having the
    wrong thoughts and something comes up and
    anger expresses itself. But I've tried to just
    put all of that behind and go on and live
    'cause in addition to that so many other
    things have happened you know: my husband
    is gone; my three brothers; my sister; my
    parents; of course I still have my kids my
    family: I have two - a son and a daughter;
    three   grandchildren   and   four   great
    grandchildren – so I have something to be
    thankful for after all."

Commentary:

Lee himself, in this section of the transcript, interviews siblings
and parents of the victims, and we see them speaking from the
perspective of the soul-God framework about God's transcendent
nature in ways that are parallel to our understanding of acausality
in the ego-Self framework, when these relatives explain that this
terrible tragedy cannot be used to question God, but must, in the
end, be accepted as part of God's unfathomable higher plan (lines
23 and 24). The lines highlighted here refer to the trans level.

In line 23 we Junie Collins the sister of one of the girls who was
killed being very careful from a soul-God perspective to distinguish
God's goodness from sources of evil other than God, when she says:
"A lot of people would think well God did this and God did that -
it's just like there's a God of good we have a god of evil too." In line
24 Maxine McNair, mother of one of the slain girls, and again from

a soul-God perspective, describes her surrender to God's plan in the midst of her loss.

Also, on the psychological level, Lee is quite curious about issues of emotional healing and the release of anger that family members of the victims might have been experiencing about the terrorist bombing of the church (lines 25-33). These and the remaining sections of the transcript look mostly at intra and inter levels of how people responded to the killings. In line 25 Alpha Robertson talks about the hard work of letting go of her anger and hatred towards the people responsible for the bombing. In line 26 we see Lee initiate a very gentle and respectful line of questioning with a view towards building empathy with Alpha. In line 27 she declares that she believes she conquered the anger and hatred through the insight that holding on to her anger and hatred would have hurt her more than it would have hurt the killers. She also indicates that although it is pretty much behind her, that sometimes it shows up again. In line 28, Lee wants to know more about how it comes out, and for some reason, Alpha's defenses go up as evidenced in line 29. In line 30 Lee reassures Alpha that he is not an aggressive "60 Minutes"-like interviewer, as he seeks to rebuild the empathic bridge between Alpha and himself. Alpha responds in line 31 with a request for further reassurance that she is safe with him, when she asks him whether or not he would be like Ed Bradley, and Lee reassures further in line 32. In line 33, Alpha explains that anger and hatred still come out sometimes in ways that she is not conscious of and that there are any number of triggers that can make this happen. She goes on to explain that the death of her daughter in the bombing has been followed by the many other deaths of people important to her, and that in the end she is grateful to have her children, grandchildren, and great grandchildren.

These three sections of the transcript of Lee's film go to the heart of the thesis of this study, that concepts about synchronicity and the miraculous should be embraced simultaneously because this enriches our experiences of both synchronicity and the miraculous. Lee's film also brings to mind intriguing questions about whether and how people deliberately make connections between synchronicity and the miraculous. Jackson's perception of the miracle of resurrection is that in the face of extreme and deadly violence towards a historically oppressed people, their spirit is not killed, nor do they themselves resort to the same violence inflicted upon them. Rather they keep on fighting for their God-given dignity and human rights as equals to their oppressors, and thereby do rise up again and again from this type of devastation.

The point being made here is that whether Lee is fully aware of this or not , his choice of material for the film, when taken all together, ends up reflecting a simultaneous embrace of synchronicity and the miraculous as well as the depth psychological concerns with the wholeness of the psyche on the one hand, and the theological concerns about God's transcendent and loving plan for us on other. It is this type of simultaneous embrace of synchronicity and the miraculous (even when it is just in small trace amounts), that this study seeks to make an on-going focus, and it is quite remarkable that a contemporary African American film maker, ostensibly with no formal psychotherapeutic or pastoral training has captured elements one of the desired end-result of this study in this film - the simultaneous embrace of synchronicity and the miraculous, within the context of the struggle for liberation from racial oppression. While this is quite a positive and encouraging finding, it certainly is just the beginning; much more explicit attention to the healing and redemptive implications of synchronicity and the miraculous together is called for.

Conclusions

The following conclusions and questions seem warranted from the foregoing explorations. It appears that in the above approaches to the Bible and biblical psychotherapy and healing in the face of oppression in relation to contemporary African American social cultural formation, that although there are no significant expressions of synchronicity as such, nor of a connection between synchronicity and the miraculous, there are trace ways in which such connections can be discerned implicitly. These understandings can certainly be enriched by further explorations into the following questions. Are there models of the ego-Self and soul-God frameworks, as well as of synchronicity and the miraculous, which are derived originally from African and African American foundations, and if there are, how are they similar to or different from those based more on white American and European sources? Does this matter? If this does matter, then how does it matter?[249] A

---

[249]Michael Vannoy Adams' *The Multicultural Imagination: "Race," Color, and the Unconscious* (New York: Routledge, 1996), is an impressive and informative presentation of definitions, conceptions, and dream material about diversity, race, the raciality of the unconscious, racial identity, racism, color, and colorism. As part of his explicit aim for the book he states that "What is distinctive about psychoanalysis is its emphasis on the unconscious. A genuinely multicultural psychoanalysis would provide us with an opportunity to inquire into the 'raciality' (as we already have done with the sexuality) of the unconscious. This book is an effort on my part to try to determine what the 'racial' contents of the unconscious have been - and are," xx. Although most of the book is focused on the "black-white" racial and cultural dynamics of the unconscious as developed through treatments of Freud and Jung, there are also references to Hillman, Klein, Kohut, and Winnicott as well. In addition to this there are illuminating references to, or treatments of, Melville's *Moby Dick*, Conrad's Heart of Darkness, Haggard's *She*, Walker's *Possessing the Secret of Joy*, and Fanon's *Black Skin, White Masks*, all of which Adams uses to exemplify, in splendid didactic style, ways in which multicultural psychoanalysis can be turned to rich multicultural depth psychological praxis. See also Edward Bruce Bynum's *The African Unconscious: Roots of Ancient Mysticism and Modern Psychology*

fuller interdisciplinary and multidisciplinary examination of the roles of depth psychology and theology, and of the ego-Self and soul-God frameworks in particular, in biblical scholarship and biblical psychotherapy in relation to African American social cultural formation is perhaps a potentially useful innovation and path of inquiry. In other words, how can depth psychology and the ego-Self framework, as well theology and the soul-God framework, when taken together, enrich the approaches of black discourses related to the Bible and vice versa? What can depth psychology and theology together, learn regarding how to address questions of race and racism from the rich resources of black psychological and biblical discourse? How can depth psychology and theology together, be adapted from a primarily white enterprise into one that is a more trustworthy tool of healing change in, and for, black communities? [250]

(New York: Teachers College Press, 1999). See also *Oedipus and Job in West African Religion* (London: Cambridge University Press, 1959), by Meyer Fortes and Robin Horton. *Oedipus and Job in West African Religion* addresses Freudian (intrapersonal), interpersonal, and transpersonal understandings of fate in the social psychology of the Akan of Ghana from a predominantly "intra" and "inter" perspective. Robert Pelton's *The Trickster in West Africa: A Study of Mythic Irony and Sacred Delight*, addresses synchronistic phenomena, also through the social psychology of the Akan, especially in the section on "Ananse: Spinner of Ashanti Doubleness." *Oedipus and Job in West African Religion* and *The Trickster in West Africa* when taken together with Gates' *The Signifying Monkey*, provide a good framework for future work on African and African American sources for aspects of the topic at hand.

[250]Reginald L. Jones, ed. *Black Psychology* (Berkeley, CA: Cobb and Henry Publishers, 1991).Alexander Thomas and Samuel Sillen, *Racism and Psychiatry* (New York: Carol Publishing Group, 1991).Vincent L. Wimbush, "The Bible and African Americans: An Outline of an Interpretive History," in *Stony the Road We Trod: African American Biblical Interpretation*, ed. Cain Hope Felder (Minneapolis: Fortress Press, 1991), and "'Rescue the Perishing':The Importance of Biblical Scholarship in Black Christianity," in *Black Theology: A Documentary History. Volume 2: 1980-1992*, ed. James H. Cone and Gayraud S. Wilmore (Maryknoll, NY: Orbis Books, 1993). Also, James H. Cone and Gayraud S. Wilmore, ed. *Black Theology: A Documentary History. Volume 1:*

It also appears that the above approaches to the Bible and psychotherapy in relation to African American social cultural formation all implicitly focus on intra, inter, and trans levels of theory and practice. However, this focus is in need of being made more explicit and holistic.

1966-1979 (Maryknoll, NY: Orbis Books, 1993); James H. Cone, *Black Theology and Black Power* (Maryknoll, NY: Orbis Books, 1997); *A Black Theology of Liberation* (Maryknoll, NY: Orbis Books, 1986); *For My People: Black Theology and the Black Church* (Maryknoll, NY: Orbis Books, 1984).

6.CONCLUSIONS

THIS STUDY HAS FOUND that here-to-fore, there have been no major studies focused on the integration of synchronicity from a depth psychological perspective, and the miraculous from a theological perspective in mainstream academia, the church world, or the clinical world. This study has also found that if there is an absence of integration regarding synchronicity and the miraculous for the mainstream arenas mentioned above, it is even more true with regard to African American social cultural formation. We have sought to address these gaps by focusing on the benefits of integrating approaches to synchronicity and the miraculous, and have attempted to establish that there is tremendous value in teaching and learning about synchronicity and the miraculous simultaneously. Synchronicities show us in startling ways how our egos are in communion with the transcendent – the Self - and yet how deeply our egos can be unaware of the Self's involvement in our everyday circumstances. Miracles, as illuminated in the language of the Bible, tell us how to cultivate and deepen our relationships with God deliberately and morally, in order to live fuller and ultimately redeemed lives. Bolstering the view that synchronicity and the miraculous are related phenomena, we have discerned six major parallels between the depth psychological definitions of synchronicity and theological definitions of the miraculous.

Initially, I identified the intra, inter, and trans levels in depth psychology, and then applied the terms more generally to theological discourses, and also to discourses in African American social cultural formation with regard to biblical counseling and psychotherapy with a focus on synchronicity and the miraculous. The value of integrating the intra, inter, and trans levels is that, together, they provide us with a hermeneutical tool with which to analyze the various ways in which the psyche and the soul seek to resist or embrace a simultaneous appreciation of synchronicity and the miraculous.

In depth psychology we examined Freud, Klein, Winnicott, Kohut, Stern, Jung and Ulanov to look at ways in which the intra, inter, and trans levels provide a window onto the simultaneous embrace of synchronicity and the miraculous. Also, in theology we explored Feuerbach, Kelsey, Kee, Hume, Easton, and Ulanov to find ways in which the intra, inter, and trans levels might enable us to engage in the simultaneous embrace of synchronicity and the miraculous. And then in African American cultural social formation we employed the work of Cleage, Wimberly, Walker, and Lee to study the ways in which the three levels support a simultaneous embrace of synchronicity and the miraculous.

The usefulness of this study about the need for greater teaching and learning about the simultaneous embrace of synchronicity and the miraculous can be illustrated further by a sermon I heard on the miracle of the multiplication of the fishes and loaves while working on this very section of the book. The preacher, an eloquent and well-prepared expositor, first read the text[251] to an audience of about 200. Then he proceeded to describe in colorful and gripping detail how a small band of about forty Christians in the former Soviet Union had managed, back in the late seventies, to generate

---

[251] John 6:9ff.

over $300 a day in donations for several years in order to keep a badly needed soup kitchen running. The soup kitchen normally fed over 500 people per day.

As he exhorted us, his listeners, to believe in the power of the miraculous, there was clarity and conviction in his voice about the tangible multiplication of the loaves and fishes in the story in the text. The preacher was taking on the miraculous so directly, so head on. Then he completely surprised me. He stated that one of the explanations he had heard about this miracle story in the Gospel narratives was that the loaves were actually multiplied because the crowd was moved to a heightened sense of generosity and sharing by the act of kindness of the little boy who had offered up his fish and loaves,[252] the preacher believed that the crowds in the biblical story were moved by the generosity of the boy to share their own fishes and loaves that they already had on them. The preacher then stated that this was his favorite, and also the most likely, explanation for how this miracle probably took place.

To my mind, what the preacher had done was to remove the trans level from his teaching about the miracle. He was in effect using his authority and great skill to reinforce for his audience what now sounded like his resistance to the trans level. It is not that what he said about the miracle – from a mostly inter level, in which people influence one another – is not valid or helpful. It is more that he was ignoring the intra and trans levels, and in subtle ways even celebrating that the inter level seemed like the only plausible way to account for the miracle. The main difficulty with this approach is that it can reinforce for the unsuspecting, that God and

---

[252]John 6:9 tells us of the boy with five loaves and two fish; the other versions of this story in Matthew, Mark, and Luke do not contain any mention of the boy, therefore on purely exegetical grounds, the preacher's interpretation of the origins of the abundance of fish and bread for the multitudes does not stand because the texts make it clear that there was an actual material lack of food.

the Self are not really present in our experiences. In other words, this study seeks to advance understandings of synchronicity in terms of the ego–Self framework, and of the miraculous in terms of the soul–God framework in simultaneous and integrated ways as a check on the types of distortion and resistance to synchronicity and the miraculous demonstrated not only in this sermon, but in many other interpretive arenas as well.

Possible Hindrances to the Fuller Embrace of Synchronicity and the Miraculous Simultaneously

Why is it that even when the trans elements of psychological reality are embraced, a fuller reporting of synchronistic and miraculous phenomena (and the relationship between them) associated with these trans elements appears to be rejected, ignored, or muted? One tentative response to this question is that the absence of reports about synchronistic and miraculous phenomena might be the result of various mechanisms of psychological repression regarding synchronistic and miraculous phenomena in particular. Also people may tend to feel funny and self-conscious about reporting such experiences.

Another set of reasons for the lack of reports and explorations regarding synchronistic and miraculous phenomena in the approaches presented above might be found in the personal, cultural, educational/professional and intellectual biases in both clients and therapists against such ways of thinking. There is a human tendency in modern society to deal mostly with phenomena we can explain.

Furthermore, the lack of reports and explorations regarding synchronistic and miraculous phenomena in the approaches presented above might be due to the ineffability of such experiences, which makes it difficult for these phenomena to be claimed and explicated more fully, let alone verbalized.

Additionally, the relative lack of reports and explorations regarding synchronistic and miraculous phenomena in the approaches presented above, and the lack of the more integrated and holistic views of the psyche and the soul that seem necessary to explore such synchronistic and miraculous phenomena, might be due to the lack of well-established and accepted methodologies for including them. People may fall into their biases against the integration explored here, because they feel it is too hard, it is not necessary, or it is not possible to be holistic in this way.

In this study, we have argued that there is great benefit in linking the resurrection of Jesus with the concept of synchronicity. As a part of the project of the simultaneous embrace of synchronicity and the miraculous, we have attempted to show how this linkage of synchronicity and the resurrection can alter and enrich our understandings of Jesus' resurrection, such that we are not simply left struggling to believe in the absurd from the perspective of the soul-God framework concerning what God requires of us. From the perspective of the ego-Self framework, synchronicities are part of the human experience especially with regard to our unconscious dynamics.

When the reality of such amazing experiences of coincidence are connected with the miracle traditions of our sacred texts, and in particular with the miracles of Jesus and of his resurrection, we have a fresh way of approaching both synchronicity and the miraculous. Synchronicity disrupts my inability to fathom the resurrection; in other words it shores up my faith in the resurrection. Synchronicities are odd, unusual, amazing, and often unanticipated, and seemingly improbable occurrences of coincidence. When I experience them, they gave me the thrilling sense that something lies behind and within every day experience which is able to disrupt my understanding of what can happen. It is not very far to go from here to a fuller embrace of the resurrection.

At the same time, the resurrection informs my appreciation of synchronicity, by reminding me that there is a loving and just God who supports, guides, and leads us to transform adversity into opportunity over and over again, and who did this very thing by raising his son, Jesus, back to life from the dead. The resurrection of Jesus is not just a myth, or a symbol, for me, it is literally the way it could have been, and it is literally the way I, and many other Christians, take it. As an example of someone for whom synchronicity does not work in this way, although he has some sense that perhaps it could, let us turn to the words of John Shelby Spong in his book *Resurrection: Myth or Reality?*, in which he argues that the resurrection of Jesus is not to be taken literally:

....I sought to understand life after death in the other religious traditions of the world. Nirvana, reincarnation, the transmigration of souls – all engaged my attention, titillated my interest for a moment, but then finally lost their appeal. I read widely in parapsychology. There is an amazing amount of material in this area of human speculation. There are also striking claims and fascinating "coincidences" that cry out to be explored. There are provocative hints about levels of communication that, by our standards today, are nonphysical. But no emerging or real consensus exists. Perhaps there are telepathic messages that humans can pass one to another, but the data is so chaotic, so lacking in verification, as to be untrustworthy. I keep an open mind, but I remain an agnostic on this approach.[253]

---

[253]John Shelby Spong, *Resurrection: Myth or Reality?*, New York: HarperSanFrancisco, 1994, 286. Spong's overall argument is that scripture was formed by way of midrash (penetrating into the spirit of texts from all sides in order to approach the future through the past), and knowing, understanding, and employing this way of studying scripture can prevent us from erroneously interpreting the miracles, and especially the resurrection, literally. Hank Hanegraaf, in his book *Resurrection*, (Tennessee: Word Publishing, 2000), argues, from scripture for a literal approach to the resurrection, yet without reference to the miraculous per se, or to synchronicity. Part of his work is directed at defending the resurrection from such claims of detractors as that the tomb was robbed, some sort of hypnosis

Spong's description here seems to contain all three causes mentioned above as to why there is a lack of integrated approaches to synchronicity and the miraculous – i.e., people may have psychological blocks and feelings of awkwardness about such experiences; these experiences can be difficult to describe and explain; and it is difficult to incorporate them into a more integrated approach to our traditional understandings of religion and depth psychology.

was involved and the like. Morton Kelsey's *Resurrection: Release from Oppression*, (New York: Paulist Press, 1985), is a blend of orthodox theological explication on the meaning of the crucified and risen Lord Jesus as real, together with psychological approaches by which we can experience the risen Lord Jesus in our own lives. In a late discovery, from the psychoanalytic side, I found in the work of Winnicott, Kohut, and Kristeva explorations of the death and resurrection of Jesus similar to the manner in which I interpreted the resurrection dream about my father in Chapter Three – i.e., these theoretical orientations give us finely nuanced ways of approaching the process of our own psychological development in terms of Jesus' death and resurrection through explorations of object permanence (Winnicott); the establishing of the nuclear self (Kohut); and through alterity (Kristeva). Yet, helpful as these treatments of the death and resurrection of Jesus are, they do not help us with fundamental questions of synchronicity and the miraculous, and indeed, consistently imply in one way or another that it is the symbolism of Jesus' death and resurrection which is most important. The miraculous elements are variously ignored, minimized, or explained away as later cultural additions. See "Jesus and Object Use: A Winnicottian Account of the Resurrection Myth," by Brooke Hopkins, "On Courage," by Heinz Kohut, and "Holbein's Dead Christ," by Julia Kristeva, all in *Freud and Freudians on Religion: A Reader*, ed. Donald Capps, (New Haven: Yale University Press, 2001).

IMPLICATIONS FOR FURTHER RESEARCH

1) The Development of an Ethnographic Project Related to Synchronistic and Miraculous Phenomena

IN ORDER TO ADDRESS these issues more fully, it seems appropriate to begin to create and continue to seek to implement an ethnographic survey instrument which investigates the wide range of potentially synchronistic and miraculous phenomena in ways related to depth psychology in contemporary society. Such an instrument might investigate a wide range of related phenomena such as the following: the miracles in the Bible; anecdotal accounts of synchronicity and the miraculous; serendipity; spontaneous healings; luck; the supernatural; the paranormal; the occult; superstition; and magic to name but a few. One example of these phenomena is the much heralded Tour de France cycling victory by Lance Armstrong in 1999. This widely covered story tells of how three years before his victory, Armstrong had been struggling with a terminal testicular cancer diagnosis. The cancer had spread to most of his vital organs and wasted his body away. It is widely considered to be a miracle not only that the cancer went into remission, but that Armstrong got himself back into top athletic condition, and that he also won the grueling Tour de France competition several times thereafter.

An interesting contemporary example of a widespread social phenomenon related to the teaching and learning of wizardry[254] and

---

[254]Again on the Bible's disapproval of sorcery and wizardry see 2 Chronicles 33:6 – "He made his son pass through fire in the valley of the son of Hinnom, practiced soothsaying and augury and sorcery, and dealt with mediums and with wizards. He did much evil in the sight of the LORD, provoking him to anger"; Nahum 3:4 - "Because of the countless debaucheries of the prostitute, gracefully alluring, mistress of sorcery, who enslaves nations through her debaucheries, and peoples through her

magic is to be found in J.K. Rowling's series of wildly popular books for children (the four books out on the market so far - a total of seven are planned for this series – have sold over 41 million copies in more than 30 countries since 1997). The central figure of each of the books is an English boy called Harry Potter. The stories revolve around Harry's dawning awareness that the world is made up of wizarding folk who are engaged in a battle amongst themselves between those of them drawn to the dark side of wizardry, and those of them who use wizardry for the good. Harry belongs to the community of good wizards and is indeed a sort of unwitting savior figure to them. Even at his tender age as a pre-teen where the first book in the series begins, he is a precocious wizard, whose nascent, and though largely as yet unrealized, supernatural powers make him the chosen one to fight and defeat the chief agent of the dark

sorcery;" also Exodus 7:11 – "Then Pharaoh summoned the wise men and the sorcerers; and they also, the magicians of Egypt, did the same by their secret arts;" Malachi 3:5 – "Then I will draw near to you for judgment; I will be swift to bear witness against the sorcerers, against the adulterers, against those who swear falsely, against those who oppress the hired workers in their wages, the widow and the orphan, against those who thrust aside the alien, and do not fear me, says the LORD of hosts;" Revelation 21:8 –"But as for the cowardly, the faithless, the polluted, the murderers, the fornicators, the sorcerers, the idolaters, and all liars, their place will be in the lake that burns with fire and sulfur, which is the second death;" Revelation 22:15 – "Outside are the dogs and sorcerers and fornicators and murderers and idolaters, and everyone who loves and practices falsehood;" Leviticus 19:31 – "Do not turn to mediums or wizards; do not seek them out, to be defiled by them: I am the LORD your God;" Leviticus 20:6 – "If any turn to mediums and wizards, prostituting themselves to them, I will set my face against them, and will cut them off from the people;" 2 Kings 21:6 – "He made his son pass through fire; he practiced soothsaying and augury, and dealt with mediums and with wizards. He did much evil in the sight of the LORD, provoking him to anger;" 2 Kings 23:24 - "Moreover Josiah put away the mediums, wizards, teraphim, idols, and all the abominations that were seen in the land of Judah and in Jerusalem, so that he established the words of the law that were written in the book that the priest Hilkiah had found in the house of the Lord."

forces, Lord Voldemort. The mere mention of Voldemort's name causes unspeakable terror in the hearts of most wizards, and yet Harry possesses an uncanny ability to defeat Voldemort at every turn.

Harry lives part of the time, in an oppressed Cinderella-like existence with his aunt, uncle, and cousin. They hate him, fear his powers, and for the most part are ignorant of what this whole realm is about. Their kind (people largely ignorant about wizardry) are referred to by wizards as "Muggles." The rest of the time, Harry attends a co-educational seven-year boarding school dedicated to the intensive training of wizards. Their required reading list in the first year includes such books as: *The Standard Book of Spells, A History of Magic, Magical Theory, A Beginners' Guide to Transfiguration, One Thousand Magical Herbs and Fungi, Magical Drafts and Potions, Fantastic Beasts and Where to Find Them,* and *The Dark Forces: A Guide to Self-Protection.*

Although most people in the mainstream may shrug or laugh dismissively at any serious mention of synchronicity or the miraculous, over 41 million readers are devouring a so-called children's book that is concerned primarily with offering access to the world of one who can manipulate the supernatural. And of the 41 million readers, a spot poll is not required to determine whether readers are identifying with Harry, (the young wizard learning the ways of the miraculous), or the Muggles, (those who fear or are ignorant in the ways of the miraculous).[255]

---

[255]From an evangelical Christian perspective, see Connie Neal's *What's a Christian to Do With Harry Potter?* (Colorado Springs: Waterbrook Press, 2001), for an attempt at a view of how Harry Potter could be an inappropriate source of inspiration about the occult phenomena on the one hand, as well as how Harry Potter could be a useful tool to teach children about the battle between good and evil on the other. Also, see Erwin W. Lutzer's *Seven Convincing Miracles*, (Chicago: Moody Press, 1999), where in a section entitled "An Analysis of the Signs and Wonders Movement," he says, " Many of these signs and wonders are more in keeping with the hyper-spirituality of

Another ethnographic survey instrument could also be implemented to investigate synchronistic and miraculous phenomena in ways related to the Bible, depth psychology, and African American social cultural formation in contemporary society. It would be one of the aims of such an investigation to begin

popular culture than the teachings of the Bible," 75. What both Neal and Lutzer try to do is help their readers discern between Godly and demonic manifestations of the supernatural in popular culture. However, this study is concerned not only with employing such careful discernment about the competing sources of the supernatural, but also with encouraging a fuller opening up to a disciplined engagement with, and discernment of, the supernatural through synchronicity to begin with, and then reaching towards the miraculous, especially for those who discount the supernatural mode of reality. For explicitly Christian novels with supernatural themes somewhat rivaling the Harry Potter phenomenon, see also the popular *Left Behind* books by Tim LaHaye and Jerry B. Jenkins which have sold over 40 million copies world-wide. This series uses the apocalyptic drama of the Book of Revelation to invent supernatural thrillers in which the deceiving and utterly evil Anti-Christ, Nicolae Carpathia, seeks to rise to dominion in a world left behind by those Christians raptured into heaven just before the Tribulation. In these stories, the Anti-Christ is battled by a band of valiant Christians who see numerous biblical prophecies about the end of the world unfold, sometimes, before their very eyes. In one such scene, the Anti-Christ figure, Carpathia comes back to life after having been assassinated: "Carpathia catapulted himself to a standing position in the narrow end of his own coffin. He turned triumphantly to face the crowd, and David noticed makeup, putty, surgical staples, and stiches in the box where Nicolae's head had lain. Standing there before now dealthly silence, Nicolae looked as if he had just stepped out of his closet where a valet had helped him into a crisp suit. Shoes gleaming, laces taut, socks smooth, suit unwrinkled, tie hanging just so, he stood broad-shouldered, fresh-faced, shaven, hair in place, no pallor...It was as if Caparthia read their minds. 'You marvel that I speak directly to your hearts without amplification, yet you saw me raise myself from the dead. Who but the most high god has power over death? Who but god controls the earth and sky?...You need never fear me, for you are my friends. Only my enemies need fear me. Why are you fearful, O you of little faith? Come to me, and you will find rest for your souls'....David nearly fainted from nausea. To hear the words of Jesus from this evil man, whom Dr. Ben-Judah taught was now....Satan incarnate, was almost more than he could take" *The Indwelling: The Beast Takes Possession*, (Wheaton, IL: Tyndale House Publishers, Inc., 2000, 366-7).

collecting and cataloguing examples of references in contemporary culture involving depth psychology and synchronistic and religio-miraculous phenomena in music, poetry, film, and general literature. As examples: A reference in *Time* by Henry Louis Gates, Jr., to the supernatural aspects of Toni Morrison's work; Mariah Carey and Whitney Houston singing a duet about the power of miracles on the soundtrack to the Disney animation feature film, "The Prince of Egypt;" the supernaturally tinged song "Hallelujah Square," by the gospel group, The Canton Spirituals; two different Miles Davis albums of recorded music, one entitled "E.S.P.," and the other entitled, "The Sorcerer," Jimi Hendrix's "Voodoo Child;" the miracle-flavored films, "The Preacher's Wife," "The Last Temptation of Christ," "Phenomenon," "The Bishop's Wife," and so forth.

Additional dialogue partners with regard to the aims of this investigation, drawn from (but not limited to) The African Americans and the Bible Research Project might include Yvonne Chireau in the area of African American folklore; Fayth Parks in African American folk healing; Jacob Olupona, Kathleen Wicker, and Kofi Asare Opoku in the area of African indigenous spirituality; Leslie King-Hammond, Richard Powell, and David Driskell in the are of African American art; Mellonee Burnim in the area of spirituals; William Lowe and Dwight Andrews in the area of jazz; Cheryl Kirk-Duggan in the area of rhythm and blues; and Hans Baer in the area of African American denominations and sects.

2) The Development of Systems of Training and Supervision Based on Synchronicity and the Miraculous

I experienced a series of synchronicities with clients during psychotherapy sessions when, as a clinical trainee, on one particular Thursday 5 years ago, I noticed I had a dull headache from not having eaten all day. In the first few minutes of my session with a client (A) I regularly see at 5 p.m., the client complained of a headache, and told me he wanted to leave the session to go home. After about 10 minutes of exploring the client's desire to end the session so early, I indicated that any decision to leave was entirely his, right after which he decided to leave, and did so. I then saw another client (B) at 6 p.m., our regularly scheduled time, and although he did not report having a headache, he told me that he would have to miss his sessions for the next two weeks. At 7 p.m., I saw another client (C), who very much like client A whom I had seen at 5 p.m., came in and almost right away complained that he had a headache and wanted to leave the session as soon as possible to go home. After exploring this with him, he left. I felt both delighted and curious about this sequence of synchronistic episodes: first there was my headache, added to which there were two of my clients, scheduled on either side of client B, who not only both reported having headaches at the same time that I was having one, but who also both strongly insisted on going home as a result of their discomfort. I had never before had even one client report a headache so dramatically in a session, let alone two of them so close together on the same day, and with the same abrupt end to their sessions. I knew this was synchronistic, but did not know what else to make of it.

In exploring it in several different supervisions, I became aware that one possible meaning of these events was that, unlike my clients, I was not taking adequate care of myself (as evidenced for example by my having ignored my headache and not eaten all day), and that perhaps like them I needed to get some rest. This synchronistic "message" seemed to become a bit clearer, when the following Thursday, I had a frightening and almost disabling flare-up of severe lower back pain - something that has never happened to me before. In any case, this sequence of headaches and departures from therapy by two clients that day, caught my attention so abruptly and led me to speculate on their meaning, that by the time my back pain started, I knew the problem was that I was over-exerting myself. Like the woman in Jung's story about the scarab, I needed a synchronicity to catch my attention about an aspect of myself I was unwilling to look at.

Here is another example of a synchronicity that occurred in a session with a client which provided me with powerful intuitive-affective knowledge, on the trans level in relation to the ego-Self framework, as well as in relation to the miraculous and the soul-God framework.

Most of our work had been focused on a particularly difficult relationship this client was struggling with. My client had been reporting, in session after session, feelings of anger, frustration, and despair about this relationship, and I had been consistently and firmly interpreting for him what I thought was his need to take greater responsibility for his feelings about this relationship, rather than continually lapsing into rage and assigning blame to his partner. In this session, I listened patiently at some length to the familiar recitation of difficulties about the relationship. When I thought it was time to provide a bit of feedback about what I was hearing – because of an abrupt crescendo of frustration from the client with his partner ending with his assigning all blame to the other - I suggested that the client might want to step back a bit from the situation lest "you become so angry that you start kicking everything in sight and stub your toe" (these were my words to him).

Right after I said this, he looked at me with surprise and a bit of a smile, and then told me I was really going to like what he was about to show me. He pulled out several sheets of paper on which were printed a reading from the ancient Chinese divination system, the *I Ching*, which he had recently consulted about his difficulties in this relationship of his.[256] His question to the oracle was this: "Is it wise to see her?" What follows is the particular portion of the reading he wanted me to see, and which he thought I would be pleased about:

Indecision in times of adversity only brings added misfortune. The image is of a man who has gone on a walk to wrestle with a personal dilemma involving a relationship with his mate. Failing to resolve the problem with his own mind, he becomes more and more frustrated. He comes across a tree whose position annoys him, so in his frustration he kicks at it, stubbing his toe (italics mine).

After I had read these sentences we both marveled at the coincidence involved around the image of stubbing one's toe, and needless to say, my client was more convinced than ever with his need to stop lunging at the problem externally through a blaming attitude.

Here we see that the client was able to read the message from the *I Ching* and correlate it with my coincidental reference about stubbing his toe, and then to take this as a sign to pay deeper attention to withdrawing inappropriately directed anger and blame from his partner. And it is important to note that, in spite of the clear message from the *I Ching*, and the client's recognition of the message, it took many additional months of concentrated and arduous effort and application in the direction suggested by the message quickly grasped in the synchronicity for us to make the actual breakthroughs in which the client's ego actually began to surrender to the essence of the message from the Self.

---

[256]See footnotes in the Introduction about distinctions between forms of divination and the miraculous which are biblically acceptable and those which are not.

In this work we have benefited tremendously from having had the synchronistic sign to refer to as irrefutable evidence that we are on the right track. This has been especially helpful in those periods when the client's ego has desired, even more fiercely at times than ever before, to remain as it was with regard to the earlier blaming disposition.

I had introduced the *I Ching* to this client in an earlier session, and the synchronicity that the client recognized upon my reference to stubbing one's toe, and which he shared with me, was important to both of us because I had not encountered that portion of the oracle before. Also the client's working with the oracle and sharing the synchronicity with me indicated to me that the client was willing to cooperate to a large extent with my interventions and interpretations, even if he did have frequent episodes of resistance to the inner transformation from blame to forgiveness.

While it would seem that, ultimately, these synchronistic situations have been of more relevance to me than my clients, nonetheless, they have motivated me to come up with the outline of a broader method by which to identify, organize, and interpret such experiences in therapy, training, and supervision.[257]

---

[257]I am naming this outline "Towards a Synchronistic and Miracle-Oriented Method in Pastoral Psychoanalytic Psychotherapy," and it currently includes the following elements:

I. Theoretical Foundations

a)Multiculturalism, Pre-Modernism, Modernism, and Post-Modernism: The East, West, and the Rest

b)A Holistic and Holographic Approach: Integrating the Intrapersonal, Interpersonal, and Transpersonal

c)Jungian and post-Jungian Formulations Regarding Synchronicity and Theological Formulations

Regarding the Miraculous

d)Classifying Types and Models of Synchronicities and Classifying Types and Models of the Miraculous

e)Critiques from counter-paradigms: Differences between Coincidences,

Also, from the side of the miraculous, in teaching, supervision, therapy and beyond, I have used and evolved the "miracle question" technique first developed by the Brief Family Therapy Center (BFTC):

The basic miracle question is: "Suppose that one night, while you were asleep, there was a miracle and this problem was solved. How would you know? What would be different?....De Shazer has said he adapted this technique from Erickson's "pseudo-orientation in time"...technique described...in de Shazer's Keys to Solution in Brief Therapy.) Contemplating this question seems to make a problem-free future more real and therefore more likely to occur. In addition, the therapist is given guidelines and concrete information to help the client go directly towards a more satisfactory future. For example, if the client says that after solving the problem he will be socializing with his friends more often, the therapist can encourage the client to go out with his friends more as part of the solution assignment.[258]

Causality, and Non-Causality and
   the Miraculous
   II.Empirical and Anecdotal Accounts from Therapists and Clients
   a)Evaluating Veracity of Reports
   III. Supervised and Non-Supervised Assessments of Synchronistic and Miraculous Events According to
   Several Possible Types of Event:
   a)When experienced only by client and reported by same
   b)When experienced by both client and therapist and remarked on by client
   c)When experienced only by therapist (remarked on or not)
   IV.Applying Assessments by Integrating them with Other Aspects of the Process Such as Working Alliance, Resistance, Transference, Countertransference, Interpretation, Dream Work, etc.
   V.On-Going Assessment of Role of Synchronicity and the Miraculous in the Case

[258]See *In Search of Solutions: A New Direction in Psychotherapy*, (New York: W.W. Norton & Company, 1989), 24, by William Hudson O'Hanlon and Michele Weiner-Davis.

It seems worthwhile to pursue ways to enhance and evolve such techniques even further.

3) The Development of a Stage Model Regarding the Integration of Synchronicity and the Miraculous

In view of the fact that I have accumulated many personal stories of synchronicity and many testimonials about the miraculous along the various stages of my spiritual and psychological evolution, it might be of some value to consider whether this material allows me to develop a stage theory of sorts regarding how we perceive synchronicity and the miraculous. At earlier stages of ego-Self and soul-God development, synchronicities and miracles frequently seem to be interpreted by those who experience as some sort of random chance or luck. At later stages of evolution, synchronicities and miracles come to be understood more fully within either the ego-Self or soul-God frameworks. Another stage is the one in which both frameworks become integrated with one another.

The following are three brief accounts of meaningful coincidences which happened to me before the more mature final stages of this study, and which at the time they happened, were more meaningful to me in terms of the ego-Self framework than the soul-God framework. Also, these coincidences, as with the other personal ones I have recounted in this study, happened for me at a time when I was less clear about the thesis of this study regarding the simultaneous embrace of synchronicity and the miraculous, as well as the method of this study about integrating synchronicity and the miraculous without reducing them to one another. These and other experiences like them that have happened to me and others, are part of the basis on which I intend to explore a possible stage approach to synchronicity and the miraculous which is organized around notions of luck and good fortune as one stage; understandings of synchronicity in terms of the ego-Self framework as another stage; the miraculous in terms of the soul-God framework as another; and the simultaneous embrace of the ego-Self and soul-God frameworks as yet another. The manner in which I first documented these stories, which is basically how they are presented here, shows a less developed separation of the ego-Self and soul-God frameworks, and shows subtle tendencies to collapse God and the Self, and synchronicity and the miraculous, and which I find to be quite common in others I discuss the subject with now. The findings of this study are that there are great benefits in teaching and learning about the simultaneous embrace and integration of synchronicity and the miraculous without collapsing them into one another, and so I believe it is important, in order to pursue effective teaching and learning about such integration, to be aware of the ways in which such integration is not achieved. These examples illustrate this.

Almost from the beginning of my studies at Union in 1992, I struggled to pass my German translation exam (a strict requirement for remaining in the program in good standing) for several years to no avail. I had taken the recommended prep courses in German at some considerable cost; I had worked with private tutors; I had engaged in a rigorous program of German reading and also had immersed myself in listening to German-related audio tapes. Nothing seemed to help. By this time I had taken the exam twice already and both times I failed it miserably. I was desperate. I hunkered down for another try and anxiously awaited the results of the third go-around. I steeled myself for yet another failing notification which indeed came along shortly. Both times before this I had received a rather impersonal and official notification that I had failed the exam. This third time I received a very personal and friendly note from a Professor by the name of Fred Weidmann. This note provided me with powerful intuitive-affective knowledge, on the trans level in relation to synchronicity and the ego-Self framework, as well as in relation to the miraculous and the soul-God framework because it signaled to me that meaningful and special help was at hand.

Professor Weidmann stated in his note that while he could not pass me based on the work I had done, he was quite confident that with a little bit more preparation I would be able to pass the exam on the next try. He invited me to come to him for some extra pointers on how to improve my translating skills and, sure enough, the next time I took the exam I knew as I was writing it that I would pass the exam. I felt myself unraveling those German sentences into English more smoothly and confidently than I had ever done before. And this time I passed.

The synchronicity in this story is multi-layered in that Professor Weidmann was the teaching assistant I had been assigned to for New Testament while I was at Yale and where we became friendly. Then, when he graded my third German exam, I had no idea he had completed his Ph.D. at Yale and was now on the faculty at Union. Then our paths crossed again in my intense struggles with German, and then his friendly re-emergence in my life helped to see me through a very difficult ordeal. Once again, the synchronicity of encountering a friendly face just when I needed it, in a place I least expected it, led me to consider the source of such a helpful synchronicity.

Again, here the dominant sense in my ego was that of fear; fear that all my efforts thus far would be wasted; that I would never get beyond this block; that my life was being ruined by my inability to get moving on to the next set of things I had to accomplish. The fear itself was the main problem, although at the time it was nearly impossible to quell for a long time. Eventually, as I deepened my sense of trust in God's ability to guide and direct me about how to endure and overcome this ordeal, bit by bit, the compensating signs in the form of Professor Weidmann's kind and supportive presence began to emerge. However, I had to work, with much effort and for a prolonged period, on addressing the fear in my ego (another manifestation of its resistance), before I could begin to allow in and experience the beneficence of the Self.

The following example is actually of yet another synchronicity, but one that, in its content, pertained to miracles and so opened me up to the miraculous more fully, and thereby motivated and led me to be more interested in miraculous possibilities. In other words, in this next example, I experienced an inspiring multi-layered synchronicity about the topic of the miraculous itself.

I was several years into my doctoral studies at Union, and deeply immersed in preparing for one of my comprehensive exams on the topic of the miraculous. One day during this preparation period, I took a break from my studying and happened to tune in to a documentary on T.V. about miraculous healings at the shrine at Lourdes. Later in that same week I took my comprehensive exam which had a question on it about healing shrines. I was able to use some of the material I had seen in the documentary in writing the exam, and while writing I had an overwhelming sense of a divine presence guiding me. In fact, the meaning of this synchronicity about the miraculous was so profound for me that I burst into tears of unspeakable joy at my desk for several minutes. In other words, this experience provided me with powerful intuitive-affective knowledge, on the trans level in relation to synchronicity and the ego-Self framework, as well as in relation to the miraculous and the soul-God framework.

In this example, I was becoming more immersed in my interest in synchronicity and the miraculous through my studies. I was paying attention to the subject in the media, and in a moment during which much pent up tension was being released as I was writing the exam, I could feel a deep and inexpressible kinship with the Self or God. This powerful sense of guidance, support, and protection even, was available to me because of my particularly charged up state of mind in which the ego became more surrendered to the Self.

Again, the ego's system of resistance is not to be underestimated, for it requires daily renewal and discipline to prevent the ego from going back into a state of cloudiness about its need for a deep, abiding, and conscious relationship with the Self. The ego has a tendency to want to avoid this relationship with the Self, and therefore it can use the mere surface amazement of such coincidences to lull itself into an avoidance of a truer and ever-deepening relationship with the Self.

On November 26, 2000, I experienced yet another example of a synchronicity that led me to be curious about what lay beyond it. This synchronicity alerted me to powerful intuitive-affective knowledge, on the trans level in relation to synchronicity and the ego-Self framework, as well as in relation to the miraculous and the soul-God framework in the following manner. I attended Christ the King Sunday at Saint Matthew Presbyterian Church in Rockville, Maryland. The pastor preached a sermon entitled "The Character of Kingship." At the time, I was wrestling deeply with the feedback I had received recently from Professors Ulanov and Fogarty on my first draft of this book. It was my first time at this church, and I quickly reviewed the program for the service to find out as much as I could about this church community. When I got to the back cover of the program this is what I saw:

Individuation is the process of the ego discovering, conversing with, and relating to the objective psyche, and realizing that it is subject to this more comprehensive psychic entity." p.71. Ann Belford Ulanov: The Feminine in Jungian Psychology and in Christian Theology (Evanston, IL: Northwestern University Press, 1971).

Somehow, in the midst of yet another set of struggles related to my academic work, I was being met with a synchronicity that led me to be more curious about the source of such timely guidance and comfort.

Here again, I was actually struggling through yet another process of shedding layers of my ego's resistance to the Self, and thereby opening myself more fully to being guided and helped. I was in the grip of an icy and lonely feeling the result of having reached another impasse in my work. When would I finish this part of my journey? Why was it taking so long? Why couldn't I adapt to the changes in this part of my program and produce complete and acceptable results faster?

No matter what my own sense of doubt and frustration about my progress, I had to accept the ultimate fact that the only thing that would really help me would be for me to seek out and respond to the messages from the Self. By dint of habits developed over the years of pursuing this rather isolating work, I began once again to ask myself how my ego might be falling back into various subtle forms of resistance to and evasion of the Self. All I could really come up with was the need for me to deepen my determination and tenacity as never before with regard to the Self.

For me to then walk into an unknown church and read those words by my advisor confirming that I needed to attend more fully to the messages from the Self; I needed to surrender more fully to the Self, no matter how uncomfortable my ego was feeling – this was nothing short of astounding, and it grabbed my attention quite firmly.

In other words, this message encouraged me to keep "discovering, conversing with, and relating to the objective psyche, and realizing that [I am] subject to this more comprehensive psychic entity." This process of surrender can feel tiring and costly to the ego but with these signs of guidance and encouragement from the Self and God it does not have to feel impossible to continue on the journey.

4) The Application of the Thesis and Method of this Study to other Discourses and Religious Systems

A central aspect of this study is that there are many phenomenological, constitutional, and methodological factors that support the idea that there is an essential ("trans") unity underlying and connecting all of the diverse manifestations of life, and that this trans factor generates miracles from the soul-God perspective, and synchronicities from the ego-Self perspective, although such emergences of the trans factor in various discourses are usually minimized, ignored, or rejected. With regard to this trans factor, in evolutionary biology there is the notion that ontogeny (individual development) recapitulates phylogeny (the entire development of a species); in certain approaches to biblical studies there is the understanding that the Christ event can be seen allegorically in every page of scripture; in philosophy there is the idea of monadism in which any discrete aspect of reality (the monad) mirrors or contains the whole of reality, a concept similar to the idea that the microcosm contains the macrocosm. In Jung's depth psychology there is the notion that all the diverse cultures throughout time are the manifestations in different symbolic forms of one underlying objective psyche, an idea with antecedents in Plato, Hegel, and Kant. In the new physics there is holography, and the quest for the unified field theory that would account for a common underlying cause for gravity, electromagnetism, and the strong, and weak subatomic forces. In psychoanalysis there is the idea of the parallel process which underlies and relates what happens between supervisor and supervisee to what happens between the supervisee and the client, and there is also Menninger's triangle of insight, which includes the use of the third ear to discern the parallels between manifest and latent content, and coordinates such content between the client's archaic material, present life circumstances outside the analytic situation, and the analytic situation itself.

From another angle, which is concerned more specifically with extending the discourse started in this study to other religions, the following questions are full of intriguing possibilities. What do the other major religions of the world teach about death and resurrection within their own systems, in ways that we might connect to this study on the integration of synchronicity and the miraculous? Also, along the same lines based on the integration of synchronicity and the miraculous, what are their best and deepest responses to the Christian belief in the death and resurrection of Jesus?

A. J. van den Blink, in an address to the American Association of Pastoral Counselors entitled, "Seeking God: The Way of the Spirit - Some Reflections on Spirituality and Pastoral Psychotherapy," integrates holistic insights from history, philosophy, Eastern religion, the new physics, theology, and psychotherapy on his way to saying the following:

I have begun to notice that there are many fleeting moments of transcendence that take place between people, as well as in therapy and supervision. I had been socialized to believe that the experience of the Holy only occurs in the intrapsychic world of a person and [is] unrelated to the interpersonal field. It took me a while, therefore, to become aware of these small, holy or sacred moments that take place not only within people but between people. The Numinous, that which brings tears of joy, feelings of wonder, and even rapture is, or can be, experienced as overcoming the distance between parts of oneself in the presence of others. To contrast these mini-experiences of transcendence [with] the classical view of the mysterium tremendum and to give them a name, I began calling these minor sparklings of the numinous mysteria parvula, or little mysteries.[259]

In many ways, Van den Blink's paragraph is the perfect encapsulation of the hermeneutical process at the root of the method in this book. In the first two sentences he illustrates his early sense of fragmentation and disparateness about the intra, inter, and trans levels of therapy and supervision. Eventually, experiences of joy, wonder, and rapture (see definitions of synchronicity and the miraculous from Ulanov and Tillich), with regard to the Numinous (the "trans" level), assist Van den Blink to realize that "these small, holy or sacred moments...take place not only within people [the "intra" level] but between people [the "inter" level]. An additional point made in the book, that Van den Blink highlights, when he says, "It took me a while...," is that the linkages between the three levels of the psyche, as well as between them and synchronicity and the miraculous are not obvious or easily experienced by us, at first.

Van den Blink's "little mysteries" are roughly equivalent to what I have emphasized here as those synchronicities in terms of the ego-Self framework, those miracles in terms of the soul-God framework, those guiding lights, which in my experience, I believe point towards the unity underlying all the diversity of life, and are a foretaste of that paradise which is our final destination.

---

[259]A.J. van den Blink, "Seeking God: The Way of the Spirit – Some Reflections on Spirituality and Pastoral Psychotherapy," 22.

APPENDIX

(Sample of Survey Used with Clients in The African Americans And The Bible Research Project)

THE AFRICAN AMERICANS AND THE BIBLE: AN INTERDISCIPLINARY RESEARCH PROJECT

Survey Questions Related to Couples Therapy as a Site of Investigation*

*Perhaps the easiest way into these questions is to think about which Bible passages have actually spoken to you as an individual, before, on any of these topics; this as distinct from trying to generate answers, in the moment, you think might be "correct" answers. Also, you might choose merely to note Bible stories or scripture verses that come to mind to make the process simpler and faster. Please use the other side of this sheet to provide additional questions, comments, and information, if you so desire, and think they might be useful to the project. Thank you very much.

1. How does the Bible influence your approach to romance?
2. How does the Bible influence your approach to sexuality and the erotic?
3. How does the Bible influence your approach to fidelity?
4. How does the Bible influence your approach to parenting?
5. How does the Bible influence your approach to communication?
6. How does the Bible influence your approach to gender roles?
7. How does the Bible speak to you regarding relationship conflicts, blame, anger, and forgiveness between couples? How does the Bible influence your approach to therapy?

8. What are your favorite Bible stories and passages as an individual?
9. What if any Bible passages do you share as a couple?
10. How often and under what circumstances do you engage the Bible?
11. How do you identify yourself? (African American – with Caribbean, African, Latino/a, European, Asian, and other emphases of race, ethnicity, and culture?).
12. What are some of your significant experiences of the miraculous and/or synchronicity (meaningful coincidences) in relation to
    a) the Bible b) therapy c) your life as a whole?
13. What is (are) your religious affiliation (s): Catholic, Protestant – Mainline, AME, Baptist,
    Non-Denominational, Other?

BIBLIOGRAPHY

A Course in Miracles. 3 vols. Mill Valley, CA: Foundation for Inner Peace, 1992.

Adams, Michael Vannoy. *The Multicultural Imagination: "Race", Color, and the Unconscious.* New York: Routledge, 1996.

Ajaya, Swami. *Psychotherapy East and West: A Unifying Paradigm.* Honesdale, PA: The Himalayan International Institute of Yoga Science and Philosophy of the U.S.A., 1983.

Appiah, Kwame Anthony. *In My Father's House: Africa in the Philosophy of Culture.* New York: Oxford University Press, 1992.

Augustine, St. *City of God.* Translated by Henry Bettenson. New York: Penguin Books, 1972.

Auld, Frank and Marvin Hyman. *The Resolution of Inner Conflict: An Introduction to Psychoanalytic Therapy.* Washington, DC: American Psychological Association, 1991.

Aziz, Robert E. *Jung's Psychology of Religion and Synchronicity.* Albany: State University of New York Press, 1990.

Barthes, Roland. *Elements of Semiology.* Translated by Annette Lavers and Colin Smith. New York: Hill and Wang, 1967.

Basinger, David Basinger and Randall. *Philosophy and Miracle: The Contemporary Debate.* Lewiston, NY: The Edwin Mellen Press, 1986.

Belford, Ann. "A Consideration of C. G. Jung's Psychology of the Feminine and Its

Implications for Christian Theology." Ph.D. Dissertation, Union Theological Seminary, 1967.

Betz, Hans Dieter, ed., *The Greek Magical Papyri in Translation: Including the Demotic Spells*, Chicago: The University of Chicago Press, 1992.

Bion, W.R. *Experiences in Groups, and Other Papers.* New York: Basic Books, 1961.

Bolen, Jean Shinoda. *The Tao of Psychology: Synchronicity and the Self.* New York: HarperCollins Publishers, 1982.

Boss, Ludwig Binswanger and Medard. "Existential Analysis and Daseinanalysis." In *Theories of Personality and Psychopathology*, ed. Theodore Millon. Chicago: Holt, Rinehart and Winston, Inc., 1967.

Boyd-Franklin, Nancy. *Black Families in Therapy: A Multisystems Approach.* New York: The Guilford Press, 1989.

Brandon, George. *Santeria from Africa to the New World: The Dead Sell Memories* Blacks in the Diaspora, ed. John McCluskey Darlene Clark Hine, Jr., and David Barry Gasper. Bloomington, IN: Indiana University Press, 1997.

Brown, Karen McCarthy. *Mama Lola: A Vodou Priestess in Brooklyn* Comparative Studies in Religion and Society, ed. Mark Juergensmeyer. Los Angeles: University of California Press, 1991.

Brown, Colin. *Miracles and the Critical Mind.* Grand Rapids, Mich.: Wm. B. Eerdmans Publishing Company, 1984.

Bulhan, Hussein Abdilahi. *Franz Fanon and the Psychology of Oppression.* New York: Plenum Press, 1985.

Burns, R. M. *The Great Debate on Miracles: From Joseph Glanvill to David Hume.* East Brunswick, NJ: Associated University Presses, 1981.

Buttrick, A.G., ed. *The Interpreter's Dictionary of the Bible.* Nashville: Abingdon Press. 1986.

Bynum, Edward Bruce. *The African Unconscious: Roots of Ancient Mysticism and Modern Psychology.* New York: Teachers College Press, 1999.

Capaldi, Nicholas. *David Hume: The Newtonian Philosopher.* Boston: Twayne Publishers, 1975.

Capps, Walter H. *Religious Studies: The Making of a Discipline.* Minneapolis: Fortress Press, 1995.

Chireau, Yvonne. "The Bible and African American Folklore." In *African Americans and the Bible: Sacred Texts and Social Textures..* New York: Continuum, 2000. Ed. Vincent L.Wimbush.

Cleage, Albert G. *The Black Messiah.* Africa World Press, 1989.

Cone, James H. *Black Theology and Black Power.* Maryknoll, NY: Orbis Books, 1997.

_____. *A Black Theology of Liberation.* Maryknoll, NY: Orbis Books, 1986.

_____. *For My People: Black Theology and the Black Church.* Maryknoll, NY: Orbis Books, 1984.

_____. *God of the Oppressed.* San Francisco: Harper & Row, Publishers, 1975.

_____. *Martin and Malcolm and America: A Dream or a Nightmare.* Maryknoll, NY: Orbis Books, 1991.

_____. *My Soul Looks Back*. Maryknoll, NY: Orbis Books, 1986.

_____. *The Spirituals and the Blues*. Maryknoll, NY: Orbis Press, 1992.

Danquah, J. B. *The Akan Doctrine of God: A Fragment of Gold Coast Ethics and Religion*. London: Frank Cass & Co. Ltd., 1968

Davies, Stevan L. *Jesus the Healer: Possession, Trance, and the Origins of Christianity*. New York: Continuum, 1995.

Derrida, Jacques. *Dissemination*. Translated by Barbara Johnson. Chicago: The University of Chicago Press, 1981.

_____. *The Post Card: From Socrates to Freud and Beyond*. Translated by Alan Bass. Chicago: The University of Chicago Press, 1987.

Devereux, George, ed. *Psychoanalysis and the Occult*. New York: International Universities Press, Inc., 1953.

Dingemans, Gijsbert D. J. "Practical Theology in the Academy: A Contemporary Overview." *The Journal of Religion* 76, no. 1 (1996): 82-95.

Docherty, Thomas, ed. *Postmodernism: A Reader*. New York: Columbia University Press, 1993.

Drewermann, Eugen. *Discovering the GodChild Within: A Spiritual Psychology of the Infancy of Jesus*, translated by Peter Heinegg. New York: The Crossroad Publishing Company, 1994.

Easton, M.G. *Easton's Illustrated Dictionary of the Bible*. Third Edition. Thomas Nelson. 1897.

Eck, Brian E. "Integrating the Integrators: An Organizing Framework for a Multifacted

Process of Integration." *Journal of Psychology and Christianity* 15, no. 2 (1996): 101-13.

Edinger, Edward F. *Ego and Archetype: Individuation and the Religious Function of the Psyche.* Boston: Shambhala, 1972.

Eliade, Mircea. *Occultism, Witchcraft, and Cultural Fashions: Essays in Comparative Religions.* Chicago: The University of

Eliade, Mircea. *Shamanism: Archaic Techniques of Ecstasy.* Translated by Willard R. Trask. New York: Bollingen Foundation, 1964.

Ellenberger, Henri F. *The Discovery of the Unconscious: The History and Evolution of Dynamic Psychiatry.* San Francisco: BasicBooks, 1970.

Elliot, Anthony. *Psychoanalytic Theory: An Introduction.* Cambridge, MA: Blackwell Publishers, 1994.

Evans-Pritchard, E. E. *Witchcraft, Oracles, and Magic among the Azande.* Oxford: The Clarendon Press, 1937.

Eze, Emmanuel Chuwudi, ed. *Race and the Enlightenment: A Reader.* Cambridge, MA: Blackwell Publishers, 1997.

_____, ed. *Postcolonial African Philosophy: A Critical Reader.* Cambridge, MA: Blackwell Publishers. 1997.

Fanon, Franz. *Black Skin, White Masks.* Translated by Charles Lam Markmann. New York: Grove Press, 1967.

_____. *The Wretched of the Earth.* Translated by Constance Farrington. New York: Grove Press, 1963.

Feuerbach, Ludwig. *The Essence of Christianity.* Translated by George Eliot. Buffalo, NY: Prometheus Books, 1989.

Feyerabend, Paul. *Against Method.* London: NLB, 1975.

Flew, Antony. *David Hume: Philosopher of Moral Science.* Oxford: Basil Blackwell Ltd., 1986.

Fogarty, Harry Wells. "Approaches to the Process of Personal Transformation: The Spiritual Exercises of Ignatius Loyola and Jung's Method of Active Imagination." Ph.D. Dissertation, Union Theological Seminary, 1987.

Fortes, Meyer and Robin Horton. *Job in West African Religion.* New York: Cambridge University Press, 1983.

Foshay, Harold and Toby Coward, ed. *Derrida and Negative Theology.* Albany, NY: State University of New York Press, 1992.

Fosshage, James, L. and Paul Olsen. *Healing: Implications for Psychotherapy.* New York: Human Sciences Press. 1978.

Frank, Jerome D. *Persuasion and Healing: A Comparative Psychotherapy.* Baltimore: The Johns Hopkins Press, 1961.

Franz, Marie-Louise von. *On Divination and Synchronicity: The Psychology of Meaningful Chance.* Toronto: Inner City Books, 1980.

_____. *Psyche and Matter.* Boston: Shambhala, 1992.

Freud, Anna. *The Ego and the Mechanisms of Defense.* Madison, CT: International Universities Press, Inc., 1966.

Freud, Sigmund. *Beyond the Pleasure Principle* The Standard Edition, ed. James Strachey. New York: W. W. Norton & Company, 1961.

_____. *Character and Culture* The Collected Papers of Sigmund Freud, ed. Philip Rieff. New York: Macmillan Publishing Company, 1963.

_____. *Civilization and Its Discontents* The Standard Edition, ed. James Strachey. New York: W. W. Norton & Company, 1961.

_____. *The Ego and the Id* The Standard Edition, ed. James Strachey. New York: W. W. Norton & Company, 1960.

_____. *The Future of an Illusion* The Standard Edition, ed. James Strachey. New York: W. W. Norton & Company, 1961.

_____. *Group Psychology and the Analysis of the Ego* The Standard Edition, ed. James Strachey. New York: W. W. Norton & Company, 1959.

_____. *The Interpretation of Dreams.* Translated by James Strachey. New York: Avon Books, 1965.

_____. *Introductory Lectures on Psychoanalysis* The Standard Edition, ed. James Strachey. New York: W. W. Norton & Company, 1920.

_____. *Moses and Monotheism.* Translated by Katherine Jones. New York: Vintage Books, 1939.

_____. *New Introductory Lectures on Psychoanalysis* The Standard Edition, ed. James Strachey. New York: W. W. Norton & Company, 1965.

_____. *Totem and Taboo* The Standard Edition, ed. James Strachey. New York: W. W. Norton & Company, 1950.

Gadamer, Hans-Georg. *Truth and Method*. New York: The Crossroad Publishing Company, 1988.

Gaskin, John Charles Addison. *Hume's Philosophy of Religion*. New York: Harper and Row Publishers, Inc., 1978.

Garrett, Susan R. *The Demise of the Devil: Magic and the Demonic in Luke's Writings*. Minneapolis, MN: Fortress Press, 1989.

Gates, Henry Louis, Jr. "The Blackness of Blackness: A Critique of the Sign and the Signifying Monkey." In *Black Literature and Literary Theory*, ed. Henry Louis Gates, Jr., 1984.

_____. ed. *The Classic Slave Narratives*. New York: Mentor Books, 1987.

_____. *Figures in Black: Words, Signs, and the "Racial" Self*. New York: Oxford University Press, 1987.

_____. *The Signifying Monkey: A Theory of Afro_American Literary Criticism*. New York: Oxford University Press, 1988.

Gay, Volney P. *Understanding the Occult: Fragmentation and Repair of the Self*. Minneapolis, MN: Fortress Press, 1989.

Geertz, Clifford. *The Interpretation of Cultures*. San Francisco: BasicBooks, 1973.

Geisler, Norman L. *Miracles and Modern Thought*. Grand Rapids: Zondervan Publishing House, 1982.

George, Carol, V. R. *God's Salesman: Norman Vincent Peale and the Power of Positive Thinking*. New York: Oxford University Press. 1993.

Gordon, Lewis, R., and Denean Sharpley-Whiting and Renee T. White. *Fanon: A Critical Reader.* Cambridge, MA: Blackwell Publishers. 1996.

Grant, Robert. *The Problem of Miraculous Feedings in the Graeco-Roman World* Protocol of the Colloquy of the Center for Hermeneutical Studies in Hellenistic and Modern Culture, ed. Irene Lawrence. Berkeley, CA: The Center for Hermeneutical Studies in Hellenistic and Modern Culture, 1982.

Greer, Rowan A. *The Fear of Freedom: A Study of Miracles in the Imperial Church,*
University Park: The Pennsylvania State University Press, 1989.

Griffen, David Ray. *Parapsychology, Philosophy, and Spirituality: A Postmodern Exploration.* Albany: State University of New York Press, 1997.

Grof, Stanislav, and Christina Grof. ed. *Spiritual Emergency: When Personal Transformation Becomes a Crisis.* Los Angeles: Jeremy P. Tarcher/Perigee Books. 1989.

Guattari, Felix and Gilles Deleuze. *Anti-Oedipus: Capitalism and Schizophrenia.* Translated by Robert Hurley, Mark Seem, and Helen R. Lane. Minneapolis, MN: University of Minnesota Press, 1983.

Guiley, Rosemary Ellen. *Harper's Encyclopedia of Mystical and Paranormal Experience.* New York: HarperCollins Publishers, 1991.

Gundaker, Grey. *Signs of Diaspora; Diaspora of Signs: Literacies, Creolization, and Vernacular Practice in*

African America. New York: Oxford University Press. 1998.

Habermas, Jurgen. *The Philosophical Discourse of Modernity: Twelve Lectures.* Translated by Frederick Lawrence. Cambridge, MA: The MIT Press, 1987.

Hall, James, A. *Jungian Dream Interpretation: A Handbook of Theory and Practice.* Toronto: Inner City Books. 1983.

Hansel, C. E. M. *ESP and Parapsychology: A Critical Reevaluation.* Buffalo: Prometheus Books, 1980.

Haraldsson, Erlendur. *Modern Miracles: An Investigative Report on Psychic Phenomena Associated with Sathya Sai Baba.* Mamaroneck, NJ: Hastings House Book Publishers, 1987.

Harland, Richard. *Superstructuralism: The Philosophy of Structuralism and Post-Structuralism.* New York: Routledge, 1987.

Hegel, G. W. F. *Phenomenology of Spirit.* Translated by A. V. Miller. New York: Oxford University Press, 1977.

Heidegger, Martin. *Being and Time.* Translated by John Macquarrie and Edward Robinson. New York: Harper & Row, Publishers, 1962.

Hemenway, Joan E. "Clinical Pastoral Education: Supervisor's Final Evaluation." Hartford, CT: Hartford Hospital, 1992.

Hendrickx, Herman. *The Miracle Stories of the Synoptic Gospels.* San Francisco: Harper & Row, Publishers, 1987.

Hill, Peter C., and Duane Kauffmann. "Psychology and Theology: Toward the Challenges." *Journal of Psychology and Christianity* 15, no. 2 (1996).

Hoeller, Keith, ed. *Dream and Existence: Michel Foucault and Ludwig Binswanger.* New Jersey: Humanities Press, 1993.

Holland, Allan Combs and Mark. *Synchronicity: Science, Myth, and the Trickster.* New York: Marlowe and Company, 1996.

Hopkins, Brooke. "Jesus and Object Use: A Winnicottian Account of the Resurrection Myth." In *Freud and Freudians on Religion: A Reader*, ed. Donald Capps. New Haven: Yale University Press. 2001.

Horney, Karen. *Neurosis and Human Growth: The Struggle Toward Self-Realization.* New York: W. W. Norton and Company, Inc., 1950.

Hoyt, Thomas, Jr. "Interpreting Biblical Scholarship for the Black Church Tradition." In *Stony the Road We Trod: African American Biblical Interpretation*, ed. Cain Hope Felder. Minneapolis: Fortress Press, 1991.

Hume, David. "An Enquiry Concerning Human Understanding." In *Essays, Moral, Political and Literary*, ed. T. H. Green and T. H. Grose. London: Longmans, Green and Co., 1875.

_____. "Of Miracles." In *Writings on Religion.* La Salle, IL: Open Court, 1992.

Hunsinger, Deborah van Deusen. "Becoming Bilingual: The Promise of Karl Barth for

Pastoral Counseling." Ph.D. Dissertation, Union Theological Seminary, 1993.

Hurding, Roger F. "Pathways to Wholeness: Christian Journeying in a Postmodern Age." *Journal of Psychology and Christianity* 14, no. 4 (1995).

Huxley, Aldous. *The Devils of Loudun.* New York: Harper and Brothers, 1952.

Hyde, Lewis. *Trickster Makes this World: Mischief, Myth, and Art.* New York: Farrar, Straus and Giroux, 1998.

Ingram, John A. "Contemporary Issues and Christian Models of Integration: Into the Modern/Postmodern Age." *Journal of Psychology and Theology* 23, no. 1 (1995).

Jaworski, Joseph. *Synchronicity: The Inner Path of Leadership.* San Francisco: Berrett-Koehler Publishers, 1996.

Jones, Reginald L., ed. *Black Psychology.* Berkeley, CA: Cobb and Henry Publishers, 1991.

Jung, C. G. *Synchronicity: An Acausal Connecting Principle.* Translated by R. F. C. Hull. 1973 ed. Bollingen Series. Princeton, N.J.: Princeton University Press, 1960.

Karasu, T. Byram. *Deconstruction of Psychotherapy.* Northvale, NJ: Jason Aronson Inc., 1996.

Kaufmann, Walter. *Freud, Adler, and Jung: Discovering the Mind.* Vol. 3. New Brunswick, U.S.A.: Transaction Publishers, 1992.

Kaye, Bruce, and John Rogerson. *Miracles and Mysteries in the Bible.* Philadelphia: The Westminster Press, 1978.

Kee, Howard Clark. *Medicine, Miracle, and Magic in New Testament Times.* New York: Cambridge University Press, 1986.

_____. *Miracle in the Early Christian World: A Study in Sociohistorical Method.* New Haven: Yale University Press, 1983.

Kegan, Robert. *The Evolving Self: Problem and Process in Human Development.*

Cambridge: Harvard University Press, 1982.

Kelsey, Morton. *Healing and Christianity: In Ancient Thought and Modern Times.* New York: Harper & Row, Publishers. 1973.

_____."Miracles: An Overview" and "Miracles: Modern Perspectives." In *The Encyclopedia of Religion.* ed. Mircea Eliade. New York: Macmillan Publishing Company. 1987.

Kerrigan, Joseph H. Smith and William, ed. *Taking Chances: Derrida, Psychoanalysis, and Literature.* Vol. 7, Psychiatry and the Humanities. Baltimore: The Johns Hopkins University Press, 1984.

Klein, Melanie. "Love, Guilt, and Reparation." In *Love, Guilt and Reparation, and OtherWorks, 1921-1945.* New York: The Free Press, 1975.

_____. "Mourning." In *Love, Guilt and Reparation, and Other Works, 1921-1945.* New York: The Free Press, 1975.

_____. *The Psycho-Analysis of Children.* New York: The Free Press, 1975.

Kohut, Heinz. "On Courage." In *Freud and Freudians on Religion: A Reader,* ed. Donald Capps. New Haven: Yale University Press. 2001.

_____. *How Does Analysis Cure?*, ed. Arnold Goldberg with Paul E. Stepansky. Chicago: The University of Chicago Press, 1984.

Kristeva, Julia. "Holbein's Dead Christ." In *Freud and Freudians on Religion: A Reader*, ed. Donald Capps. New Haven: Yale University Press. 2001.

LaHaye, Tim, and Jerry B. Jenkins. *The Indwelling: The Beast Takes Possession.* Wheaton, IL: Tyndale House Publishers. 2000.

Larmer, Robert A., ed. *Questions of Miracle.* Montreal, Canada: McGill-Queen's University Press, 1996.

_____. *Water into Wine: An Investigation of the Concept of Miracle.* Montreal, Canada: McGill-Queen's University Press, 1988.

Larue, Gerald A. *The Supernatural, the Occult, and the Bible.* Buffalo, NY: Prometheus Books, 1990.

Latourelle, Rene. *The Miracles of Jesus and the Theology of Miracles.* Translated by Matthew J. O'Connell. Mahwah, New York: Paulist Press, 1988.

Levine, Michael P. *Hume and the Problem of Miracles: A Solution.* Boston: Kluwer Academic Publishers, 1989.

Levi-Strauss, Claude. *The Savage Mind.* Chicago: University of Chicago Press, 1966.

Livingstone, F. L. Cross and E. A., ed. *The Oxford Dictionary of the Christian Church.* New York: Oxford University Press, 1983.

Long, Charles H. *Significations: Signs, Symbols, and Images in the Interpretation of Religion.* Philadelphia: Fortress Press, 1986.

Lutzer, Erwin W. *Seven Convincing Miracles.* Chicago: Moody Press. 1999.

MacGregor, Geddes. *Dictionary of Religion and Philosophy.* New York: Paragon House. 1991.

_____. *Reincarnation in Christianity: A New Vision of the Role of Rebirth in Christian Thought.* Wheaton: Quest Books. 1978.

Main, Roderick, ed. *Jung on Synchronicity and the Paranormal.* Princeton: Princeton University Press. 1997.

Makaryk, Irena R., ed. *Encyclopedia of Contemporary Literary Theory: Approaches, Scholars, Terms.* Toronto: University of Toronto Press, 1993.

Martinez, Diane. "Pains and Gains: A Study of Forced Terminations." *Journal of the American Psychiatric Association* 37, no. 1 (1989): 89-115.

McGoldrick, Monica, Joe Giordano, and John K. Pearce, ed. *Ethnicity and Family Therapy.* New York: The Guilford Press, 1996.

McGuire, William, ed. *The Freud/Jung Letters: The Correspondence Between Sigmund Freud and C. G. Jung.* Cambridge, MA: Harvard University Press, 1974.

Meadow, Mary Jo. "Yogic Chakra Symbols: Mirrors of the Human Mind/Heart." *Journal of Religion and Health* 32, no. 1 (1993).

Meissner, W. W. *Psychoanalysis and Religious Experience.* New Haven: Yale University Press, 1984.

Middleton, John. *Magic, Witchcraft, and Curing.* Garden City, NY: Natural History Press, 1967.

Miller, Alice. *For Your Own Good: Hidden Cruelty in Child-Rearing and the Roots of Violence.* Trans H. and H. Hannum. Toronto: McGraw-Hill Ryerson Ltd., 1983.

Millon, Theodore, ed. *Theories of Personality and Psychopathology.* Chicago: Holt, Rinehart and Winston, Inc, 1983.

Mitchell, Stephen A. *Relational Concepts in Psychoanalysis: An Integration.* Cambridge, MA: Harvard University Press, 1988.

Monick, Eugene. *Phallos: Sacred Image of the Masculine.* Toronto, Canada: Inner City Books, 1987.

Moore, Robert L., ed. *Carl Jung and Christian Spirituality.* Mahwah, NY: Paulist Press, 1988.

Mossner, Ernest Campbell. *The Life of David Hume.* Oxford: Oxford University Press, 1980.

Mullin, Robert Bruce. *Miracles and the Modern Religious Imagination.* New Haven: Yale University Press, 1996.

Myers, William H. "The Hermeneutical Dilemma of the African American Biblical Student." In *Stony the Road We Trod: African American Biblical Interpretation*, ed. Cain Hope Felder. Minneapolis: Fortress Press, 1991.

Neal, Connie. *What's a Christian to Do with Harry Potter?* Colorado Springs: Waterbrook Press. 2001.

Nelson, John E. *Healing the Split: Integrating Spirit Into Our Understanding of the Mentally Ill.* Albany: State University of New York Press, 1994.

Newsom, Carol A. "Bakhtin, the Bible, and Dialogic Truth." *The Journal of Religion* 76, no. 2 (1996): 290-306.

Nichols, Sallie. *Jung and Tarot: An Archetypal Journey.* York Beach: Samuel Weiser, Inc. 1980.

O'Collins, Gerald, Stephen T. David, and Daniel Kendall.eds. *The Resurrection: An Interdisciplinary Symposium on the Resurrection of Jesus.* New York: Oxford University Press, 1997.

Oduyoye, Mercy Amba. *Hearing and Knowing: Theological Reflections on Christianity in Africa.* Maryknoll, NY: Orbis Books, 1986.

Oduyoye, Mercy Amba and Virginia Fabella, ed. *With Passion and Compassion: Third World Women Doing Theology.* Maryknoll, NY: Orbis Books, 1996.

O'Hanlon, William Hudson, and Michele Weiner-Davis. *In Search of Solutions: A New Direction in Psychotherapy.* New York: W.W. Norton & Company.1989.

Ouspensky, P.D. *The Symbolism of the Tarot: Philosophy of Occultism in Pictures and Number.* New York: Dover Publications, Inc. 1976.

Peat, F. David. *Synchronicity: The Bridge Between Matter and Mind.* New York: Bantam Books, 1987.

Peek, Philip M., ed. *African Divination Systems: Ways of Knowing.* Edited by Charles S. Bird and Ivan Karp, African Systems of Thought. Bloomington, IN: Indiana University Press, 1991.

Pelton, Robert D. *The Trickster in West Africa: A Study of Mythic Irony and Sacred Delight*. Los Angeles: University of California Press, 1989.

Peters, Ted. *The Cosmic Self: A Penetrating Look at Today's New Age Movements.* SanFrancisco: HarperSanFrancisco. 1991.

Philp, H.L. *Freud and Religious Belief.* London: Rockliff Publishing Corporation, 1956.

Pontalis, J.-B and J. Laplanche. *The Language of Psychoanalysis.* Translated by Donald Nicholson-Smith. New York: W. W. Norton & Company, 1973.

Porter, Stanely E., Michael A. Hayes, and David Tombs.eds. *Resurrection*, Journal for the Study of the New Testament Supplement Series 186. Sheffield, England: Sheffield Academy Press, 1999.

Radin, Paul. *The Trickster: A Study in American Indian Mythology.* New York: Shocken Books, 1972.

Rank, Otto. *Art and Artist: Creative Urge and Personality Development.* New York: W.W. Norton & Company. 1932.

Rattray, R. S. *Akan-Ashanti Folk Tales.* New York: AMS Press, 1983.

Richo, David. *Unexpected Miracles: The Gift of Synchronicity and How to Open It.* New York: Crossroad Publishing Company. 1999.

Ricoeur, Paul. *The Conflict of Interpretations* Northwestern University Studies in Phenomenology and Existential Philosophy, ed. Don Ihde. Evanston, IL: Northwestern University Press, 1974.

_____. *Freud and Philosophy: An Essay on Interpretation.* Translated by Denis Savage. New Haven, CT: Yale University Press, 1970.

_____. *From Text to Action: Essays in Hermeneutics, II.* Translated by Kathleen Blamey and John B. Thompson Northwestern University Studies in Phenomenology and Existential Philosophy, ed. James M. Edie and John McCumber. Evanston, IL: Northwestern University Press, 1991.

_____. *Interpretation Theory: Discourse and the Surplus of Meaning.* Fort Worth, TX: The Texas Christian University Press, 1976.

_____. *Philosophical Hermeneutics and Theological Hermeneutics* Protocol of the Colloquy of the Center for Hermeneutical Studies in Hellenistic and Modern Culture, ed. Wilhelm Wuellner. Berkeley, CA: The Center for Hermeneutical Studies in Hellenistic and Modern Culture, 1976.

_____. *The Rule of Metaphor: Multi-disciplinary Studies of the Creation of Meaning in Language.* Translated by Robert Czerny with Kathleen McLaughlin and John Costello, SJ. Toronto: University of Toronto Press, 1975.

Robertson, Pat with William Proctor. *Beyond Reason: How Miracles Can Change Your Life.* New York: William Morrow and Company, Inc, 1985.

Rowe, William L.. *Philosophy of Religion: An Introduction.* Encino, CA: Dickenson Publishing Company, Inc., 1978.

Rowe, William L., and William J. Wainwright, eds. *Philosophy of Religion: Selected Readings.* New York: Harcourt, Brace Jovanovich, Inc., 1973.

Samuels, Andrew. *Jung and the Post-Jungians.* New York: Routledge. 1985.

Sanders, James A. *Canon and Community: A Guide to Canonical Criticism* Guides to Biblical Scholarship: Old Testament Series, ed. Gene M. Tucker. Philadelphia: Fortress Press, 1984.

Saussure, Ferdinand de. *Course in General Linguistics.* Translated by Roy Harris, ed. Charles Bally, Albert Sechehaye, and Albert Riedlinger. Chicago: Open Court, 1996.

Scotton, Bruce W., Allan B. Chinen, and John R. Battista, eds. *Textbook of Transpersonal Psychiatry and Psychology.* New York: BasicBooks, 1996.

Segal, Hanna. *Introduction to the Work of Melanie Klein.* New York: BasicBooks, 1974.

Segal, Robert A., ed. *The Allure of Gnosticism: The Gnostic Experience in Jungian Psychology and Contemporary Culture.* Chicago: Open Court, 1995.

Sekyi-Otu, Ato. *Fanon's Dialectic of Experience.* Cambridge, MA: Harvard University Press, 1996.

Sexson, Michael. *The Quest of Self in the Collected Poems of Wallace Stevens.* New York: The Edwin Mellen Press. 1981.

Shainberg, Diane. *Healing in Psychotherapy: The Process of Holistic Change.* Philadelphia: Gordon and Breach Science Publishers, 1983.

De Shazer, Steve. *Words Were Originally Magic*. New York: W. W. Norton & Company, 1994.

Smith, Morton. *Jesus the Magician*. SanFrancisco: Harper & Row, Publishers. 1978.

Smith, Theophus H. *Conjuring Culture: Biblical Formations of Black America*. New York: Oxford University Press, 1994.

Some, Malidoma Patrice. *Of Water and the Spirit: Ritual, Magic, and Initiation in the Life of an African Shaman*. New York: G. P. Putnam's Sons, 1994.

Spong, John, Shelby. *Resurrection: Myth or Reality?* New York: HarperSanFrancisco. 1994.

Starhawk. *Dreaming the Dark: Magic, Sex and Politics*. Boston: Beacon Press. 1988.

Stern, Daniel N. *The Interpersonal World of the Infant: A View from Psychoanalysis and Developmental Psychology*. New York: Basic Books, Inc., Publishers, 1985.

Stevens, Anthony. *On Jung*. New York: Routledge, 1990.

Stolz, Anselm. *The Doctrine of Spiritual Perfection*. New York: The Crossroad Publishing Company, 2001.

Swinburne, Richard, ed. *Miracles*. New York: Macmillan Publishing Company, 1989.

Talbot, Michael. *The Holographic Universe*. New York: HarperPerennial, 1991.

Tart, C. D. *Transpersonal Psychologies*. New York: Harper & Row, 1975.

Taussig. Michael T. *Shamanism, Colonialism, and the Wild Man: A Study in Terror and Healing*. Chicago: University of Chicago Press, 1986.

Taylor, Mark C. *Altarity*. Chicago: The University of Chicago Press, 1987.

_____. *Erring: A Postmodern A/theology*. Chicago: The University of Chicago Press, 1984.

Thomas, Alexander, and Samuel Sillen. *Racism and Psychiatry*. New York: Carol Publishing Group, 1991.

Thomas, Keith. *Religion and the Decline of Magic*. New York: Charles Scribner's Sons, 1971.

Tillich, Paul. *Systematic Theology*. 3 vols. Chicago: University of Chicago Press, 1951.

Ulanov, Ann Belford. "Jung and Religion: The Opposing Self." In *The Cambridge Companion to Jung*, ed. Polly Young-Eisendrath and Terence Dawson. Cambridge, UK: Cambridge University Press, 1997.

_____. *The Feminine in Jungian Psychology and in Christian Theology*. Evanston, IL: Northwestern University Press, 1971.

_____. "The Holding Self: Jung and the Desire for Being." In *The Fires of Desire: Erotic Energies and the Spiritual Quest*, ed. Fredrica R. Halligan and John J. Shea. New York: Crossroad, 1992.

_____. *The Functioning Transcendent*. Wilmette, IL: Chiron Publications, 1996.

_____. *The Wisdom of the Psyche*. Cambridge, MA: Cowley Publications, 1988.

_____. *The Wizard's Gate: Picturing Consciousness*. Einsiedeln, Switzerland: Daimon, 1994.

Ulanov, Ann and Barry Ulanov. *Cinderella and Her Sisters: The Envied and the Envying*. Philadelphia: The Westminster Press, 1983.

_____. *The Healing Imagination: The Meeting of Psyche and Soul*. Daimon Verlag. 1999.

_____. *Primary Speech: A Psychology of Prayer*. Atlanta: John Knox Press, 1982.

_____. *Religion and the Unconscious*. Philadelphia: Westminster Press, 1975.

_____. *Transforming Sexuality: The Archetypal World of Anima and Animus*. Boston: Shambhala, 1994.

_____. *The Witch and the Clown: Two Archetypes of Human Sexuality*. Wilmette, IL: Chiron Publications, 1987.

Ulanov, Barry. *Jung and the Outside World*, ed. Barry Ulanov. Wilmette, IL: Chiron Publications, 1992.

Vice, ed. *Psychoanalytic Criticism: A Reader*. Edited by Sue Vice. Cambridge, UK: Polity Press, 1996.

Van den Blink, A.J. "Seeking God: The Way of the Spirit – Some Reflections on Spirituality and Pastoral Psychotherapy." (Address to the American Association of Pastoral Counselors).

Von Franz, Marie-Louise. *Psyche and Matter*. Boston: Shambhala Publications, Inc. 1992.

Walker, Clarence. *Biblical Counseling with African Americans: Taking a Ride in the Ehiopian's Chariot*. Grand Rapids: Zondervan Publishing House, 1992.

Ward, Graham. *Barth, Derrida, and the Language of Theology*. New York: Cambridge University Press, 1995.

_____. ed. *The Postmodern God: A Theological Reader*. Edited by L. Gregory Jones and James J. Buckley, Blackwell Readings in Modern

Theology. Malden, MA: Blackwell Publishers, 1997.

Weber, Max. *The Sociology of Religion*. Boston: Beacon Press, 1963.

Weidmann, Frederick W. *Polycarp and John: The Harris Fragments and Their Challenge to the Literary Tradition.* Christianity and Judaism in Antiquity Series. Ed. Gregory E. Sterling. Vol. 12. Notre Dame: University of Notre Dame Press, 1999.

Weinstock, Allan. *Psychotherapy East and West: A Unifying Paradigm.* Honesdale, PA: The Himalayan International Institute of Yoga Science and Philosophy of the U.S.A., 1983.

West Cornell. *Prophecy Deliverance! An Afro-American Revolutionary Christianity.* Philadelphia: Westminster Press. 1982.

Westkott, Marcia. *The Feminist Legacy of Karen Horney.* New Haven:Yale University Press, 1986.

Whitton, Joel, and Joe Fisher. *Life Between Life: Scientific Explorations into the Void Separating One Incarnation from the Next.* Garden City: Doubleday & Company, Inc. 1986.

Wieseltier, Leon. *Kaddish*. New York: Vintage Books. 1998.

Wilber, Ken. *The Spectrum of Consciousness*. Wheaton: The Theosophical Publishing House, 1977.

Williams, Delores S. *Sisters in the Wilderness: The Challenge of Womanist God-Talk*. Maryknoll, NY: Orbis Books, 1993.

Williams, Lena. *It's the Little Things: Everyday Interactions that Anger, Annoy, and Divide the Races.* New York: Harcourt, 2000.

Williams, T. C. *The Idea of the Miraculous: The Challenge to Science and Religion.* New York: St. Martin's Press, 1990.

Wilmore, Gayraud S. *Black Religion and Black Radicalism: An Interpretation of the Religious History of Afro-American People.* Maryknoll, NY: Orbis Books, 1983.

Wilmore, Gayraud S. and James H. Cone, ed. *Black Theology: A Documentary History.* 2 Vols. Maryknoll, NY: Orbis Books, 1993.

Wimberly, Edward P. *African American Pastoral Care.* Nashville: Abingdon Press, 1991.

Wimbush, Vincent L. "Ascetic Behavior and Color-ful Language: Stories about Ethiopian Moses." *Semeia* 58 (1992): 81-92.

_____. "Biblical Historical Study as Liberation: Toward an Afro-Christian Hermeneutic." *In African American Religious Studies: An Interdisciplinary Anthology,* ed. Gayraud S. Wilmore. Durham, NC: Duke University Press, 1989.

_____. "Reading Darkness, Reading Scriptures." In *African Americans and the Bible: Sacred Texts and Social Textures.* New York: Continuum, 2000, ed. Vincent L. Wimbush.

_____. "Reading Texts through Worlds, Worlds through Texts." *Semeia* 62 (1993): 129-40.

_____. "Rescue the Perishing": The Importance of Biblical Scholarship in Black Christianity." In

Black Theology: A Documentary History. Volume 2: 1980-1992, ed. James H. Cone and Gayraud S. Wilmore. Maryknoll, NY: Orbis Books, 1993.

_____. *The Bible and African Americans: A Brief History*. Minneapolis: Fortress Press. 2003.

_____. "The Bible and African Americans: An Outline of an Interpretive History." In *Stony the Road We Trod: African American Biblical Interpretation*, ed. Cain Hope Felder. Minneapolis: Fortress Press, 1991.

Wimbush, Vincent L. and Leif E. Vaage. *Ascetism and the New Testament*. New York: Routledge, 1999.

Wink, Walter. *Cracking the Gnostic Code*. Society of Biblical Literature. Atlanta, GA: Scholars Press, 1993.

Winnicott, Clare, Ray Shepherd, and Madeleine Davis. eds. *Winnicott: Psychoanalytic Explorations*. Cambridge, MA: Harvard University Press, 1989.

Winnicott, D. W. "The Aims of Psycho-Analytical Treatment," in *The Maturational Processes and the Facilitating Environment: Studies in the Theory of Emotional Development*. Madison, CT: International Universities Press, INC., 1965.

Wolf, Fred A. *The Eagle's Quest: A Physicist's Search for Truth in the Heart of the Shamanic World*. New York: Summit Books, 1991.

Wulff, David M. *Psychology of Religion: Classic and Contemporary Views*. New York: John Wiley & Sons. 1991

Woolger, Roger, J. *Other Lives, Other Selves: A Jungian Psychotherapist Discovers Past Lives.* New York: Bantam Books. 1988.

Wyschogrod, Edith. *Saints and Postmodernism: Revisioning Moral Philosphy* Religion and Postmodernism, ed. Mark C. Taylor. Chicago: The University of Chicago Press, 1990.

_____. *Spirit in Ashes: Hegel, Heidegger, and Man-Made Mass Death.* New Haven: Yale University Press, 1985.

Wyschogrod, Edith, David Crownfield, and Carl A. Raschke, eds. *Lacan and Theological Discourse.* Albany, NY: State University of New York, 1989.

Young, Josiah U. *Black and African Theologies: Siblings or Distant Cousins?* Maryknoll, NY: Orbis Books, 1986.

PRECIS

THIS BOOK HAS AS its purpose research into the inter-disciplinary connections between synchronicity and the miraculous on the interface between depth psychology and religion. This research process is conducted through a hermeneutic of integration which embraces sacred texts and experiences of divine healing, as well as deliverance in relation to the psychology of oppression.

The method of integration used in the book is applied to three levels of depth psychological theory - the intra, the inter, and the trans levels of theory - to explore the relationship between synchronicity and the miraculous in the following areas of focus: 1) a depth psychological focus to address synchronicity; 2) a focus on theology to address the miraculous; and 3) a focus on African American social cultural formation with regard to the Bible and biblical psychotherapy.

The thesis of this book is that synchronicity and the miraculous are best approached simultaneously and enrich one another tremendously when this is done. Although synchronicity and the miraculous are related phenomena, understandings about the relationship between them are relatively unexplored by scholars and healers in the various fields of depth psychology and theology in particular. More specifically, synchronistic events possess their own gently marvelous effects, and prepare us to sense the more powerfully transcendent dimension of life, which miracles so brilliantly display.

One of the major conclusions of the book is that although trans elements of psychological reality are embraced in certain important approaches of depth psychology, theology, and African American approaches to the Bible and biblical psychotherapy, the fuller reporting of synchronistic and miraculous phenomena (and the relationship between these phenomena) in these various approaches appears to be rejected, ignored, or muted. The study concludes by proposing a number of exciting and challenging new areas of research to explore.

About the Author

DAVE ASOMANING'S scholarly focus is the interdisciplinary study of synchronicity and the miraculous at the interface of religion and depth psychology. He employs an integrative and practical method which embraces sacred texts, signs, and experiences of divine deliverance in relation to the psychology of oppression and adversity. He applies this method to Western, Eastern, African, and African-American spirit-mind-body wellness, self-help, and leadership development strategies.

He supports leaders in foundational engagement with Jung's depth psychological ego-Self framework regarding synchronicity, in parallel with a theological soul-God framework regarding the miraculous from *A Course in Miracles.* He believes these frameworks individually make for fascinating study, but together they lead to powerful processes for healing and leadership development.

Dave is a graduate of Yale University where he majored in biology. He has graduate degrees from Hartford Seminary and the Yale Divinity School; a diploma in Anglican Studies from Berkeley Divinity School at Yale; and a teaching certificate from Southern Connecticut State University. He received clinical training in individual, family, and group psychotherapy and spirituality at The Blanton-Peale Graduate Institute in New York City, where his clinical work focused on synchronicity and the miraculous. He completed a Ph.D. in depth psychology (psychoanalysis) and religion at Union Theological Seminary also in New York City.

Dave has served in the Episcopal Church, as well as at Riverside Church in New York City and has enjoyed attending Unity. He is the founder of SynchroMind, an executive coaching, consulting, and seminar company dedicated to using the principles underlying synchronicity and the miraculous to support clients in transforming adversity into opportunity, and designing and achieving lives of health, wealth, love, and enlightenment.

His next book is entitled *Nightmares to Miracles: Miracle Mindsets for CEOs, Executives, and Entrepreneurs to Transform Adversity into Success in Health, Wealth, Love, and Enlightenment.*

Dave studies guitar music of all kinds (especially blues, jazz, and fusion), and fantasizes about learning to dance one day. He is an avid reader and watcher of movies and loves to travel.

Website
https://www.synchromind.com/

Contact
dasomaning@sychromind.com

Made in the USA
Middletown, DE
15 February 2019